Charles Wesley on
Sanctification

Charles Wesley on Sanctification

A Biographical and Theological Study

JOHN R. TYSON

FRANCIS ASBURY PRESS
of Zondervan Publishing House

Grand Rapids, Michigan

CHARLES WESLEY ON SANCTIFICATION
Copyright © 1986 by John R. Tyson

FRANCIS ASBURY PRESS
is an imprint of
Zondervan Publishing House
1415 Lake Drive S.E.
Grand Rapids MI 49506

Library of Congress Cataloging in Publication Data

Tyson, John R.
  Charles Wesley on sanctification.

  Bibliography: p.
  Includes index.
  1. Wesley, Charles, 1707–1788—Contributions in doctrine of
sanctification. 2. Sanctification–History of doctrines–18th century. I.
Title.
BT765.W45T97   1986   234'.8   86-4050
ISBN 0-310-75131-4

All Scripture quotations, unless otherwise noted, are taken from the
King James Version.

Edited by Joseph D. Allison
Designed by Louise Bauer

Printed in the United States of America

86 87 88 89 90 91 92 93 / 9 8 7 6 5 4 3 2 1

Contents

Preface and
Acknowledgments

It is difficult to imagine a cofounder and shaper of any religious tradition who is less known among his descendants than Charles Wesley is among the Wesleyans. My own investigation of the youngest Wesley brother began several years ago, without any clear sense of who he was or what he was about—apart from the obvious fact that he wrote many of the hymns of the Methodist churches. So, I began this project more or less on a dare, "Why don't you take a look at the other Wesley?" This present volume is written out of my excitement about Charles Wesley, about what he means to modern Christians in general and to Wesleyans in particular, and out of a clear conviction that this man deserves to be better known among us than he has been up to now. We shall meet Charles in the theological construction that he considered to be the Methodists' most significant doctrine; but that encounter cannot be true to the full-orbed explication he gave sanctification unless our treatment is rooted in an examination of his life and set in the larger context of his theology of redemption.

But before we begin our excursion into the life and thought of Charles Wesley, a few words must be said about the slippery terminology involved in this topic. First of all, when I use the terms *Methodist* or *Wesleyan*, I am referring to the movement begun by the Wesleys and the theological tradition they epitomize; thus, the terms are used without their popular denominational connotations.

Second, I shall strive for some clarification in the panoply of words used to describe the Wesleyan doctrine of sanctification. Although we shall undertake an examination of the biblical and Wesleyan use of each of the key terms, by *sanctification* I mean that work of Christ in the Christian that begins with justification and extends beyond it in a lifelong process of purging sin. *New birth* or *regeneration* describes the inward transformation that occurs at justification and makes the process of sanctification a reality within the Christian. When words such as *full* or *entire* are added to *sanctification* (or *salvation,* for that matter), our attention shifts from the durative process of purification to the realization of its ultimate goal—actual sanctity, wholeness, or sinlessness. *Christian perfection* describes the Wesleyan conception of what full salvation or entire sanctification implies; and, as we shall see, each of the Wesleys had a distinctive emphasis on this matter. Throughout this book, remember that the words *Christian perfection* refer to the Wesleyan doctrine of Christian perfection or "perfection in love," not *perfection* as we are more accustomed to applying that word. *Holiness* is generally taken to refer to the personal or moral qualities that come to Christians through sanctification; and while I will continue to use the term in that fashion, I shall also use it as a synonym for *sanctification.*(Just why I believe that is appropriate will be discussed later.) Each of these themes receives extensive treatment and clarification in the following sections, but it seems useful to establish some common ground prior to entering into Charles Wesley's life and faith.

Many people have contributed to the completion of this project. Although it does not seem possible to name them all, I want to thank them en masse and identify a few who have given freely of their time. I am grateful to my mentor and friend, James H. Pain, of Drew University, whose insistence that I do something different in Wesley studies got me interested in Charles Wesley; further, I thank Kenneth Rowe and Bard Thompson who joined James Pain on my Ph.D. dissertation committee and hashed over a portion of the contents of this book in a rather different form. I am grateful to my friends and colleagues David Howard, professor of history, Houghton College, for investing so much of his time in the laborious task of proofreading my manuscript; and Carl Schultz, chairman, Department of Religion and Philosophy, Houghton College, for his insightful interaction with my conclusions. While I am indebted to each of these individuals, I bear full responsibility for the interpretations and analyses carried herein.

Many others have contributed material that made this project possible. I am indebted to William Leary and the Methodist Church Committee on Archives and History, England, for allowing me to print so much unpublished manuscript material from their holdings. Furthermore, I must thank D. W. Riley and his staff at the John Rylands Library of the University of Manchester for their help in locating the manuscript treasures of the Methodist Archives. I am grateful to S. H. Mayor and the Cheshunt College Foundation, Westminster College, Cambridge, for use of their manuscript volume of Charles Wesley's hymns.

My thanks to Thomas Albin and Oliver Beckerlegge for permission to cite the manuscript version of their *Charles Wesley's Earliest Sermons: Six Manuscript Shorthand Sermons Hitherto Unpublished*, which will soon appear as an occasional publication of the Wesley Historical Society. I am also grateful to Bethany House Publishers for permission to quote extensively from their 1946 edition of Henry Scougal's *Life of God in the Soul of Man*, edited and introduced by Winthrop Hudson; to Abingdon Press for similar use of Frederick Gill's *Charles Wesley: The First Methodist* (1964); to William B. Eerdmans Publishing Company for extensive use of G. Schrenk's article "Eloga," in *Theological Dictionary of the New Testament*, vol. 4, edited by Gerhard Kittel and translated by Geoffrey Bromiley, and for the use of Irenaeus' "Against Heresies," from *The Ante-Nicence Fathers*, vol. 1, edited by Alexander Roberts and James Donaldson; to Banner of Truth Trust, Edinburgh, for permission to quote from their 1960 edition of *George Whitefield's Journals*; to Epworth Press for permission to use material from their 1931 "Standard Edition" of *The Letters of John Wesley*, edited by John Telford; and to Oxford University Press for quotations from Albert Outler's *John Wesley* (1964). My thanks are also extended to Joyce Moore and her staff at the Willard Houghton Memorial Library of Houghton College for such extensive use of the Wesleyana collection.

I would like to thank my family and friends for their encouragement in this project, and most especially my wife, Beth Milner Tyson, without whose "partnership" this work could not have been completed. Finally, I extend my appreciation to the laymen and laywomen of Methodist churches in New York, Pennsylvania, and Texas who listened so patiently and shared some of my excitement about Charles Wesley and the faith that was in him.

JOHN R. TYSON
Houghton College
Houghton, New York

A Chronology of Charles Wesley

1707	Dec. 18	Born at Epworth
1716	April	Enters Westminster School
1726	June 13	Enters Christ Church College, Oxford
1729		Formation of the Holy Club
1731–36		George Whitefield's involvement in the Holy Club and his subsequent conversion
1735	Sept. 21	Ordained deacon (Church of England)
	Sept. 24	Appointed secretary to Oglethorpe
	Sept. 28	Ordained priest
	Oct. 14	Sails for Georgia
1736	Feb. 5	Lands in Georgia
	Mar. 9	Begins ministry in Frederica
	Mar. 14	Preaches "The Single Eye" in Frederica
	July 25	Resigns secretaryship in Georgia
	July 26	Begins return trip to England
	Sept. 26	Preaches "The One Thing Needful" in Boston
	Dec. 3	Lands in England
1738	Apr. 3	Resigns his secretaryship (second time)
	May 21	His "evangelical conversion"
		"Where Shall My Wondering Soul Begin?"
		"And Can It Be That I Should Gain?"
	May 24	John Wesley's "conversion"
		"What Morn on Thee with Sweeter Ray"
1738–39		Assists at St. Mary's Church, Islington
1739	May 29	First field preaching
	Oct. 28	Begins his work in Bristol
1739–42		Three collections of *Hymns and Sacred Poems*
1741		*Hymns on God's Everlasting Love*
1742	Apr. 4	Preaches "Awake Thou That Sleepest" before the University at Oxford

1744	June 25	First Methodist Conference
1745		*Hymns on the Lord's Supper*
1746		*Hymns of Petition and Thanksgiving for the Promise of the Father*
1747		*Hymns for those that seek and those that have Redemption*
	Sept. 9	Arrives to plant Methodism in Ireland
1748	Aug. 13	Second visit to Ireland
1749		*Hymns and Sacred Poems,* 2 Vol.
	Apr. 8	Marries Sarah Gwynne
1752	Aug.	A son, John Wesley, born
1756	Sept.	Last evangelistic tour of the north of England; begins a rather settled life in Bristol
	Nov. 5	His published *Journal* ends
1757	Dec. 11	A son, Charles Wesley, Jr., born
1759	Apr. 1	A daughter, Sarah Wesley, Jr., born
1761	Dec. 29	Beginnings of perfection controversy in the London Methodist society
1762		*Short Hymns on Select Passages of Scripture* published in 2 vols., with the "Preface" on Christian perfection. Charles continues to write thousands of these hymns through 1766, most of which remain unpublished.
	Aug. 23	Arrives in London to supply in John's place
	Sept. 15	John's letter to Dorothy Furly
	Dec. 23	Charles back home in Bristol
1763	Jan. 23	Schism in the London society
	Feb. 21	Thirty "sinless ones" leave the society
	Feb. 28	The end of the world, according to G. Bell
	May	Charles returns to London
	Nov. 30	At least 170 people leave on Maxfield's account
1764–66		*Ms. Luke,* full of polemical poems on Christian perfection
1764	May	Back in London, reconciling the brethren
1765		John's *Christian Perfection* published
1766	Feb. 24	A son, Samuel Wesley, born
	July 7	John's letter accuses Charles of setting perfection "too high"
1767	Jan. 27	John's letter: "If it be possible, let you and I come to a good understanding."
1771		Charles moves to London

1772		Hymns in "Preparation for Death"
1786		Attends his last Annual Conference
1788	Mar. 29	Dies at the age of 82
	Apr. 5	Buried in Marylebone churchyard
1822	Dec. 22	Death of his wife, Sarah

Introduction:
The Grand Depositum

Charles Wesley (1707–88) was the eighteenth child born to Samuel and Susanna. He arrived prematurely and spent his earliest months of life wrapped in wool, neither opening his eyes nor raising his voice. But his fine voice would not always be silent! For fifty years it would announce, in sermon and in song, the Good News of God's redemption through faith in Christ.

Five years younger than the more famous brother he called "Jacky," Charles often stood in his older brother's shadow. What began in them as an accident of temperament has become an accident of history, as John Wesley still overshadows his brother in the remembrances of the Wesleyan tradition.

There was a shy and retiring side to Charles. He had to force himself to stand before the ten thousand people who came to Moorfields on July 8, 1739, to hear him preach on the text, "Thou shalt call his name Jesus; for he shall save his people from their sins." Both preacher and congregation were deeply affected. He walked over an open field (a deed that brought him a lawsuit for trespass) to his next preaching post at Kennington Common. There he "preached 'Christ our wisdom, righteousness, sanctification, and redemption,' to double my morning congregation; and the Lord Almighty bowed their hearts before him" (*C.W. Journal*, 1:157). But the obvious evidence of his successful service could not quell Charles's inner turmoil, and he confided to his friend George Whitefield, in a letter of August 10, "I am continually tempted to leave off preaching, and hide myself. . . . Do not reckon on me, my brother, in the work God is doing: for I cannot expect he should long employ one who is ever longing and murmuring to be discharged" (C.W. Journal, 1:159). But Whitefield knew better, and so did Charles Wesley. The mystic William Law had said that when the populace wagged their tongues about him the way they did about Whitefield, Law would run away and hide himself. "You might," Charles retorted, "but God would bring you back like Jonah."[1] His words had a ring of experience about them. The revival committed the younger Wesley to a cause larger than his own, and by God's grace he overcame the natural inclinations of his temperament in ministerial service that eventually eclipsed his involvement in it.

The unsigned editor of Charles's published collection of sermons (1816) remembered him as a man who "seemed formed by nature to repose in the bosom of his family. Tender, indulgent, kind, as a brother, a husband, a father . . . warmly and unalienably devoted to his friend" (C.W. Sermons, p. xxxii). This recollection is all the more remarkable since it seems to have come from Charles Wesley's wife, Sarah.[2]

When John Wesley characterized himself as a man "full of business," he made a fair analysis of one side of his character (J.W. Letters, 1:43). Methodist tradition has remembered the older Wesley as a singularly humorless man, who considered his earnestness a virtue. Full of drive and discipline, John expended himself in herculean efforts that readily wore out those who chose him for a role model. But John also seemed to hurry through life in a way that robbed it of its richness. Though he was also an ardent evangelist, Charles was the sort of man who could pause to pen a poem, "Written at Land's End," while watching the sun set by the sea (P.W., 5:133; cf. C.W. Journal, 1:329–30). Comparing Charles's published journal with his private correspondence, we glimpse him writing a sermon as well as a warm letter to his "best beloved Friend"—the woman who later became his wife—from a wilderness retreat he called his "Prophet's Chamber" (C.W. Journal,

2:17). The younger Wesley was a family man whose sacred hymnody also reached the heights and depths of everyday life. He wrote hymns "For Young Men" and "For Maidens" that betray the eye of a doting father; his hymns "For a Child Cutting His Teeth" and "For the Death of a Child" signal Charles's attempt to find God's grace at work in almost any circumstance (*P.W.*, 7:82, 85, 89, 150).

In contrast to the intensity of his brother, Charles was an easygoing person. His natural reserve and affection often caused him to choose compliance over conflict, and this choice was certainly the norm when dealing with his brother John. Late in his life, Charles intimated to his friend William Chandler that it was the force of John's insistence that took the younger Wesley to the New World as a missionary; his older brother Samuel Wesley had made a similar assessment the year his brothers left for Georgia, although Charles would not hear it from him at the time.[3] Through that rather inauspicious beginning, the Wesley brothers established what they both called their "partnership" in ministry, and their partnership was so successful in their day that it has paid dividends into our own.

A warm and somewhat shy man, Charles Wesley also had an iron will. It was a tremendous feat for this frail, undersized lad to become captain of his school at Westminster. As a youth caught in the trap of grinding poverty, Charles refused an offer to become the heir of a wealthy Irish cousin, Garret Wesley, since it meant his removal from the love-bonds of family and friends. A cousin from the other side of the family went in Charles's stead, and Richard Colley became Richard Colley Wesley—the grandfather of Marquis Wellesley, who colonized India, and of the Duke of Wellington, who defeated Napoleon at Waterloo. How much history hung on a small boy's decision! Yet, Charles Wesley also left a heritage, one more permanent than any empire and larger than any army.

If Charles was a man of warmth, he could also generate some heat. There was an explosive side to his personality, and John's private correspondence occasionally inquired whether Charles "was all off the hooks again," or was he merely arguing for the sake of "his humor" (stubbornness)? If the latter were the case, John lamented, he might as well "blow against the wind" as argue with Charles (*J.W. Letters*, 5:19). The younger Wesley could be impetuous. Dealing harshly with the ineptness of the Methodist lay preachers, Charles sometimes fired them as quickly as John appointed them. Charles's rash intervention cost John what seemed to be the love of his life, when the older brother became betrothed to lovely Grace Murray.

Methodist biographers have preserved a rather variegated recollection of Grace Murray.[4] She was a pious, attractive widow who was the leader of a Methodist class at Newcastle. Grace became John Wesley's housekeeper in that city. She nursed him through a serious illness, and they became fast friends and traveling companions. Eventually they were (somewhat secretly) engaged to be married during John's preaching tour of Ireland in the spring of 1749. As their relationship matured, it became public knowledge that Grace had previously agreed to marry another Methodist preacher, John Bennet. Popular gossip made it seem that she played one suitor against the other, creating a sort of love triangle that covered the Methodists with a cloud of scandal. As the rumors ran rife, Charles made a forced march from Bristol to Newcastle so that he could have a fatherly talk with Grace Murray. (She had been one of his first converts, so the metaphor is an especially apt one.) The result of his visit was that Grace Murray suddenly married John Bennet, with Charles Wesley performing the service before John Wesley could arrive on the scene. The incident caused quite a chasm between the Wesley brothers, and only much prayer and the intervention of their friend George Whitefield bridged the distance at all. Certainly, a portion of the blame for John Wesley's subsequent unhappy marriage to the widowed Mrs. Vazeille can be traced to his wounded effort to rebound from the Grace Murray incident.

Charles could take an independent course in theological matters as well; we see evidence of this in the Wesleyan revival, as he battled the forces that sought to separate the Methodists from their mother church, the Church of England. The explosive younger brother stormed out of the 1755 Annual Conference, vowing never to return to the Methodists if they passed an act of separation. As John tried to extricate Charles from "the bosom of this family" and keep him riding circuits, Charles left his brother's directive unanswered—except for a cryptic note on the back of John's letter: "Trying to bring me under his yoke!"[5] And, as the following study will show, Charles was able to strike out on his own direction when it came to the formulation of at least one important Wesleyan doctrine.

He had an uncanny gift for seeing the unvarnished truth about people and accepting them for what they were; he was "discerning in the character of men," as the 1816 edition of his *Sermons* described him (*C.W. Sermons*, p. xxxii). It was well that Charles had that talent, since John did not and, on more than one occasion, was duped into believing feigned miracles, honesty, or friendship. Hence, Charles remembered his brother as one "born for the benefit of knaves." He had a sense of reality about him that his older brother sometimes lacked.[6]

If Wesleyans do not know Charles Wesley as well as they should, it has to do—at least in part—with his temperament. The unnamed editor of his early sermons identified Charles's humility as "his most striking excellence," since it "extended to his talents as well as virtues; he acknowledged, pointed out, and even *delighted* in another's superiority, and if there was ever a human being who disliked power, avoided pre-eminence, and shrunk from praise, it was Charles Wesley" (*C.W. Sermons*, p. xxxiii). If his family withheld his papers from the prying eyes of an adoring public, as John Telford reports, it was probably in deference to his humility, if not his express wishes.[7] Nor was Charles likely to be the hero of the second-generation Methodists. He was "an unbending Churchman" (to borrow one of their descriptions) and opposed the ordinations that began the Methodist separation from the Church of England.[8] The Methodists did separate, and they traced their lineage from John Wesley, even though it could be said just as reasonably that Charles gave birth to the movement.[9] There is a sense in which the Methodists' lack of identification with Charles is appropriate, since it was John who organized and led the movement almost from its inception and who continued to undergird it as Charles's ill health and family responsibilities forced him to withdraw gradually from the more active work of their earlier shared ministry. John was certainly the architect of the American Methodist church, laying those foundations despite his brother's opposition. Yet, none of these factors can justify the almost total silence among Wesleyans about Charles Wesley.

Charles, however, has not been silent among us! His hymns have remained as a monument to his ministry and God-given talents. Of course, a few of his sermons, many of his letters, and his journal have survived; but it is chiefly through his hymns that the younger Wesley still takes voice among us. He wrote over nine thousand hymns, a figure that must place him near the top—if not at the very top—of the list of composers, in terms of literary productivity. This level of production sets Charles a pace of writing one finished hymn every two days, year in and year out, for the fifty years of his ministry. It was an ambitious task for any person! It is an incredible achievement for the poet who was also a busy Methodist evangelist, claimed by the responsibilities of family, flock, and almost incessant travel. More noteworthy, however, is the enduring significance of so much of what he wrote. Nearly five hundred of his hymns are still used in the worship of numerous Christian churches.[10]

The younger Wesley was a talented musician, though he never reached the level of either of his sons in that regard.[11] His hymnological gifts lay chiefly in the realm of his poetic muse. John and Charles composed no tunes; they borrowed their music from sources as diverse as the Anglicans, the German Moravians, the Roman Catholics, and the wags in English pubs. This music touched the whole range of human emotions, from the uplifting adoration of the great cathedrals to the simple joy of the jig that was popular in the dance halls of the Wesleys' day. It was this ability to capture the broad sweep of human experience that made Wesleyan hymns so effective; the hymns lived in the music of traditional worship, as well as in the melodies that people hummed as they worked or whistled as they walked down the street. Wesley's joyous meters made his lyrics abide in the hearts and minds of the common folk of England, and therein lies the clue to the role Wesleyan hymnody played in the revival.

These poems are the work of an evangelist; throughout his life, Charles Wesley wrote primarily as a preacher.[12] Charles's somewhat sad preface to his 1762 *Short Hymns on Select Passages of Scripture*, which he wrote in his declining years, indicates that he understood himself as exchanging pulpit for poem: "My desire is, rightly to divide the word of Truth; but who is sufficient for these things? . . . Reader, if God ministers grace to thy soul through any of these hymns, give Him the glory, and offer up a prayer for the weak instrument, . . . " (*P.W.*, 13:viii). In earlier years, his hymns were a significant counterpoint to Wesleyan evangelism. Charles often greeted the multitudes that had gathered for preaching by singing a hymn that announced the opening of worship. He must have had a strong pair of lungs, since he believed he could be heard by crowds numbering in the thousands—in a day before electronic amplification. He wrote in a letter of August 1739, "God enabled me to lift up my voice like a trumpet so that all distinctly heard me. I concluded with singing an invitation to the sinners."[13] His evangelistic service often ended the same way it began, with Charles Wesley singing an invitation or leading the multitude in a familiar hymn of dismissal. Many of his hymns were written to dovetail with his favorite sermons, so that these closing hymns completed and vivified his preaching.[14]

He occasionally used his powerful voice for crowd control; on more than one occasion, Charles sang noisy opponents into silence or marched a singing procession of Methodists out of the midst of their attackers, "out of the den of the Lion," as Charles described it (February 4, 1744, *C.W. Journal*, 1:347). Thus, there are several Wesleyan hymns that celebrate God's providential care in the face of danger and persecution.[15] His journal records persecution of nearly apostolic proportions; he was pelted with stones and garbage, clubbed, punched, ridden down by men on horseback, and thrown into a roaring river— and he accepted the fact that it was all in a day's work (*C.W. Journal*, 1:307–75)! There is even a Wesleyan hymn entitled "Thanksgiving for Deliverance in the Fall of a House," since a mob in Wednesbury (certainly one of Charles's tougher audiences) literally tore a house down in order to get at him (*P.W.*, 5:381–82)!

In the Methodist societies, Charles's hymns met with greater appreciation. The Wesleys' three dozen or so hymnbooks had their main application in the societies, in Methodist preaching houses, and in private devotions. The connection between the Methodists and their hymns is probably best seen in the literally hundreds of funeral hymns that Charles composed for people under his pastoral care. Common folk, as well as a few famous ones, were eulogized in hymns that celebrated the vitality of their Christian faith; one of these hymns, "Come, Let Us Join Our Friends Above," continues to appear in our modern hymnals.[16] Even more revealing than the victorious lyrics were the meters of Wesley's funeral hymns. They will not work with dirges; these hymns were written to fit tunes of triumph. Most can be sung to Azmon (the tune of "O For a Thousand Tongues to Sing"). Such tunes were not-so-subtle reminders that even death could be defeated in the victory of Christ's cross and resurrection.

Charles's lyrics had a catechetical intention. They were designed to teach basic Christian beliefs to the unlettered masses. While his hymns were poetry, and generally poetry of good quality, Wesley did not think of himself primarily as a poet; in hymn as in homily, he was a Methodist preacher. Thus, as John Rattenbury pointed out, much of Wesley's earliest verse—written in the harried days of the revival—was rushed into print without the polish of numerous revisions.[17] The message mattered more to him than literary polish; yet many of his most enduring hymns come from that earliest period. James Dale, who made an extensive comparison of Charles's poetry to that of his contemporaries, came to the conclusion that the Wesleyan hymns participated in a literary style that "stressed the primacy of meaning" and was "always didactic in aim."[18] Several of Charles's hymnals will pass for formal theology, since they set forth and explain important Christian doctrines (e.g., *Hymns on the Lord's Supper*, 1745, and *Hymns on the Trinity*, 1768). But in the larger sense, almost all of his hymns had a theological intention behind their composition.

John Wesley certainly saw Charles's hymns as theological statements; he cited them illustratively in his *Standard Sermons*, published many of them as appendices to his theological writings (as in *An Earnest Appeal to Men of Reason and Religion*, 1743), and used them to define what he regarded as the most important Methodist doctrine, in his treatise on Christian perfection.[19] His famous preface to what was to become the standard Methodist hymnbook, *A Collection of Hymns for the Use of the People Called Methodists* (1780), called the book's contents "a little body of experimental and practical divinity" (*J.W. Works*, 14:340). By "experimental," he meant they were experiential. These hymns communicated a lived body of Christian theology; they had grown in the fertile soil of the Methodist revival and had been tested in the Methodist societies. By "practical," he pointed to the polar opposite of speculative theology.

Charles Wesley's hymns are theological pieces; but they are not, to use the Wesleyan idiom, "speculative divinity." They are "practical divinity," basic Bible doctrines vivified in religious experience. Both Wesley brothers wrote theology as general practitioners; they were well educated, well trained, and astute enough to know that England would not be won for God in the ivy-covered citadels of learning. They wrote, as John said, *ad populum*, "to the bulk of humanity."[20] This is not to say that their work would not bear close scrutiny; for in fact it did, and continues so to do. Nor is it to suggest that there was something theologically inferior in their writings; in fact, it was rather courageous of these diminutive Oxford Dons to venture to the coal pits and prisons to explain the rudiments of religion to the irreligious. But to set the brothers Wesley in the context of their task and times, we should understand that they could not produce works like Thomas Aquinas's expansive *Summa Theologica* or Karl Barth's massive *Church Dogmatics*; and their work, while satisfying enough in its own right, will compare disfavorably to the formal or systematic theologies of other eras written to meet different aims. Their writings do not set forth the Wesleys' doctrine in a closely marshaled fashion. Any modern attempt to perceive the Wesleys' system of thought is further complicated in the case of Charles Wesley, since the bulk of the resources he has bequeathed to us are in the form of hymns.[21]

John gives further insight into the rationale of the Wesleyan hymns in another portion of his preface to *A Collection of Hymns for the Use of the People Called Methodists*, as he says that the hymnbook "is large enough to contain all the important truths of our most holy religion, whether speculative or practical; yea, to illustrate them all and prove them both by Scripture and reason" (*J.W. Works*, 14:340).

That Charles's hymns were scripturally based is beyond question. Few people have been as saturated with Scripture as the Wesley brothers. The Bible flowed naturally from them—not only in sermon and song, but also in the phrasing of their daily speech and expression. The Wesleyan hymns are mosaics of biblical words and phrases, cemented together by master craftsmen. (They also communicate the thoughts of the great writers of Christian history; here we find a few words borrowed from Augustine, there an echo of Athanasius, elsewhere from Martin Luther.[22]) Over five thousand of Charles's compositions were direct expositions of biblical passages; he called these *Short Hymns on Select Passages of Scripture*, and the title is characteristically descriptive. Short, poetic commentaries on various verses, they are no less a Bible commentary than John Wesley's more famous *Notes Upon the Old and New Testaments*. Even those hymns that do not present themselves as explicit expositions of scriptural passages show Charles's hermeneutical pattern; he explained one biblical passage or theme by drawing together a montage of biblical phrases and allusions cut from other portions of the Scripture and joined together to form Wesley's own theological expressions.[23]

While the language of poetry is not the language of philosophical syllogism or theological diatribe, it is religious language—a language of experience, affirmation, and adoration. It unites heart and mind in affirmations that, while sung, take the form of confession or creed; Methodists sing as well as say their credo. There is a sense in which Methodist hymnology reaches a dimension of the person that formal theology does not address, or at least does not address as directly. It applies scriptural pictures and images to capture the larger sense of the Bible's truth. Uniting the heart and the mind's eye, the Wesleys' hymns cause the singer to participate in and experience the gospel in a way that sterile theological definitions do not. Charles wrote his hymns, as T. S. Gregory has said so well, "not only to express but to induce the experience they reveal."[24] Charles intended not only to communicate biblical teaching, but also to cause us to replicate biblical experience. To this end, Charles Wesley never narrated biblical accounts in his poetry, as was the fashion of Milton, Bunyan, or Isaac Watts;[25] instead, he turned the singer of his hymns into an actor in the biblical drama he is recounting. By singing Wesley's poetical renditions of Scripture, we become "wrestling Jacob," struggling for "the blessing." We are the traveler, set upon by thieves and robbed of our original righteousness, but restored by Christ, our Good Samaritan. Blind Bartimaeus's affliction becomes our own until we turn from our sin and are healed of our wanderings. We are the woman taken in adultery, guilty, yet by grace no longer accused.

The rather scant record of Charles's preaching suggests that he preached many of the biblical texts in almost the same imaginative way that his hymns sang them.[26] In these hymns we touch the foundation of the Wesleyan revival; they communicate the practical, experiential connections of basic Bible doctrines.

When considering the theological distinctives of the Methodists, John Wesley pointed to "full salvation," which he termed "the grand depositum which God had lodged with the people called Methodists; and for the sake of propagating this chiefly He appeared to have raised us up" (*J.W. Letters*, 8:238). "Full salvation," as we shall see at length, was a Wesleyan phrase for sanctification, a doctrine that the Wesleys intended to set in the larger context of their entire soteriology. To examine Charles Wesley's concept of sanctification is doubly significant: It is to look at Methodism's most distinctive doctrine as well as the one that most notably distinguished Charles's theology from that of his brother John. The inquiry leads us into Charles's theology of redemption, since he esteemed "Universal Redemption and Christian Perfection as the two great truths of the everlasting Gospel" and established them as the poles around which his entire theology revolved (*C.W. Journal*, 1:286).

The younger Wesley's understanding of salvation and sanctification is significant for us, not only because he is one of the founders of the Wesleyan tradition, but also because his hymns are alive among us, perpetuating the Methodist distinctives in our own age. It is significant, as hymnologist F. J. Gilman suggests, that "John preached and organized, whilst Charles sang. It is a significant fact that today the sermons are forgotten except by the select few, while the hymns remain to bring daily inspiration, comfort, and refreshment to countless struggling people."[27] The vitality of the Wesleyan tradition depends upon the work of the more famous Wesley *and* also upon the vibrant hymns of his younger brother. In Charles Wesley's hymns, we still hear and participate in the heart of the Wesleyan revival!

CHAPTER ONE:

"Awake Thou That Sleepest!"

Holiness did not come suddenly or easily for Charles Wesley. During his first year at Oxford, he was so successful at the popular diversions that his family became concerned about his religious and academic diligence (*J.W. Oxford Works*, 25:230, 233, 234, 237). John Wesley, who was then serving as their father's curate at Wroot, visited Charles during that first year at Oxford University; many years later, the elder brother remembered that Charles "pursued his studies diligently, and led a regular, harmless life; but if I spoke to him about religion he would warmly ["heatedly"] answer, 'What! would you have me be a saint all at once!'" (*C.W. Letters*, p. 10). Charles's lack of seriousness in matters of religion became an issue between the two brothers; but by the end of that same year, he had begun a lifelong pilgrimage that set him on a different course:

> My first year at college I lost in diversions. The next I set myself to study. Diligence led me to serious thinking. I went to the weekly Sacrament, and persuaded two or three young scholars to accompany me, and to observe the method of study prescribed by the University. This gained me the harmless nick-name of 'Methodist.'[1]

Here we have Charles Wesley's description of the origin of that famous "Holy Club," where Methodist piety was born.[2] A little group quickly gathered around Charles; first William Morgan and Robert Kirkham, then John Gambold of Christ Church College. Gambold left a remarkable description of young Charles Wesley, the chief mover behind the Oxford group:

> He was a man made for friendship; who, by his cheerfulness and vivacity, would refresh his friend's heart; with attentive consideration, would enter into and settle all his concerns; so far as he was able, would do anything for him, great or small; and, by a habit of openness and freedom, leave no room for misunderstanding.[3]

George Whitefield, future fiery evangelist but then student of Pembroke College, was another of the young men drawn to Charles and the Holy Club. The younger Wesley remained Whitefield's lifelong friend and was the instrument of his conversion.[4]

By the end of 1729, John Wesley was back at Oxford: "In half a year," Charles wrote, "my brother left his curacy at Epworth, and came to our assistance. We then proceded regularly in our studies, and in doing what good we could to the bodies and souls of men."[5] The Oxford Methodists' piety combined rigorous academic study with a demanding regimen of devotions and service activities; it had the obvious intention of "spiritual formation"—exploring and expanding the whole person for commitment to and service of God. The "method of study" included close examination of the Bible as well as books of practical theology and devotional piety. It combined these readings with disciplines such as early rising, shared fellowship, frequent communion and prayers, and philanthropic service to weld those students into a small group that closely resembled the Pietists' *collegia pietatis* ("colleges of piety"); both types of groups were centers of study, fellowship, spiritual development, and social service.[6] Henry Scougal, author of the formative little book *The Life of God in the Soul of Man*, had been president of a similar sort of religious society during his student days in the 1660s.[7] William Law's *Serious Call to a Devout and Holy Life,* which appeared in 1728, the same year as Wesley's Holy Club, urged individuals interested in vital religion to "unite themselves into little societies professing voluntary poverty, virginity, retirement, and devotion, living upon bare necessities, that some might be relieved by their charities and all be blessed with their prayers and benefited by their example."[8]

As founder of the Holy Club and ardent "Methodist" at Oxford, Charles Wesley was intimately interested in personal piety and sanctification. Like his brother John and the other members of the Oxford group, Charles immersed himself in the Bible and books on practical Christianity. They read a wide variety of authors, from the church fathers to the Puritans, always with an eye toward inward purity. Beside the Church Fathers (especially the Eastern fathers), books such as Jeremy Taylor's *Holy Living and Holy Dying* and Thomas à Kempis's *Imitation of Christ* were among their favorites. The former book taught John Wesley an interest in purity of intention: "In reading several parts of this book," he wrote, "I was exceedingly affected; that part in particular which relates to purity of intention. Instantly I resolved to dedicate all my life to God, all my thoughts, and words, and actions; being thoroughly convinced that there was no medium; but that every part of my life (not some only) must be either a sacrifice to God, or myself, that is in effect to the devil" (*J.W. Works,* 11:366). Bishop Taylor's book also motivated John to keep scrupulous records of his use of time: "It was in Pursuance of an Advice given by Bp. Taylor, in his *Rules for Holy Living and Dying,* that about fifteen years ago, I began to take more exact Account than I had done before, of the manner wherein I spent my Time, writing down how I had employed every Hour. This I continued to de [*sic*] whereever I was, till the Time of my leaving England" (*J.W. Journal,* 1:83). These detailed lists of Wesley's daily regimen, subdivided even to the quarter hour, have survived in John's Oxford diaries (*J.W. Journal,* 1:36–70).[9]

While reading à Kempis, John remarked, "The nature and extent of inward religion, the religion of the heart, now appeared to me in a stronger light than it ever had done before" (*J.W. Works*, 11:366). Inward purity remained the focal point of his interest: "I saw that giving even all my life to God (supposing it possible to do this, and go no farther) would profit me nothing, unless I gave my heart, yea, all my heart to Him. I saw that 'simplicity of attention,' and purity of affection, one design in all we speak or do, and one desire ruling all our tempers. . . ." (*J.W. Works*, 11:366–67).

Henry Scougal's *Life of God in the Soul of Man* was another of these devotional books that passed from hand to hand among the Oxford Methodists. Charles loaned it to George Whitefield, and it became the means of his conversion![10] Next to the Bible, however, William Law seems to have been the most formative force behind the Wesleys' early quest for holiness. John remembered Law's *Serious Call to a Devout and Holy Life* and *On Christian Perfection* (1726) as being formative factors in his own spiritual life: "These convinced me, more than ever, of the absolute impossibility of being half a Christian; and I am determined, through his grace . . . to be all-devoted to God, to give him all my soul, my body, and my substance" (*J.W. Works*, 11:367). Law became their "oracle," and the Wesleys made several visits to his home in nearby Putney to discuss matters of spiritual development and holiness.[11] Under William Law's direction, the brothers Wesley continued to search for sanctification and social holiness; under his tutelage, they were grasped by a vision that never let them go. But John and Charles parted ways with their former mentor.[12] From the vantage point of his postconversion life in Christ, Charles identified a fundamental error he saw in Law's soteriology: "I told him," Charles remembered, "he was my school master to bring me to Christ; but the reason I did not come sooner to Him, was my seeking to be sanctified before I was justified" (*C.W. Journal*, 1:159).[13] John Wesley's early sermon, "The Circumcision of the Heart," first preached in 1733, shows some of this same type of confusion. In that instance, John defined inward "circumcision" as Christian perfection:

> that habitual disposition of the soul which, in the sacred writings, is termed holiness; and which directly implies, the being cleansed from sin, 'from all filthiness both of flesh and spirit'; and, by consequence, the being endued with those virtues which were in Christ Jesus; the being so 'renewed in the image of our mind,' as to be 'perfect as our Father in heaven is perfect' (*J.W. Works*, 11:367).

Also in this sermon, John Wesley described sanctification as "perfect love":

> 'Love is the fulfilling of the law, the end of the commandment.' It is not only 'the first and great' command, but all the commandments in one. 'Whatsoever things are just, whatsoever things are pure, if there be any virtue, if there be any praise,' they are all comprised in this one word, love. In this is perfection, and glory, and happiness" (*J.W. Works*, 11:368).

This is standard Wesleyan sanctification language, yet the soteriology set forth in the "Circumcision of the Heart" is about as backwards as the order of salvation that Charles lamented in William Law! John's early sermon is full of the mystical call to self-denial, influenced no doubt by Law, but is relatively silent on the issue of justification by faith in Christ, the very theme that later preceded and formed the foundation of the Wesleys' doctrine of sanctification (*J.W. Works*, 5:210–11).[14]

Charles Wesley's published journal opens with his entry for March 9, 1736, the day he and his brother arrived in Georgia for their famous missionary endeavor (*C.W. Journal*, 1:1).[15] Charles, no doubt because of his skill in letters and shorthand, had hired on as secretary to General Oglethorpe, leader of the expedition. No precise description of Charles's reason for going to the New World has survived, though John Wesley wrote a rather detailed account of his reasons for going to Georgia to his friend and benefactor, the Reverend John Burton:

But you will perhaps ask, Can't you save your own soul in England as well as in Georgia? I answer, No; neither can I hope to attain the same degree of holiness here which I may there; neither if I stay here knowing this, can I reasonably hope to attain any degree of holiness at all: for whoever, when two ways of life are proposed, prefers that which he is convinced in his own mind is less pleasing to God, and less conducive to the perfection of his soul, has no reason from the gospel of Christ to hope that he shall ever please God at all, or receive from him that grace whereby alone he can attain any degree of Christian Perfection (*J.W. Letters*, 1:190–91).

Thus, John Wesley saw the Georgia adventure as a logical extension of the Methodists' work at Oxford; it had to do with their quest for holiness and concerns for spiritual formation. John Burton also understood the project in this same way: "Dr. Burton keenly appreciated the piety, zeal and High Church proclivities of the Holy Club. He acted in the matter as a Trustee of the Colony, and in friendly alliance with General Oglethorpe and the S. P. G. [Society for the Propagation of the Gospel, an Anglican missionary agency]. It appears that one time he seriously hoped to capture, the whole Club for the service of this mission" (*J.W. Journal*, 1:30). Charles's correspondence, recollecting the adventure nearly fifty years later, indicates that he felt the force of brother John's personality as much as (if not more than) his arguments:

I took my Master's degree, and only thought of spending all my days at Oxford. But my brother, who always had the ascendant over me, persuaded me to accompany him and Mr. Oglethorpe to Georgia. I exceedingly dreaded entering into holy orders: but he overrulled me here also, and I was ordained Deacon by the Bishop of Oxford, Dr. Potter, and the next Sunday, Priest, by the Bishop of London, Dr. Gibson.[16]

Charles's shipboard correspondence indicates that his spirits had sunk quite low during the Atlantic crossing.

Writing to his friend and confidante, Sally Kirkham, he lamented: "God has brought an unhappy, unthankful wretch hither, through a thousand dangers, to renew his complaints, and loathe the life which has been preserved by a series of miracles. . . . Could I hide me from myself too in these vast impervious forests, how gladly would I fly to 'em as my last asylum, and lose myself for ever in a blessed insensibility and forgetfulness!"[17]

Charles's journal indicates that upon arriving in Georgia and embarking upon the mission, he had a "revived spirit," but the day-to-day struggles and obdurate colonists quickly dampened his mood once again. By Sunday, March 21, 1736, after fifteen days in the country, he wrote: "Fain and weary with the day's fatigue, I found my want [lack] of true holiness, and begged God to give me comfort in his Word" (*C.W. Journal*, 1:5). Their mission in Georgia became a part of the quest for, but did not signal the arrival of, the holiness for which the Wesleys hoped.

Charles Wesley's Georgia mission was even more troubled and beset by controversy than that of his brother John. The younger brother's duties combined, perhaps in an unhappy way, the work of pastor to the colonists and clerk-secretary to the commander of the expedition, General Oglethorpe. Charles's work was focused in Frederica, while John labored in Savannah, some sixty miles to the north. The separation and double duty did not weather well on Charles. Frederica was a dismal, isolated place,

> little more than a place on the map, a wretched outpost of Empire, as yet poorly organized, consisting of a fort, huts, and tents, with only its storeroom for a church and no other facilities for pastoral work. The surrounding territory was a wilderness of wood, swamp and prairie, of prowling . . . Indians and wild life.[18]

Such an environment was a stark contrast to the setting Charles left behind at Oxford and must have been a disappointment to his romantic notions of what life would be like on the American frontier. Charles's twin tasks made him the target of arrows of gossip and village intrigue; and those arrows found their mark!

Charles Wesley had a sensitive nature; he took to heart the small-town gossip and petty criticism. His chief adversary was the seemingly deranged Mrs. Hawkins, who duped Charles into believing malicious slander against the company's commander while she whispered Wesley's supposed "mutiny and sedition" to Oglethorpe (*C.W. Journal*, 1:8, 20). The woman's animosity toward Charles stemmed from his testimony against her husband, the company's doctor, in a case of Sabbath-breaking. Dr. Hawkins had fired his gun during Charles's Sunday sermon. The young preacher also remembered another occasion in which "Providence . . . had turned me from that end of the walk, which the shot flew through; but I heard them pass close by me" (*C.W. Journal*, 1:4). Since there was no clear evidence that his parishioners were taking up arms against him, Charles attributed these incidents to the "carelessness" of the people (*C.W. Journal*, 1:3). Mrs. Hawkins slandered Wesley to her neighbors and berated him to his face in a manner he considered too scandalous to record verbatim; "I cannot write, and thought no woman, though taken from Drury-lane, could have spoken" (*C.W. Journal*, 1:5).

His falling out with the settlers of Frederica was virtually complete not twenty days after arriving in Georgia: "My few well-wishers are afraid to speak to me. Some have turned out of the way to avoid me. Others desired I would not take it ill, if they seemed not to know me when we should meet. The servant that used to wash my linen sent it back unwashed" (*C.W. Journal*, 1:15).

The refusal of clean linen was more than a symbolic act; it marked the end of the last vestige of civilized comfort Wesley would know in Frederica. Since he was working directly under General Oglethorpe, Charles had supposed that he was to have room and board with his employer:

> Knowing I was to live with Mr. Oglethorpe, I
> brought nothing with me from England, except my
> clothes and books; but this morning, asking a servant
> for something I wanted, (I think a tea-kettle,) I was
> told that Mr. Oglethorpe had given orders that no one
> should use any of his things. I answered, that order, I
> supposed, did not extend to me. 'Yes, Sir,' says she,
> 'you was excepted by name.' Thanks be to God, that
> it has not yet been made [a] capital [crime] to give me
> a morsel of bread! (*C.W. Journal*, 1:14).

But the very next day, Charles found himself "being forbid
the use of Mr. Oglethorpe's things, and in effect barred of
most of the conveniences, if not necessaries, of life" (*C.W. Journal*, 1:15).

By the end of his first month in Frederica, the
younger Wesley's spirits had sunk low. He wrote: "I
sometimes pitied, and sometimes diverted myself with, the
odd expressions of their contempt; but found the benefit of
having undergone a much lower degree of Obloquy at
Oxford" (*C.W. Journal*, 1:15).

Sleeping on the dirt floor in the corner of Mr. Reed's
hut, and then eventually on the floor of his own hut, caused
Charles's frail health to quickly deteriorate. He was soon ill
with fever and "distemper," and sickness plagued nearly
half the days he remained in Georgia. A visit from brother
John was necessary to melt Charles's stubbornness: "My
brother," Charles wrote, "brought me off a resolution
which honor and indignation had formed, of starving
rather than ask for necessities" (*C.W. Journal*, 1:20–21).
During the same visit, the breach with the general was
somewhat repaired, but only after Charles reported to
Oglethorpe the gossip the company was circulating about
its allegedly adulterous commander. In a flourish of
melodrama, Oglethorpe protested his innocence and gave
Wesley a ring to be taken to the trustees of the colony as a
sign of his favor.

The general then ventured forth to do battle with the
Spaniards. "With this sword," he said, "I was never yet
unsuccessful." "I hope, Sir," Charles replied, "you carry

with you a better, even the sword of the Lord, and of Gideon" (*C.W. Journal*, 1:20).

Upon returning from his adventure, the general treated Charles with kindness; but Wesley's continued illness and growing sense of ineffectiveness caused him to resign his "secretary's place" and begin to make arrangements to return to England. The date of his resignation was July 25, 1736, less than four months after he first set foot in the New World. The two parted amicably; Oglethorpe for his part made Charles the bearer of the company's dispatches to the trustees of the colony, which had the effect of giving a guise of honor to Charles's departure and offering another opportunity for him to reconsider his resignation: "Then you may either put in a deputy or resign." The commander also had some fatherly advice for the young pastor: "On many accounts I should recommend to you marriage, rather than celibacy. You are of a social temper, and would find in a married state the difficulties of working out your salvation exceedingly lessened, and your helps increased" (*C.W. Journal*, 1:35). Even Oglethorpe had observed the toll that loneliness and separation had taken upon young Charles Wesley.

His voyage back to England took Charles first to Savannah and then on to Boston, where he preached several times (including the sermon, "The One Thing Needful") and succumbed to illness once again. Wesley landed in England on December 3, 1736, and spent the next three months awaiting Oglethorpe's arrival from the Georgia colony. His days were divided between visiting family and old friends and meeting with dignitaries, trying to relieve the problems of the Georgia colony. Charles finally resigned his post with the company a second time on April 3, 1738. Initially he had intended to return to Georgia, as a chaplain and not as a secretary; but his continuing illness and the impending return of John Wesley made that plan seem unsuitable (*C.W. Journal*, 1:69). Those intervening months, between Charles's return to England and his eventual resignation of his post with the colony, were full of soul-searching and also a bit of self-recrimination. There were also very pleasant times at Epworth, Oxford, and in the parlors of close friends. Yet, the spring of 1738 saw his health deteriorate once again, and with that same spring came a restless quest for a sense of God's forgiveness.

On February 18, 1738, Charles met his brother John at Mr. Sarney's and with them were a few friends, "some scholars and a Moravian" (*C.W. Journal*, 1:82). The unnamed Moravian was Peter Böhler, and he would press Charles with the issues of justification and faith that he later enforced upon John Wesley (*J.W. Journal*, 1:442, 447, 454, 471). An additional conversation with Böhler on February 22 found him using metaphors of "waking" and "sleeping" to describe the way of salvation to Charles Wesley (*C.W. Journal*, 1:82).

Although Charles's journal does not report his reaction to Böhler's remarks on that evening, Wesley would later return to the imagery of "waking" and "sleeping" to describe the process of conversion or coming to faith in Christ. This description became the foundation for Charles's most famous sermon, "Awake Thou That Sleepest" (*J.W. Works*, 5:25–36). The sermon, now carried among the published works of John Wesley, was the most frequently published and purchased Methodist tract during the lifetime of the Wesleys (*C.W. Letters*, p. 35–36), a particularly significant fact in view of the huge number of sermons, tracts, and hymnbooks they made available to the Methodists.

Charles first preached "Awake Thou That Sleepest" on April 4, 1742. The sermon was based on Ephesians 5:14, "Awake thou that sleepest, and arise from the dead, and Christ shall give thee light." The setting was rather formal, since the sermon was delivered at Oxford University, so Charles followed the clearly defined three-point pattern common in that day (and still, to some degree, in ours). His outline was clear and direct: "First, Describe the sleepers, to whom [these Bible words] are spoken: Secondly, Enforce the exhortation, 'Awake, thou that sleepest, and arise from the dead': And thirdly, Explain the promise made to such as do awake and arise: 'Christ shall give thee light'" (*J.W. Works*, 5:25).

Charles's sermon declared that the "sleepers" are those who remain "in the natural state of man; that deep sleep of the soul, into which the sin of Adam hath cast all who spring from his loins; that supineness, indolence, and stupidity, that insensibility of his real condition, wherein every man comes into the world and continues till the voice of God awakens him." The person who "sleeps" in this soteriological sense is "a sinner satisfied in his sins, contented to remain in his fallen state, to live and die without the image of God" (*J.W. Works*, 5:25–26). Charles equated this deadly slumber with the danger of being ignorant, which was the focus of his sermon "The One Thing Needful": "He [the sinner] sees *no necessity* for the *one thing needful*, even that inward universal change, that 'birth from above,' figured out by baptism, which is the beginning of that total renovation, that sanctification of spirit, soul, and body, 'without which no man shall see the Lord'" (*J.W. Works*, 5:26). As Charles's sermon on "sleepers" moved toward his "enforcement" of the text's exhortation for "total renovation" or "sanctification of spirit, soul, and body" (Part Three), a foreshadowing of another important Wesleyan theme emerged—"The Promise of the Father" (*J.W. Works*, 5:33).

In that third step of the sermon, Charles moved from the "light" promised in the Ephesians passage to the promise Jesus gave His disciples regarding the coming of the Holy Spirit (John 14:17).[19] Wesley wove together themes of christology, inner renewal, and the presence of the Holy Spirit to describe the nature of this "light" that Christ bestows upon those who forsake their sins to live in Him: "God is light, and will give himself to every awakened sinner, that waiteth for him: And thou shalt then be a temple of the living God, and Christ shall 'dwell in thy heart by faith.' And 'being rooted and grounded in love, thou shalt be able to comprehend with all saints, what is the breadth, and length, and depth of that love of Christ which passeth knowledge" (*J.W. Works*, 5:30, 32). This profound inner renovation could alternately be understood as being made "a partaker of the divine nature," being made "a temple of the Holy Ghost," or "having the life of God in the soul of man; Christ formed in the heart" (*J.W. Works*, 5:27). In each instance, the "promise" and intention of salvation from sin is described as renovation of the *imago Dei* (image of God) within the person who does "awake" and "arise" in faith. This explanation of the results of salvation is especially interesting, not only because it decisively identifies several important themes in Charles Wesley's soteriology, but also because this sermon picks up his preconversion language about "awaking" and "sleeping" and applies it in a specifically evangelical, postconversion manner. The sermon also carries a foreshadowing of Charles's growing interest in the doctrine of the Holy Spirit and its connection to sanctification, an interest that would emerge powerfully in his hymns of 1746.

Charles's sermon before the university demonstrates his tendency to move easily from justification (Christ's work *for* us) toward sanctification (Christ's work *in* us). In his sermon, as in his hymns, these theological categories seem a bit artificial when one tries to describe Charles Wesley's approach to the theology of redemption. The renewal of the inward person, along with the undoing of the ill effects of the first Adam through the work of the second Adam, emerges as the main thrust of his soteriological thought:

> Even as it is written, 'By one man sin entered into the world, and death by sin; and so death passed upon all men,' not only temporal death, but likewise spiritual and eternal. 'In that day that thou eatest,' said God to Adam, 'thou shalt surely die'; Not bodily, (unless as he then became mortal,) but spiritually: Thou shalt lose the life of thy soul; . . . thy essential life and happiness. Thus first was dissolved the vital union of our soul with God; insomuch that 'in the midst of natural life,' we are now in spiritual 'death.' And herein we remain till the Second Adam becomes a quickening Spirit to us, till he raises the dead, the dead in sin (*J.W. Works*, 5:27).

In Charles Wesley's theology of redemption, the distinction between justification and sanctification is indistinct and blurred; in other words, redemption flows quickly and powerfully through justification toward its logical and theological completion in sanctification—"The One Thing Needful." Thus, as Charles wrote: "Receive this, 'not as the word of man; but as it is indeed the word of God': and thou art justified freely through faith. Thou shalt be sanctified also through faith which is in Jesus, and shalt set to thy seal, even thine, that 'God hath given unto us eternal life, and this life is his Son'" (*J.W. Works*, 5:33).

"Awake Thou That Sleepest" closed with a strong note on the importance of assurance of our salvation. As the homily surged toward its conclusion, Wesley urged his listeners to receive forgiveness of sin in Christ and to know this comfort of "forgiveness," "assurance," or "liberty of conscience": "Your conscience beareth you witness in the Holy Ghost, that these things are so, if so be ye have tasted that the Lord is gracious. 'This is eternal life, to know the only true God, and Jesus Christ whom he hath sent.' This experimental knowledge, and this alone, is true Christianity" (*J.W. Works*, 5:33).

The issue of assurance (or "witness in the Holy Ghost," to use the phraseology of the sermon) had long been an important element in Charles Wesley's own religious quest. It was certainly one of the elements that shook his life in the spring of 1738! By February 28, his illness had once again become life-threatening, and Charles's journal is almost apologetic about allowing his health to fall so far without seeking professional treatment. Yet, one can only wonder whether eighteenth-century medicine did more to cure or kill the patient. As Charles wrote, "I took my illness for the flux, and so never thought of sending for a physician. T. Bentham fetched him against my will, and was probably the instrument of saving my life a second time. Dr. M[iddleton] called in Dr. Fruin. They bled me three times, and poured down draughts, oils, and apozems without end. . . . Ever since I have been slowly gathering strength" (*C.W. Journal*, 1:83). Peter Böhler, the Moravian, was at Charles's bedside during his recovery, and on April 28 Wesley recalled:

> In the morning Dr. Cockburn came to see me; and a better physician, Peter Böhler, whom God detained in England for my good. He stood by my bedside, and prayed over me, that now at least I might see the divine intention, in this and my late illness. I immediately thought it might be that I should again consider Böhler's doctrine of faith; examine myself whether I was in the faith; and if I was not, never cease seeking and longing after it, till I attained it (*C.W. Journal*, 1:84).

After receiving the sacrament from a visiting clergyman, Mr. Piers, Charles remembered: "I felt a small anticipation of peace, and said, 'Now I have demonstration against the Moravian doctrine that a man cannot have peace without assurance of his pardon. I now have peace, yet cannot say of a surety that my sins are forgiven" (*C.W. Journal*, 1:85).

Throughout his Christian pilgrimage, Charles Wesley used his sense of peace and acceptance as a sort of spiritual barometer for measuring the vitality of his faith. In later years this reliance on an inner experience of assurance would drive him toward perfection; but in May 1738 this inward quest set Charles, as he described it, "seeking Christ as in an agony." The month of May was spent praying and searching the Scriptures with Mr. Bray—a braizer—whom Wesley described as "a poor ignorant Mechanic, who knows nothing but Christ" (*C.W. Journal*, 1:88). Martin Luther's *Galatians Commentary* found its way into Charles's hands, and the personal appropriation of Christ was made plain to him. "I laboured," he wrote, "waited, and prayed to feel 'who loved *me*, and gave himself for *me*.'"

On Pentecost Sunday, May 21, 1738, Charles Wesley's journal began with the words "I waked in hope and expectation of His coming." The day closed with those hopes and expectations being realized (*C.W. Journal*, 1:90). Charles's sense of assurance continued, rising and falling several times, into the next week; "Tues., May 23rd., I waked under the protection of Christ, and gave myself up, soul, and body, to him. At nine I began an hymn upon my conversion, but was persuaded to break off for fear of pride" (*C.W. Journal*, 1:94). John Bray prevailed upon Charles to finish the hymn, which he did by the next evening: "At eight I prayed by myself for love; with some feeling, and assurance of feeling more. Towards ten, my brother was brought in in triumph by a troop of our friends, and declared, 'I believe.' We sang the hymn with great joy, and parted with prayer" (*C.W. Journal*, 1:95).

Although there is some question about which of their hymns the Wesleys sang at Charles's bedside in celebration of their conversions in that May of 1738, the traditional identification of "Christ the Friend of Sinners" seems to be accurate. It has linguistic support from the phraseology that Charles's journal used to describe his conversion experience.[20] "Christ the Friend of Sinners" also offers an apt description of Charles's foremost concerns during the week prior to his conversion: "I longed to find Christ, that I might show him to all mankind; that I might praise, that I might love him" (*C.W. Journal*, 1:87). Verses one and two of the hymn are full of Wesley's praise and wonder at finding a gracious God:

> 1. Where shall my wondering soul begin?
>   How shall I all to heaven aspire?
>   A slave redeem'd from death and sin,
>   A brand pluck'd from eternal fire,
>   How shall I equal triumphs raise,
>   And sing my great Deliverer's praise!
>
> 2. O, how shall I the goodness tell,
>   Father, which Thou to me hast show'd?
>   That I, a child of wrath and hell,
>   I should be call'd a child of God!
>   Should know, should feel my sins forgiven,
>   Blest with this antepast of heaven! (*P.W.*, 1:91)

The hymn follows Charles's intention of showing Christ to "all mankind," as it closes with an invitation for other "guilty brethren" to come to Christ by faith alone:

7. Come, O my guilty brethren, come,
   Groaning beneath your load of sin!
      His bleeding heart shall make you room,
   His open side shall take you in.
      He calls you now, invites you home:
   Come, O my guilty brethren, come!

8. For you the purple current flow'd
   In pardons from His wounded side:
      Languish'd for you the 'eternal God,
   For you the Prince of Glory died.
      Believe, and all your guilt's forgiven;
   Only believe—and yours is heaven.
            (*P.W.*, 1:92–93)

Justification by faith was a foundational Wesleyan doctrine; the events of May 1738 pushed it into the forefront of the lives of John and Charles Wesley. They sought justification and a sense of acceptance by God in the Bible, in prayer, in the writers of the Christian past, and in godly conversation with men and women of faith; but justification was more than a theological doctrine with them—it was a doctrine vivified with experience. Hence, it is not surprising to find that justification by faith in Christ, and the constellation of soteriological themes that orbit around that central concept, were sung all across the Wesleyan hymnological galaxy.

CHAPTER TWO:

"The One Thing Needful"

Charles Wesley is most famous for his composition of many fine hymns. Recent research suggests that he wrote over nine thousand hymns and sacred poems, though fewer than half that number were published in his lifetime.[1] It was John Wesley, however, who began the Methodist hymnological tradition. He described the beginnings of the Methodist hymnbooks—from the distance of half a century—in his standard sermon no. 108, "On Knowing Christ After the Flesh":

> It was between fifty and sixty years ago that, by the gracious providence of God, my brother and I in our voyage to America, became acquainted with (so called) Moravian Brethren; we quickly took knowledge of what spirit they were of. . . . We were not only contracted by much esteem but a strong affection, for them. Everyday we conversed with them, and consulted them on all occasions. I translated many of their hymns, for the use of our own congregations (*J.W. Works*, 7:293).

Those translations from the German, along with a few adaptations of English hymns by Isaac Watts and George Herbert, appeared in John's *Charlestown Hymnbook* of

1737. As B. C. Drury observed, "It was John, not Charles, therefore, who started the eighteenth-century hymnodic revolution. Charles followed a path already marked out, and . . . John did his best to see that [Charles] followed it closely."[2]

The earliest Wesleyan hymnbooks, five in number, were either published jointly by John and Charles or under John's name alone; the *Charlestown Hymnbook* is noteworthy in this regard since it appears that Charles had no hand in it at all.[3] Thus, from 1737 through 1745, the Wesleys published a total of seven hymnals, and over seven hundred hymns, without any *clear* indication of which ones were composed by Charles. There is evidence, from the diary of Mrs. Olgethorpe (ca. 1735) and Charles's own manuscripts, that he was writing poetry on the American expedition.[4] The Wesleys' habit of not claiming authorship of any specific hymn has created what Frank Baker aptly terms "the vexed problem of joint authorship."[5] It seems that the brothers worked together on the hymnbooks. After their conversions in May 1738, Charles took over the creative side of the enterprise and John assumed an editorial role. John's editorial control altered Charles's hymns in significant ways, so that the hymns published up to 1749 were a synthesis of the talents of both of the Wesleys.[6]

Since there is no clear ascription of authorship for the hymns in those early hymnals, we shall attribute only those hymns to Charles that can be linked to him through his journal, sermons, or letters. Although this approach restricts the number of pre-1749 hymns that we may use to discover Charles Wesley's theology, it does guarantee that we are reading Charles's hymns (and not John's) in order to examine his theology. This method avoids an earlier—and I think haphazard—process of identification that merely assumed that John made all the translations, and assigned all of the original compositions to Charles. It is now clear that Charles made a few of the translations from German hymns and that John Wesley authored a few of the original compositions.[7]

With the appearance of Charles's *Hymns and Sacred Poems* in two volumes (1749), the process of identifying the author of the Wesleyan hymns became easier. Charles was now publishing his own hymnals, and John Wesley—displeased with some of the contents of the 1749 book—lamented not having a chance to exercise his editorial prerogatives: "As I did not see these before they were published, there were some things in them I did not approve of" (*J.W. Works*, 11:391).

Charles's *Hymns and Sacred Poems* of 1749 was his bride-price hymnal. It was hastily constructed out of his notebooks in order to raise the £100 necessary to convince the mother of lovely Sarah Gwynne that this young Methodist preacher had sufficient financial resources for the support of a wife (*C.W. Journal*, 2:50–51). With the exception of the 1780 *Collection of Hymns for the Use of the People Called Methodists*, edited by John Wesley, all of the Wesleyan hymns published after 1749 were the work of Charles.[8] The solution to "the vexed problem of joint authorship" focuses our attention not only on the 5,100 published and over 1,200 unpublished later hymns (post-1749) that can assuredly be attributed to Charles Wesley but also on nearly half a hundred published hymns of pre-1749 vintage that can historically be traced to his hand. This "assured collection" of hymns provides a solid foundation for our inquiry into Charles's theology of sanctification.

Charles's hymns were religious poetry, and generally they were poetry of superior quality; but it was their message that mattered most to him. James Dale summarized Wesley's use of the vehicle of poetry in this way: "The hymns say something, and thereby participate in the character of a poetry which stressed the primacy of meaning."[9] Or again, Dale suggested that Charles's verse "is fundamentallly doctrinally concerned with the communication of ideas."[10]

We noted earlier the interesting statement that John Wesley made in *A Collection of Hymns for the Use of the People Called Methodists*: "It [the hymnal] is large enough to contain all the important truths of our most holy religion, whether *speculative* or *practical*; yea, to illustrate them all and to prove them both by Scripture and reason" (*J.W. Works*, 14:340).

That Charles's hymns were scriptural is beyond question; they were brimming with biblical words, phrases, allusions, and ideas. But John's inclusion of "reason" in this brief epistemology is a bit puzzling. Rattenbury felt this same incongruity: "Why he wrote 'reason' is hardly clear; . . . Perhaps John meant that the Scripture phrases out of which the hymns were woven were, in themselves, reasons. However that may be, he rightly claimed in his defense of the hymns, 'we speak common sense, whether in prose or verse.'[11] It might further be suggested that "reason" here refers to the logical, coherent, and flowing development that Charles gave biblical words, images, and ideas in his hymns. John perhaps meant that the hymns were "reasonable" in contrast to haphazard or disorderly, or as opposed to "enthusiastic" (which in eighteenth-century parlance meant witless religious fanaticism or rampant emotionalism).

Charles's hymns were both conceived and applied as theological pieces; in an age of cold, formal, establishment religion, the hymns vivified biblical doctrine with religious experience and put basic Christian teaching on the lips and hearts of the common folk of England. As Rattenbury has written, Charles's "verses were a popular instrument for fixing the doctrines of the revival in the minds of men as nothing could, but they were not formed theological documents, but heart felt songs of personally expressed doctrine and aspiration."[12]

BASIC DOCTRINES

Charles's hymns tended to stay close to the basic doctrines of the Christian faith, emphasizing the "practical" more than the "speculative" issues. In this sense, he was an essentialist, preferring to stress the saving death of

Christ and its meaning for those who believe through justification and sanctification by faith. And while it is apparent to the careful reader that these sacred poems were written by a trained classicist and theologian, it is also clear that Wesley preferred to emphasize the main themes of the Bible—important doctrines, such as sin and salvation, and significant metaphors, such as "sleeping" and being "awakened" from that deadly slumber.

Charles Wesley often began his poetic presentations of the doctrine of redemption by first pointing his readers to the dire situation in which they found themselves. Apart from God's grace, they were dead in their trespasses; their sin cut them off from a saving relationship with their God and Father. Wesley's basic definition of sin was rather traditional; he often described sin by using traditional theological terms such as *concupiscence* and *pride*.[13] Both terms refer to that inner sense of rebellion that causes one to make self the center of one's universe, rather than give God His proper glory and place in one's life. Charles also used rather unflattering words to describe those who were not seeking and, therefore, not finding redemption; one of his favorite designations for those lost in their sin was *worms* (*P.W.*, 5:2, 18, 20, 23, 56, 77, 81, 112, 185, 223, 413). This phraseology, framed perhaps on the pattern of Job 25:6 or Psalm 22:6, was the language of self-deprecation. It was Wesley's way of pointing out—graphically—the true state of the sinner, of reminding the singer that a person's best efforts or finest qualities are nothing but "filthy rags" apart from God's grace. The evangelist's intention in this drastic description was to strip one of pride or self-reliance in order to cause one to rely solely upon Christ.

Charles also occasionally defined sin as the loss of original righteousness (*P.W.*, 12:86–87). His intention in this connection was to press for a return to the state of perfection that was lost in the Edenic fall into sin. The counterpoint to this sinful state was the restitution of the *imago Dei* (image of God) within the Christian.[14] On other occasions Charles emphasized the volitional aspect of human sin:

> Loved for a time, they might have been
>   For ever loved by Thee:
> Nothing can separate but sin
>   Betwixt my God and me:
> From sin, from *wilful sin* alone,
>   Saviour, my soul defend,
> And Thou who freely lov'st Thine own,
>   Shalt love me to the end.
>
> (*P.W.*, 10:78, no. 1443, italics added)

Charles's stress upon the willful nature of sin was standard Wesleyan doctrine. John Wesley also taught it:

> By sin, I here understand outward sin, according to the plain common acceptation of the words; *an actual voluntary transgression of the law*; of the revealed, written law of God; of any commandment of God, acknowledged to be such at the time it is transgressed [italics added].[15]

For both Wesleys, sin was a problem of the human will; it involved an inward rebellion and a knowledgeable transgression. Hence, sin "properly speaking" (*J.W. Letters*, 5:341, 322, 255) was never a matter of human finitude or sheer ignorance; it was always and primarily a problem of a bent or corrupted will. Since this conception emphasized sin as a willful or voluntary transgression, both Wesleys believed that sin implied gross irresponsibility on the part of the sinner.

It was this same emphasis upon the volitional character of sin that caused the Wesleys to develop their doctrine of sanctification in connection with texts such as 1 John 3:9, "Whosoever is born of God doth not commit sin."[16] If we are to think of sin in terms of mere creatureliness or finitude, then it cannot be overcome in this life. If, however, sin is considered to be a problem of the human will, then a complete renovation of the will should result in sinlessness—it would bring a cessation of willful sin. Thus, the Wesleys' emphasis on the volitional nature of sin formed an important connection with their conception of Christian perfection. John made this point clearly in his sermon entitled "The Privilege of the Children of God":

'Whosoever is born of God,' while he abideth in faith
and in the spirit of prayer and thanksgiving, not only
doth not, but cannot thus commit sins. So long as he
thus believeth in God through Christ, and love him,
and is pouring out his heart before him, he cannot
voluntarily transgress any command of God, either by
speaking or acting what he knows God hath forbidden
(*J.W. Sermons*, p. 185).

Charles's homily, "The Single Eye" (discussed below), carried this same sort of emphasis. The title-phrase
was a euphemism for "singleness of intention," or unmixed
and undivided motives about doing God's will. So long as
one's will (or "eye") was "single," a person would
"improve in his [God's] ways of holiness, in the love of
God, and of thy neighbour, so long shalt thou clearly
perceived what is conducive to it" (*C.W. Sermons*, p. 128).
Contrariwise, "no sooner shalt thou divide thy heart, and
aim at any other end but holiness, than the light from
which thou turnest away being withdrawn, thou shalt not
know whither thou goest: ignorance, sin and misery, shall
overspread thee, till thou fallest into utter darkness" (*C.W.
Sermons*, pp. 128–29). In John's sermon, the "privilege" of
the children of God was sinlessness—defined in this
volitional sense—which belonged to the person who was
"pouring out his heart before God." Its corollary in
Charles's "Single Eye" was a "singleness of intention,"
which created an inner conformity with the divine will. In
both instances, sanctification meant a radical renovation in
the volitional center of a person, and a change of heart and
will that unified heart and will so that willful transgression
became unthinkable. An undivided intention meant "holiness," whereas divided loyalties brought "ignorance, sin,
and misery."

Another important metaphor that Charles Wesley
used to explain his concept of sin was to liken it to dirt or
impurity, which was then to be cleansed or washed away.
Generally, this cleansing process was accomplished by
"Jesus' blood" (*P.W.*, 5:242, 243, 273; 13:178, no.
3361).[17] This imagery graphically communicates the way in

which faith in Jesus' saving death purifies a person of all
unrighteousness:

> I want the gospel purity,
>   Th' implanted righteousness of God;
> Jesus reveal thyself to me,
>   And wash me in thy hallowing blood;
> Enter, thyself and cast out sin,
>   Thy nature spread thro' every part,
> And nothing common or unclean,
>   Shall ever more pollute my heart.[18]

Charles also explained his doctrine of sin by parallel-
ing it with illness or disease. Salvation was then allegorically described as the cure of that same sickness: "Thou shalt
cleanse me from all sin, / And all my sickness cure" (*P.W.*,
2:158, "The Good Samaritan"). In this, as in the previous
metaphors, the utter seriousness of sin is emphasized in a
way that points quite naturally to its remedy.

Wesley strongly emphasized the doctrine of original
sin, and he had a colorful collection of clichés for
describing it. It was "the sinful nature," "my bosom sin,"
"inbred sin," or "inbred stains" (*P.W.*, 5:48; 7:13; 10:3,
13, 82, 83; 12:89, 90). In each case, the emphasis fell upon
the inward element of the sinful nature; yet, Charles saw no
permanent distinction between original "sin" and actual or
personal "sins." The former led immediately and invariably to the latter. Thus he wrote: "For my double sin I
grieve" (*P.W.*, 10:3, no. 1272; 5:48, no. 41). And while
Wesley was quite concerned to explain Christ's blood
washing his sins away (*P.W.*, 4:273–74, no. 49), his focus
was upon the renewal of the inner, sinful nature. His
conception of redemption was wholistic; both the actual
and original aspects of sin were taken together, both were
remedied in his soteriology. Salvation, to use Charles's
words, was "full" or "complete salvation"; it meant
salvation from both the "guilt and power of sin" (*P.W.*,
12:152, no. 2389). The effects of this redemptive process
were described as "canceling" past sin and "breaking the
chains of sin."[19] Redemption's final result was "perfect
love":

Jesus, the first and last,
  On Thee my soul is cast:
Thou didst Thy work begin
  By blotting out my sin:
Thou wilt the root remove,
  And *perfect* me in *love.*
           (*P.W.*, 13:221, no. 3445, italics added)

The same sanctifying process could also be explained as salvation from "inbred sin" and its effects, along with a corresponding visitation by God's Spirit. As Charles wrote:

Thy blood can save from inbred sin
  And make my leprous nature clean:
If Thou Thy Spirit impart,
  Anger, concupiscence, and pride
Shall never with Thy Spirit reside,
  Or lodge within my heart.

No evil thought shall there remain,
  Pass through Thy temple, or profane
The place of Thy abode,
  (Where all Thy glory is reveal'd,)
With the majestic presence fill'd
  Of an indwelling God.
           (*P.W.*, 10:13, no. 1292)

Charles Wesley took sin seriously. His theology of redemption was grounded in a rigorous affirmation of the reality of human sin, both in its original and actual aspects. He expressed this conviction about sin in colorful and dramatic imagery that was designed to strip off layers of pride and self-centeredness and to cast the reader or singer wholeheartedly upon Christ. Charles Wesley's soteriological optimism in propounding a theology of "full salvation" or Christian perfection was an optimism not about human nature per se but about God's grace and redemptive power.

Quite naturally, terms such as *saved* and *salvation* figured largely in Charles Wesley's hymns. In the later hymns alone, words from this etymological family occurred over six hundred and forty times! The biblical heritage of these terms is a rich one. The Hebrew word *YSHA* meant "to enlarge," "to be or make more spacious, roomy, or broad"; hence, the word also came to carry connotations of "deliverance," since it clearly implied the opposite of "confinement."[20] Since in its secular application this deliverance from confinement was legally secured through the payment of a redemption or ransom price, the Hebrew words for *ransom, deliverance, redemption,* and *salvation* became synonymous. The Old Testament uses these terms to refer as readily to spiritual as physical deliverances; the secular and religious connotations are tightly woven together in a way that anticipates and is supportive of the Wesleys' notion of the "full redemption" touching all avenues of life. The Greek equivalent for *YSHA* is most often found in words of the *sōzō* family. The idea of "save/salvation" communicates both physical and theological connotations; hence, *sōzō* can easily describe the saving of physical life, as in Paul's shipwreck (Acts 27:30f.), as well as apply to the theological sense of saving someone from sin, death, and judgment.[21]

Charles Wesley followed the biblical application of these salvation words with the eye of an Oxford linguist. He occasionally paralleled the word *save* with *deliverance,* as a way of elaborating the meaning of both terms (*P.W.,* 10:102, no. 1508); on other occasions, he paired these *sōzō* terms with *atonement*[22] or "redemption" (*P.W.,* 5:142, no. 1). Frequently, the word *salvation* was attached to perfectionist ideas, and extended into the idea of full salvation or being saved to the uttermost (*P.W.,* 4:135, no. 5; 4:138, no. 7; 10:131, no. 1595; 11:384, no. 1764; 11:425, no. 1861; 12:89, no. 2262; 13:191). Both phrases evidenced Charles's wholistic and integrating tendencies in approaching the doctrine of redemption. He sought to merge so completely justification (Christ *for* us) and sanctification (Christ *in* us) that these two categories became inseparable. He taught that salvation meant being "saved *from*" something—generally, in his view, salvation *from* sin:

> Salvation to our souls brought in,
>   Salvation from our guilty stains,
> Salvation from the power of sin,
>   Salvation from its last remains.
>   (*P.W.,* 4:285)[23]

Occasionally, Wesley elaborated the word *sin* as being original sin ("bosom sin") or sin in its totality, as when he described freedom "From the guilt and power of sin" (*P.W.*, 4:310; 4:373; 12:152, no. 2389; 13:22–23). Often Wesley used the word *salvation* to mean being saved from death (*P.W.*, 11:363, 481) or "from hell" (*P.W.*, 12:21, 321). In other instances, *salvation* referred to salvation "from the wrath of God" (*P.W.*, 4:157, no. 4; 4:321, no. 2740). Stated negatively, *salvation* meant deliverance from the "tyrants" of sin, death, and hell:

> Jesus from Thee I surely know
>   The streams of full salvation flow,
> Confiding in Thy death posess
>   The pardon and the holiness,
> The double life Thy wounds impart,
>   The peace and purity of heart.
>   (*P.W.*, 12:89, no. 2262; 9:439, no. 1205)

Charles Wesley's understanding of salvation yet shows remarkable symmetry. He maintained the biblical emphasis upon a salvation that can be stated positively as well as negatively. On the positive side of the equation, Charles believed that salvation means being saved *for* complete renovation. *Salvation* in this sense means always straining toward "full salvation." It leads directly to the renewal of the *imago Dei* within a person.

A similar balance is evident in Charles's presentation of the timing of this salvation. He said that salvation, while being rooted in the past reality of the Christ event, is also a present reality; a Christian is "Saved from the present guilt," or "in me reveal the grace / Which present sure salvation brings" (*P.W.*, 2:321, no. 2740; 7:226, no. 34).

THE WESLEYS' SERMONS

In addition to Charles's hymns, a rather sketchy published journal, a number of his letters, and a few published sermons have also survived; each of these contributes significantly to our understanding of the man and his search for sanctification. The only published collection of his sermons appeared in 1816, long after his death. Of the thirteen sermons included in that collection, Charles's journal records only three of them as actually being preached by him.[24] The unsigned editor of the 1816 collection of sermons (probably Charles's wife) gave an accurate description of the setting of those homilies: "Most of these sermons were delivered in his early youth, when he was in America: the thirteenth sermon, by the Rev. John Wesley, was never published amongst his works" (*C.W. Sermons*, p. xxxiv).

Richard Heitzenrater has concluded that all thirteen of these sermons published under Charles's name in the 1816 edition were actually written by John Wesley.[25] This suggestion seems startling at first glance, but it is nonetheless clear that Heitzenrater is correct. The editor of the 1816 collection, perhaps not entirely familiar with Dr. Byrom's complicated system of shorthand (which Charles used), misread a note on the manuscript: "Transcribed from my brother's copies."[26]

While the modern reader might wonder why a preacher-scholar the caliber of Charles Wesley would use his brother's sermons, it has become increasingly apparent that the eighteenth-century writers had few of our contemporary compunctions about plagiarism. In fact, we can often detect the Wesleys' borrowing from other writers. This is apparent in John's abridged versions of Christian classics in his *Christian Library,* and it also emerged subtly in the brothers' hymns and sermons.[27] Their hymns borrowed from the German Moravian hymnbooks, the Anglican writer George Herbert, and a host of other authors both ancient and contemporary, religious and secular.[28] Charles's journal admits that he used John's sermons. The entry for June 21, 1738, nearly a month after Charles's conversion, reports an approach to preaching that might seem surprising from a Methodist evangelist: "I read my brother's sermon on faith" (*C.W. Journal*, 1:97). In those days, material in the public domain was precisely that: It belonged to anyone who cared to compliment the author through the generous application of his or her ideas, and so much more the case when the source was borrowed for the propagation of the gospel of Christ. It was in this same sense that Henry Bett described the Wesleys as "great plagiarists," though "in an honorable sense."[29]

The Wesleys' life situation in early 1736 also aids our understanding of this curious interconnection in their sermons. Having been ordained scarcely a month before leaving for America, Charles probably had not preached or written a sermon prior to embarking; and he spent much time during the Atlantic crossing working on his homiletical storehouse (*J.W. Journal*, 1:112-13). It was quite natural for him to rely on the work of his older brother—who had been preaching regularly for almost ten years. Charles continued to rely on John's compositions, though not exclusively so, even after they returned to England.

That Charles Wesley did not compose these early sermons preached in America and in the first years of his ministry, and eventually published in the 1816 collection, does not devalue them as resources for studying his theology. The sermons became Charles's through his preaching of them. Probably he preached all thirteen sermons carried in the early collection, and almost certainly he preached three sermons mentioned repeatedly in his journal. Two of those provide particularly important insights into his early theology of sanctification.

Charles's first (surviving) public presentation of his views on sanctification appeared in the early sermon entitled "The One Thing Needful." The sermon was first reported to have been preached in Boston on September 26, 1736, and it was later used on both sides of the Atlantic (*C.W. Journal*, 1:45). It describes the restoration of "the image of God in man" (*imago Dei*) as that "One Thing Needful." The goal of salvation is the undoing of the effects of the Fall into sin: "the likeness of our destroyer'—i.e., Satan—must be erased and we must be remade "anew after the likeness of our Creator" (*C.W. Sermons*, p. 86). Creation and redemption are tightly woven together; in one panoramic sweep, Wesley's thought moves from paradisaical perfection, through the Fall into sin, and back again toward re-creation of that original divine likeness.

While Charles Wesley gave us no clue for the source of his approach to sanctification, nor is it apparent from his sermon text in Luke 10:42, the connection of creation and redemption is well supported in Paul's "two Adams" schema (Rom. 5; 1 Cor. 15). But it is clear that Charles used this theme of re-creation as the basic structural device for his theology of redemption. He took justification and sanctification together as two moments in God's strategy to counteract the effects of Eden's Fall; and his approach to the theology of redemption bears a striking resemblance to what the Eastern church fathers called "recapitulation."

The concept of recapitulation is generally traced to roots in the writings of Irenaeus (d. 198?) and through him to other important fathers of the Eastern church such as Athanasius, Clement of Alexandria, and John Chrysostom. It emphasized Christian perfection through love; devotional piety; a robust reliance upon Word, Spirit, and sacrament; and other means that would have been attractive to Wesley. Like Charles, Irenaeus began his theology of redemption with the need to recreate the righteousness of Adam through the restoration of the *imago Dei*. This re-creation was the goal of Christ's coming into the world:

> For never at any time did Adam escape the hands of God to whom the Father speaking said, 'Let us make man in our image, after our likeness.' And for this reason in the last times, not by the will of the flesh, nor by the will of man, but by the good pleasure of the Father, His hands formed a living Man, in order that Adam *might be created after the image and likeness of God.*[31]

The Pauline pairing of the first and second Adams may have been Irenaeus's fulcrum, but the force of his theology of redemption was to be found in the restoration of the image of God or the image of Christ within the Christian: "But following the only true and steadfast Teacher, the Word of God, our Lord Jesus Christ, Who did, through His transcendent love, become what we are *that he might bring us to be what he is himself.*"[32] According to the great church father, Christ became a human being to enable people to become what He Himself is. This simple yet daring idea was not lost upon Charles Wesley; it became the centerpole of his theology.

Albert Outler in his classic study, *John Wesley*, has pointed to John's dependence upon the writers of Eastern Christianity as he developed and articulated his doctrine of sanctification or Christian perfection:

> What fascinated him in these men was their description of 'perfection' (*teleiowsis*) as the goal (*skopos*) of the Christian life. Their concept of perfection as a process rather than a state gave [John] Wesley a spiritual vision quite different from the static perfectionism envisaged in Roman spiritual theology of the period, and the equally static quietism of those Protestants and Catholics whom he deplored as 'the mystics.' . . . Thus it was that the ancient and Eastern tradition of holiness as *disciplined* love became infused in Wesley's mind with his own Anglican tradition of holiness as *aspiring* love, and thereafter was developed in what he regarded to the end of his life as his own most distinctive contribution.[33]

The influence of the Eastern fathers can easily be traced through John's writings, and it gave his conception of sanctification a depth and vitality that was lacking in writers like Taylor, Scougal, and Law. But this connection with the patristic past cannot be demonstrated directly from Charles Wesley's writings. His journals and letters make few direct references to his reading habits or the sources of his ideas. While Irenaeus must have been included in the Wesleys' curriculum for the Oxford M.A. in classics, that fact cannot be clearly proved. It is clear, however, that reminiscences and echoes of most of the major (and a few of the minor) church fathers emerge in Charles's hymns and journal.[34] It further seems that this patristic concept of redemption was replicated in Charles Wesley's soteriology. His approach was thoroughly anchored in his basic theological concern for the restoration of original righteousness as the "one thing needful" in those who trusted Christ.

A close examination of "The One Thing Needful" confirms that it was composed in early years of the Wesleys' ministry, because it has a different character from the sermons Charles Wesley preached after his conversion in 1738. Its style is decidedly formal, and the presentation follows the standard two-point homiletical formula common to that period. Charles began by explaining his intended approach: "It cannot . . . be an improper employment, First to observe what this one thing is; and secondary to consider a few of the various reasons that prove this to be the One Thing Needful" (*J.W. Works*, 4:27–37). Absent from this sermon are those long chains of Bible words, phrases, and images that dominated his later preaching. Missing too are the excitement and the vivid imagery of a Methodist evangelist; even Charles's more formal, later sermons (such as "Awake Thou That Sleepest") were peppered with exclamation points.

The answer to Charles's first rhetorical question ("what this *One Thing Needful* is") opened the door to a characteristically Wesleyan theme—inward renewal.

> To recover our first estate from which we are fallen is *the one thing needful*: to re-exchange the image of Satan for the image of God, bondage for freedom, sickness for health! Our one great business is to erase out of our souls the likeness of our destroyer, and to be born again, to be formed anew after the likeness of our Creator (*C.W. Sermons*, p. 86, italics added).

This message would become a familiar one, but the method would not. Restoration of the image of God within us was one of Charles's most constant themes, carried over into his later hymns and sermons; but the mature Charles Wesley would always insist that justification by faith must precede a "full salvation" or sanctification. This sermon seems to reflect the early days when Wesley was confused about the order of salvation. The early Charles Wesley looked for sanctification or inward piety as a way toward justification or acceptance before God; but his postconversion writings reversed this order, placing justification prior to sanctification.

In "The One Thing Needful," Charles's approach was strongly moralistic. He called for inner renewal but not for salvation. The reader or hearer of this sermon could easily conclude that the re-creation proclaimed in the sermon could be caused or attained by one's own inner resources. Thus, the early Charles Wesley seemed to expound sanctification as renewal of the divine image (*imago Dei*) within a person, and yet Charles explained it in a way that was more like his mentor William Law than the later preacher of the Wesleyan revival.

Using the metaphor of healing (which would later become a standard theme in his hymns), he wrote: "The one work we have to do is to return from the gates of death, to have our diseases cured, our wounds healed, and ourselves restored to *perfect soundness*" (*C.W. Sermons*, p. 86, italics added).

His hymns often associated purity or inner cleansing with healing imagery. His poetic exposition of the parable of the Good Samaritan is a fine example of this usage; in that instance, Charles turned the parable into a description of the process of redemption. The biblical account became our own saving event. A Christian is the wounded traveler, healed by the care of the Good Samaritan (Christ), and his complete recovery results in "healing" from the "mortal wound" of Adam's sin:

> 11. Perfect then the work begun,
>   And make the sinner whole;
> All Thy will on me be done,
>   My body, spirit, soul.
> Still preserve me safe from harms,
>   And kindly for Thy patient care;
> Take me, Jesu, to Thine arms,
>   And keep me ever there.[35]

"The One Thing Needful" was still preached after Charles's conversion in May 17–21, 1738 (*C.W. Journal*, 1:80–92). The last recorded use of the sermon is found in Wesley's journal entry for Sunday, October 15, 1738. Charles indicated that first he read "One Thing Needful" several times, then later preached it at Islington and

"added much extempore" (*C.W. Journal*, 1:132). While we
have no way of knowing exactly what was "added extempo-
rae," one might conjecture that the additions brought the
earlier written sermon into harmony with the perspective
Charles learned through his conversion, with his new
conception of Christ as One to be received by personal faith
as "Christ *for me*" (*C.W. Journal*, 1:88).

A second sermon from the 1816 collection, "The
Single Eye,"[36] returned to this same foundational theme:
"If thou aimest at any thing but *the one thing needful*,
namely a recovery of the image of God in thy soul, thy
whole body shall be full of darkness" (*C.W. Sermons*, pp.
127–28, italics added). Once again, the published homily
(no. 8 in the collection) was much more formal than the
fluid expositions of the revival. The preconversion character of Charles's sermon is evident even when compared to
John Wesley's published exposition of the same passage
(Matt. 6:22–23). John's later sermon is more of a line-by-
line exposition of the passage than a rhetorically tailored,
two-point homily. Likewise, the John Wesley sermon on
"The Single Eye" is a mosaic of Bible words and phrases,
an aspect noticeably absent from this earlier rendition
preached by Charles.

The sermon found in Charles's 1816 collection followed the same two-step pattern observed in "The One
Thing Needful": The preacher sought first to explain the
passage and then to apply it. The theme of the sermon was
inward renewal, but this time focusing squarely on the
matter of purity of intention:

> Every thing that proceeds from, and is suitable to,
> this intention, is holy, just and good; and every thing
> which does not proceed from an upright and single
> eye is so far evil and unholy (*C.W. Sermons*,
> p. 130).[37]

The sermon began with an invitation to introspection:
"Consider well what ought to be your conduct; now choose
whether you will serve God or not: but consider that if you
do serve him, you must do it with all your mind; . . . either

you must give to God your whole heart, or none. He cannot, will not, have a divided heart" (*C.W. Sermons*, p. 125–26). "The Single Eye" became a synonym for unqualified commitment, a wholehearted dedication to God; and wholeheartedness would produce intentions and motives that are not divided between God and self, or between God and mammon.

Charles described the "single eye" as a life of holiness and love:

> The sum is this: as long as thou hast but one end in all thy thoughts, and words, and actions, to please God, or, which is the same thing, to improve in His ways of holiness, in the love of God, and of thy neighbour, so long shalt thou clearly perceive what is conducive to it. Thy God, whom thou servest, shall so tenderly watch over thee, that light, and love, and peace, shall guide all thy ways, and shine upon all thy paths (*C.W. Sermons*, p. 128).

The converse of this "single eye" is a divided heart, and Wesley warned of its results: "But no sooner shalt thou divide thy heart, and aim at any other end but holiness, than the light from which thou turnest away being withdrawn, thou shalt not know whither thou goest; ignorance, sin and misery, shall over-spread thee, till thou fallest into utter darkness." The theme was standard Wesley—for both John and Charles—and they would later call it "inward and outward holiness"; but this early manner of handling the theme would not be vintage Wesley. Absent from Charles's sermon was any clear mention of justification or sanctification by faith in Christ alone; the invitation to holiness was clear, but its evangelical foundation had not yet been realized.

A careful consideration of Charles's Oxford years and early preaching establishes several matters that are important for the balance of our study. First, it is clear that Charles Wesley was vitally concerned about holiness or sanctification from the outset of his second year at Oxford; his hungering and thirsting after righteousness was contagious, and soon others joined him in his quest. His earliest (extant) sermons located this same theological concern at the foundation and center of his proclamation, and that emphasis would remain with him always. Second, Charles preferred to explain sanctification as a restoration of the image of God within a person, an obvious and seemingly complete reversal of the effects of Eden's Fall; this pattern continued into his later sermons such as "Awake Thou That Sleepest" (*J.W. Works*, 5:27). And finally, Charles's replication of the Eastern fathers' conception of sanctification caused him to consider salvation in its fullest context; even in these earliest sermons, he equated "born again" with the restoration of the *imago Dei* within. In his mind, the word *salvation* implied a "full salvation" that was larger than justification or a new relationship with God. It meant nothing less than a restoration of paradisaical righteousness, or a creation of the mind of Christ within the Christian. Charles's radical insistence upon this "One Thing Needful" brought an emphasis that distinguished Wesleyan theology. It was also an indication of the beginning of a theological development that would eventually distinguish Charles's understanding of sanctification even from that of his brother John.

CHAPTER THREE:

"Freely Justified"

Charles Wesley's conversion in May 1738 began in him a tidal wave of spiritual energy and activity. As spring became summer, he began to recover from the serious illness that had kept him bedridden most of that year. As strength returned, he began "to inculcate the doctrine of present salvation by faith . . . " (*C.W. Journal*, 1:98).

His ministerial efforts began simply enough, as Charles told his friends of his recovery from illness and connected it with the arrival of his newfound faith. His journal entry for June 10, less than three weeks after his conversion, shows him involved in Christian conversation and the cure of souls. Mr. Piers, an Anglican cleric, and his wife visited Charles and soon became targets of personal evangelism. Along with John Bray, a Moravian mechanic who had been instrumental in Charles's own conversion, Wesley used the account of the paralytic (Luke 5:23–25) to press Piers regarding faith:

> In the morning lesson was that glorious description of
> the power of faith: 'Jesus answering said unto them,
> Have faith in God. For verily I say unto you, That
> whosoever shall say unto this mountain, Be thou
> removed, and be thou cast into the sea; and shall not

doubt in his heart, but shall believe that those things which he saith shall come to pass; he shall have whatsoever he saith. Therefore I say unto you, What things soever ye desire, when ye pray, believe that ye receive them, and ye shall have them.' We pleaded this promise in behalf of our friends, particularly [Charles's sister] Hetty and Mr. Piers. . . . The day before our coming he had been led to read the Homily on Justification, which convinced him that in him dwelt no good thing. Now he likewise saw that the thoughts of his heart were only evil continually, forasmuch as whatsoever is not of faith is sin.

He asked God to give him some comfort, and found it in Luke 5:23, &c.: 'Whether it is easier to say, Thy sins be forgiven thee, or to say, Rise up and walk? But that ye may know that the Son of Man hath power upon earth to forgive sins, (he saith unto the sick of the palsy,) I say unto thee, Arise, and take up thy bed, and go unto thine own house. And immediately he rose up before them, and took up that whereon he lay, and departed to his own house, glorifying God. And they were all amazed, and they glorified God, and were filled with fear, saying, We have seen strange things to-day.'

This was the very miracle, I told him, from which God had shown his intention to heal me; and it was a sign of the like to be done by him. Mr. Bray moved for retiring to prayer. We prayed *after God*, again and again, and asked [Piers], whether he believed Christ could just now manifest himself to his soul. He answered, 'Yes.' . . .

Seeing the great confidence of Mr. Bray and the deep humility of Mr. Piers, I began to think the promise would be fulfilled before we left the room. My fellow-worker with God [Bray] seemed full of faith and the Holy Ghost, and told [Piers], 'If you can but touch the hem of His garment, you shall be made whole.' We prayed for him a third time, the Spirit greatly helping our infirmities, and then asked if he believed. He answered, 'Yes.' The Spirit witnessed

> with our spirits, that his heart was as our heart. . . .
> We were all filled with joy; returned thanks, and
> prayed for a blessing on his ministry; and then
> brought him down in triumph. Miss Betsy was
> greatly strengthed hereby, and bold to confess 'she
> believed.' All her speech now was, 'I only hope that I
> shall never lose this comfort.'

The incident was typical of Charles's early ministry; his
days were full of Christian conversation and personal
evangelism. He began to witness and pray with seekers
after Christ long before he addressed multitudes with a
similar message. Several important themes emerged in this
earliest encounter which would become theological constants in Charles's evangelism: First, Charles's application
of the Luke 5:23 text suggests his willingness to connect a
person's inner and outer life in wholeness and equilibrium;
a similar hint is found in his willingness to understand his
recovery from illness as an acted parable of his reception of
faith. Second, in Piers's conversion account we detect a
meeting of several important religious resources: Scripture,
tradition (the Anglican homily), experience (the repeated
emphasis upon a sense of comfort accompanying the
reception of saving faith), and practical piety (as seen in
prayer and other personal religious disciplines). Each of
these emphases continued and was enhanced throughout
Charles's ministerial endeavors.

JUSTIFICATION

Charles Wesley's understanding of justification was
built upon his knowledge of the etymology of the biblical
terms used to describe it and their biblical application.
While Wesley recognized that the heritage of the word
justification (and related terms) lay in law court imagery, he
looked beyond a merely legal, forensic, or outward understanding of justice or justification. For Charles, *justification*
implied more than a judge's decree of pardon or a change of
status that did not touch the inward life of a person. The
biblical usage seemed to suggest no formal distinction

between the inward and outward dimensions of the doctrine. It had wholistic connotations of being "put right," which suggested that one's relationship with God and one's inner state were both undergoing renovation. Since the same biblical terms could be translated either *justification* or *righteousness*, Charles's development of the doctrine stood on solid ground; yet it pushed beyond static categories to the excitement of inner renewal.

Charles regularly turned to justification as a sermon topic. In fact, he wrote that it was his favorite subject: "I rode with Deschamps to Publow, where I preached from 'God so loved the world.' I spake with great boldness on my favorite subject, justification by faith only; and triumphed in the irresistible force of that everlasting love" (*C.W. Journal*, 1:169). His journal is filled with references to preaching justification, certainly a subject suitable for an evangelist. But Charles Wesley's hymns studiously avoided the terms *justify* and *justification*; those words appeared only forty-five times in the five thousand hymns designated for our study, whereas Charles's nineteen surviving sermons apply these same theological terms nearly two hundred times! This startling contrast has its basis not in differing doctrines in the hymns and sermons, but in the tendency of his hymns to depict the experience of a doctrine instead of analyzing it. Charles's hymns were full of action words; they utilized a graphic, sensate, imaging approach to theology and studiously avoided static conceptual words.

Charles's journal entry for Monday, September 17, 1739 suggests that in his theological vocabulary *justification* had become a synonym for instantaneous conversion:

> This afternoon, I conferred with Tomas Tucker and Eliz. Shindock, both clearly justified. Matthew Davis, a notorious drunkard, ie., till last Saturday was se'n nigh, come then to the green [where Charles was preaching], and was justified *in a moment* (*C.W. Journal*, 1:91, italics added).

This was a marked departure from Charles's preconversion concept of the doctrine. One month prior to his spiritual awakening of May 1738, when Charles and John Wesley had a heated discussion about whether conversion was instantaneous, Charles insisted that it was *not*:

> We sang, and fell into a dispute whether conversion was gradual or instantaneous. My brother was very positive for the latter, and very shockingly; mentioned some late instances of gross sinners believing in a moment. I was much offended at his worse than unedifying discourse. Mrs. Delamotte left us abruptly. I stayed, and insisted a man need not know when first he had faith. His obstinacy in favouring the contrary opinion drove me at last out of the room (*C.W. Journal*, 1:84–85).

If May of 1738 made instantaneous conversion a theological option for Charles, it was also a sort of watershed in his repudiation of William Law's soteriological schema. September of 1737 finds him recommending Law's writings on redemption as an accurate and useful pattern (*C.W. Journal*, 1:75, 80). But by October 19, 1739, Wesley's attitude toward the oracle of Putney had changed:

> I read part of Mr. Law on Regeneration to our Society. How promising the beginning! How lame the conclusion! *Sensi hominem!* Christianity, he rightly tells us, is a recovery of the divine image; . . . After this, he supposes it possible for him to be insensible to such a change; to be happy and holy, translated to Eden, renewed in the likeness of God, one with Father, Son and Holy Ghost, and yet not know it. Nay, we are not to expect any such consciousness, if we listen to one who too plainly demonstrates, by this wretched inconsistency, that his knowledge of the new birth is mostly in theory (*C.W. Journal*, 1:191).

Charles's break with Law was based in the latter's tendency to emphasize perfection as the path toward, rather than a fruit of, acceptance before God (justification). The increasing distance between Charles Wesley and William Law was symptomatic of Charles's growing appreciation for Pauline Christianity, as read through Martin

Luther's *Galatians Commentary*, with its emphasis upon "justification by faith alone" (*C.W. Journal*, 1:88). John Wesley trod a similar path away from his former mentor toward evangelical Anglicanism.[1] The brothers' conception of the "new birth" shows the lifelong effect the mystics and church fathers had upon them. For the Wesleys, as for Law, the new birth was more than a change of status before God; it was "a great work which God does *in us*, in renewing our fallen nature" (*J.W. Sermons*, p. 447). Yet, unlike Law, the Wesleys believed this change had clear experiential referent; it brought a sense of assurance, happiness, and holiness into the Christian's life.

Charles came close to giving a formal definition of justification in a manuscript sermon based on Luke 18:9. It was written in the complicated shorthand of Dr. Byrom and has only recently been discovered and transcribed.[2] Interacting with the Gospel passage, Wesley wrote: " 'I tell you, this man went down to his house justified, rather than the other.' *justified*, that is, *forgiven*, and *accounted righteous*."[3] It is clear that Charles sees the terms "forgiven" and "accounted righteous" as synonymous with *justification*. All of these redemption words maintain the legal or forensic imagery of the biblical term, which emphasizes a change in one's status before God: The guilty have been forgiven, God's enemies have been made children through faith in Christ, and those who have stood afar off are drawn near and made God's friends. This traditional legal element occasionally emerged in Charles's hymns, as in his poetic exposition of Abraham's call (Gen. 15:6):

> Father, in *Abraham's* steps I tread,
>   Receive Thine evangelic word,
> Who gav'st to suffer in my stead
>   Thine only Son, My God and Lord:
> The faith, which now I act on Thee,
>   Who didst again my Surety raise,
> Is counted righteous love,
>   And I am saved through Jesu's grace.
>   (*P.W.*, 9:17, no. 83)

Charles often made justification or "justification by faith only" the topic of his preaching, and he typically expounded that theme from classic passages such as Romans 3:23–24; 8:23; Galatians 2; and Isaiah 54 (*C.W. Journal*, 1:133, 144, 145, 178). He occasionally read the standard Anglican *Homily on Justification* to eager crowds and wove the church's soteriological standards into his own free-flowing expositions of justification from various biblical passages (*C.W. Journal*, 1:126).

The most complete (extant) example of Wesley's proclamation of justification by faith is found in his shorthand manuscript sermon based on Romans 3:23–24. Charles first preached the law and then he offered the gospel; he laid his listeners low by reminding them: "Every sinner deserves to be damned, every man is a sinner, therefore, every man deserves to be damned. Which of the promises can be denied without denying the Scriptures? 'The wages of sin are death; the wrath of God is revealed against all unrighteousness of men, and there is none righteous, no, not one.' The Scriptures hath concluded all under sin."[4] Because of the sinfulness of the human situation, justification is received "by faith only." Charles found this "offending doctrine," which refutes all attempts at self-salvation, not only in Scripture but also "in the words of our own excellent Church, as they are plainly set forth in the homilies." The "only" of Wesley's phraseology emphasizes that justification is the office of faith alone:

> Because all men are sinners and offenders against God, and breakers of His law and commandments, therefore can no man by his own acts, works or deeds, seem they ever so good, be justified or made righteous before God; but every man of necessity is constrained to seek for another righteousness or justification to be received at God's own hand, that is to say, the forgiveness of his sins and trespasses. And this justification or righteousness which we so receive of God's mercy and Christ's merits embraced by faith, is taken, accepted and allowed of God for our perfect and full justification.[5]

As to the cause of our salvation, Charles identified three concurrent causes that "must go together in our justification":

> Upon God's part, His great mercy and grace; upon Christ's part justice, that is the satisfaction of God's justice, or the price of our redemption by the offering of His body and shedding of His blood with fulfilling of the law perfectly and thoroughly; and upon our part, true and lively faith in the merits of Jesus Christ, which yet is not ours but by God's working in us.[6]

He attacked the notion that human works or merits contribute to one's redemption:

> Justification is not the office of man, but of God; for man cannot make himself righteous by his own works, neither in whole nor in part; . . . justification is the office of God only, and is not a thing which we render unto Him, but which we receive of Him, by His own free mercy and by the only merit of His most dearly beloved Son, our only Redeemer, Saviour, Justifier, Jesus Christ.[7]

Following the synergistic mood of the Anglican homilies, Charles described justifying faith as being both a gift of God and a genuine human response:

> St. Paul declareth here nothing upon the part of man concerning his justification, but only a true and lively faith, which nevertheless is the gift of God. And yet this faith doth not shut out repentance, hope, love, and the fear of God in every believer that is justified; but it shutteth them out from the office of justifying. So that although they be all present in him that is justified, yet they justify not all together.[8]

Yet Wesley does not propound a free-will approach to redemption, since this "true and lively faith" remains "a gift of God"; while it creates "repentance, hope, love, and the fear of God," it likewise "shutteth them out from the office of justifying." For Charles, the "gift" or bestowal nature of faith is of primary importance, and it stands against all schemes of self-salvation:

> The faith which justifies is not purely an assent to things credible as [being] credible; it is not that speculative, notional, eerie shadow which floats in the heads of some learned men; it is not a lifeless, cold, historical faith, common to devils and nominal Christians; it is not learnt of books or men; it is not a human thing, but a divine energy. . . . [Faith] can only be wrought in the soul by Him who made it. . . . God [who] commanded the light to shine out of the darkness, must shine in our hearts to give the knowledge of the glory of God in the face of Jesus Christ.[9]

One of Charles Wesley's favorite descriptions of justification was found in his phrase "freely justified."[10] The foundation of this conception was laid in what the Protestant Reformers called "alien righteousness"—that is to say, the idea that acceptance before God has its basis in Christ's righteousness and that it comes to us freely, not because of anything we are or can do:

> First let us insist that we are justified freely, that is forgiven and accepted for Christ's sake, not our own; justified in our sins, and in our blood [i.e., "guilt"]; justified as ungodly by faith only without works. And then upon this sure foundation let us build the gold and silver, precious stones of good works, and inward holiness.[11]

"Freely justified" was the Wesleyan counterpart to the sixteenth-century Reformation's "justification by faith alone." It meant that justification comes from nothing else but God's grace and man's faith in Jesus Christ. It is "free" in the sense of being unmerited and unearned. In Charles's parlance, "freely justified" is the same as being "saved by grace" or "having peace with God" (*P.W.*, 6:3; 10:15, no. 1297).

"Justification" was Charles Wesley's language of Christian initiation; it marked the beginning of a person's lifelong pilgrimage with Christ. This justification was a real beginning; it came with renewal, assurance, and the presence of the "Comforter" (*Paracletos*), or Holy Spirit, within. Hence, the concept of justification often blended with Wesley's concept of sanctification or Christian perfection:

> Only while we offer up
>   Our dearest blessings here,
> Bless us with our heavenly Hope,
>   The constant Comforter;
> While our faith by works we prove,
>   While the furnace we abide,
> Speak us perfected in love,
>   For ever justified.
>   (*P.W.*, 7:88, no. 74)

For Charles Wesley, any final distinction between justification and sanctification would be a false one. In his soteriology, justification marked the beginning of that long process of being remade in God's image, a pressing toward and yearning for that "one thing needful." Thus, justification was deemed to be wrought by faith alone; but that faith was "a lively faith" that produced holiness of heart and life:

> By faith accounted just,
>   By faith to God we live,
> With patience wait His time, and trust
>   His fulness to receive;
> That finish'd holiness
>   We must at last obtain:
> And faith shall then in vision cease,
>   And love triumphant reign.
>   (*P.W.*, 10:102–3, no. 1511)

GRACE ALONE

Just as Charles Wesley's doctrine of justification followed the Reformation's "faith alone" emphasis, it adhered to the idea of "grace alone." *Grace* was one of Charles's favorite redemption words; it occurred over fifteen hundred times in his later hymns alone. He often described grace as God's "favour" or kindness toward humanity (*P.W.*, 7:7, 214, 317, 360, 411; 10:5, 70; 12:45). The following unpublished verse illustrates this.

> Saviour of a rebellious race,
>   My ever-loving Saviour
> How have I forfeited the *grace*,
>   Slighted Thy frown and *favour*!
> How have I rose against the Lord;
>   Strong in my provocation,
> Weary of waiting on my God
>   Ever mourning for salvation.[12]

Hence, one of Charles's favorite and most common synonyms for *grace* was *mercy,* as in the lines: "Mercy doth every soul embrace, / that receives the God of grace" (*P.W.,* 11:111, no. 160; cf. 1:105; 2:154; 4:6; 10:333, 337, 338). *Favour* and *mercy* often appeared in parallel construction (suggesting that they are equivalents), as in the unpublished hymn based on John 18:27:

> Though I have the Spirit grieved,
>   Have so often relaps'd again,
> In thy mercy's arms receiv'd,
>   Favour I may still obtain:
> Peter give me back my hope;
>   After frequent fall restor'd,
> I shall soon be lifted up,
>   Praise again my pardoning Lord.[13]

The poet-evangelist continually affirmed that the grace of God is ours in Christ, and through Christ we receive God's grace and His benefits:

> The grace of our Head His members receive,
>   The Spirit is shed On all that believe,
> With Jesus the favour Of God we regain,
>   And join'd to our Saviour, Eternally reign.
>   (*P.W.,* 11:129, no. 1204; cf. 9:221, 229;
>   10:70; 13:242)

Grace, in the Wesleyan conception, was no empty gift; it had "virtuous power" and "vigorous energy."[14] This grace both saves and sanctifies (*P.W.,* 7:317, 411; 10:487; 12:284–85; 13:17, no. 3060). It cleanses, heals, and "stamps [Christ's] image on my breast" (*P.W.,* 10:131; cf. *C.W. Journal,* 2:175, letter no. 6). "Undeserved and free," grace allows a mere sinner to participate in the blessings of the kingdom of God:

> Who comes unto Thee
>   A mere sinner like me,
> Shall acknowledge Thy grace undeservèd and free,
>   While astonish'd he buys
> Without money or price
>   A kingdom on earth, and a throne in the skies.
>   (*P.W.*, 9:444, no. 1216)

Salvation comes not by works but grace (*P.W.*, 4:460; 11:202; *Ms. Luke*, p. 6); hence, "from first to last, O Lord, / Thy work is all thine own" (*P.W.*, 9:461, no. 1255). Our imparted righteousness, like the "goodness" that saves us, is not ours:

> 3. Good of Himself [Jesus] only is;
>   And if He makes us good,
>   Our goodness is not ours, but His,
>   For Jesu' sake bestow'd.
>   (*P.W.*, 6:426)

Another characteristically Wesleyan emphasis is the universality of grace. God's grace is all-encompassing in its saving sufficiency; hence, Charles wrote of an "*all* sufficient grace" and the "*all* atoning Lamb" (*P.W.*, 5:12; 12:311, italics added). In terms of the scope of its application, this grace invites all to come to God through faith in Christ. Thus, in a hymn written "Before Preaching at Cornwall," Charles Wesley prayed:

> Teach me to cast my net aright,
>   The gospel net of *general grace*,
> So shall I all to Thee invite,
>   And draw them to their Lord's embrace,
> Within Thine arms of love include,
>   And catch a willing multitude.
>   (*P.W.*, 5:126, no. 202, italics added)

Closely associated with the universal scope of God's grace was Wesley's doctrine of "preventing" or prevenient grace. Both brothers thus described the *prepartio evangelica* (the preparation for receiving the gospel) (*J.W. Works*, 5:7–17; 6:43–53). Prevenient grace is God's enabling sinners receive saving grace. The genius of the doctrine is that it maintains a robust conception of original sin, yet places responsibility upon the individual to apply preventing grace so as to receive salvation. Prevenient grace is bracketed by Charles's view of the universal sufficiency of Christ's death and by his belief that sinners can resist God's grace—to their own destruction.

Charles occasionally used the term "preventing grace" (*P.W.*, 9:274–75; 10:142, 390), though he never seems to have used "prevenient grace." He generally described this grace as a form of divine assistance:

> Assisted by preventing grace,
> I bow me toward the holy place,
> Faintly begin my God to fear,
> His weak, external worshipper:
> But if my Lord His blood apply,
> Entering into the holiest I
> Boldly approach my Father's throne,
> And claim Him all in Christ my own.
> (*P.W.*, 9:274–75, no. 820)

Charles Wesley believed this assisting grace was absolutely necessary for our salvation, since

> Unassisted by Thy grace,
>   We can only evil do;
> Wretched is the human race,
>   Wretched more than words can show,
> Till Thy blessing from above
> Tells our hearts that God is love.
> (*P.W.*, 6:383, no. 13)

In the narrative of Matthew 2:2ff., which describes the nativity of Jesus, Wesley found an allegory of the way that prevenient grace raises up followers of the Lord:

> 1. Mine eyes have seen His orient star,
>   And sweetly drawn I come from far,
>   Leaving the world behind;
>   His Spirit gently leads me on
>   A stranger in a land unknown,
>   A new-born King to find.
>
> 2. The word of all-preventing grace
>   Marks out the Saviour's natal place;
>   And follower of the word,
>   I keep His glimmering star in sight,

> Which by its sure unerring light
> Conducts me to my Lord.
> (*P.W.*, 10:142, no. 10)

Two important issues emerge in these verses; the first has
to do with the dimensions of prevenient grace, and the
second is the connection Wesley established between the
Word and the Spirit as the *modus operandi* of prevenient
grace. Charles was convinced that preventing grace was
granted to all people:

> Do we not all from Thee receive
> The dreadful power to seek, or leave?
> The dreadful power through grace I use,
> And chose of God, my God I choose.
> (*P.W.*, 9:203, no. 638)

Thus, those who fail to find the grace of God and perish do
so because of their unwillingness to apply the grace granted
them. Applying the image of Matthew 25:26, Wesley
compared the perishing to the slothful servant who buried
the talent in a field:

> The harmless inoffensive man
>   Is cast before the bar of God,
> Cast by his own excuses vain
>   For not performing what he could:
> And, burying that preventing grace,
>   Who justly perish unforgiven,
> Shall mix'd with fiends in groans confess
>   They might have sung with saints in heaven.
> (*P.W.*, 10:390, no. 642)[15]

The danger of falling from grace was a persistent note
in Charles's hymns, warning Christians to exercise responsible discipleship. Commenting on the phrase "if the salt
have lost his savour" (Matt. 5:13), he exclaimed:

> Ah, Lord with trembling I confess
> A gracious soul may fall from grace,
> The salt may lose its seasoning power,
> And never, never, find it more! . . .
> (*P.W.*, 10:165, no. 68)

In an interesting journal entry, dated August 17,
1741, Wesley made a similar suggestion that justification

could be lost and regained. He reported: "I visited one who was forsaking the fellowship, when God arrested her in her flight by sickness, convicted, condemned and justified her again" (*C.W. Journal*, 1:174). His hymns "For One Fallen From Grace" reflect a similar theological mood:

> Jesus, let Thy pitying eye
>   Call back a wandering sheep,
> False to Thee like *Peter* I
>   Would fain like *Peter* weep;
> Let me be by grace restored,
>   On me be all longsuffering shown;
> Turn, and look upon me, Lord,
>   And break my heart of stone.
>   (*P.W.*, 4:405, no. 14)[16]

Grace, in Charles Wesley's application of the term, is aptly described in the biblical imagery of the waiting Father:

> I believe Thy pardoning grace
>   As at the beginning, free:
> Open are Thy arms to' embrace
>   Me, the worst of rebels me;
> *All in me the hindrance lies,*
>   Call'd, I still refuse to rise.
>   (*P.W.*, 4:416, no. 19, italics added)

Since he believed it was possible for a person to reject God's grace, Charles warned his contemporary audience of their eschatological anguish through Jesus' rebuke of inhabitants of Bethsaida (Luke 10:11):

> Then, then ye shall with anguish own
>   Ye might have took the proffer'd grace,
> Ye might have God in Jesus known,
>   And lived the life of righteousness,
> Ye might have felt your sins forgiven,
>   Ye once were at the gates of heaven.
>   (*P.W.*, 11:192, no. 1348)

Grace, as understood in Charles Wesley's soteriology, is "free"; that is to say, it is unmerited and accessible to everyone. Justification is by "grace alone" since no human goodness or merit contributes to one's salvation; there is no "grace and . . . ," only grace *alone*. Thus, it can be said that grace is "imputed" to a person; it is Christ's righteousness (appropriated by faith) and not the believer's own righteousness that saves. This idea is classical Protestant soteriology; Charles Wesley's contribution to this discussion is found in his emphasis that, though beginning with imputed grace, moved quickly and insistently toward an imparted grace and an accompanying proper righteousness within the Christian.

Charles occasionally wrote that grace was "infused" into the believer, and the infusion was generally described as a visitation of empowering love (*P.W.*, 7:367, no. 15; 9:328, no. 944). His favorite phrasing referred to a grace or righteousness that God would "impart" to the believer's "heart."[17] The rhyme between *impart* and *heart* probably explains why Wesley preferred *impart* to *infuse*; it is clear that those terms were synonyms in his usage. In a few instances, Charles stacked *impart* and *impute* one upon the other, as if to suggest a progression in the order of salvation—that the first moment (justification) anticipated a second (sanctification). This development was certainly consonant with his theological posture:

> But canst Thou account me just,
>   And yet never make me so?
> Grafted into Christ, I trust
>   Holy as the Root to grow;
> Holy then my works shall be,
>   Then my fruit is found of Thee.
>   (*P.W.*, 13:204, no. 3408)

The progression from imputed (accounted) righteousness toward imparted (or actual) righteousness was an obvious corollary to Wesley's treatment of justification; the forensic or declared acceptance must be actualized within the Christian to produce genuine fruits of righteousness.

Charles developed several poetic images for describing this movement from imputed toward imparted and actual righteousness. In his comment on John 15:14, he pressed into service the image of the vine and its sap:

But freely justified
  In Jesus we abide,
The Spirit's fruits we show,
  In true experiences grow;
Daily the sap of grace receive,
  And more and more like Jesus live.
        (*P.W.*, 12:20, no. 2108)

The poetic picture of Jesus declaring the juridical word of pardon served the same purpose:

Reserved for this alone
  To know as I am known,
Come with Thy salvation, Lord,
  Let my sins no longer part,
Speak the reconciling word,
  Speak Thyself into my heart.
        (*P.W.*, 7:145–46, no. 121)

Christ dwelling within the Christian is the agent of this infusion and inner renewal; but Christ has ascended. His presence therefore is made manifest through the work of the Holy Spirit:

The purchased Comforter *is* given,
For Jesus is return'd to heaven,
  To claim, and then the grace impart;
Our day of Pentecost is come,
And God vouchsafes to fix His home
  In every poor expecting heart.
        (*P.W.*, 4:165, no. 1)

This connection between grace imputed and Christ formed within the Christian was the basis of one of Charles's most important theological contributions: an identification of grace with the indwelling of the Holy Spirit.[18] His "Short Hymn" based on 1 Corinthians 16:14 located this identification at the center of his soteriology:

1. Let all be done in love!
  That thus we all may do,
Jesus, the enmity remove,
  Create our souls anew:
  The gift unspeakable,
  The grace to us impart,
And O, vouchsafe Thyself to dwell

> In every longing heart.
>
> 2. If Thou in us reside
>   Who Thy commands receive,
> And steadfastly in Thee abide,
>   And in Thy Spirit live;
>   Then, only then we prove
>   The perfect charity,
> And all our works are wrought in love,
>   When all are wrought in Thee.
>   (*P.W.*, 13:43, no. 3114)

The hymn presents a basic Wesleyan theology of redemption in three points: (1) reconciliation through Christ, (2) re-creation of the Christian because of "grace imparted" or Christ's Spirit dwelling within, and (3) the ensuing renewal actualized in a life of love as Christ is formed in those who belong to Him.

Charles often identified the infusion of grace with the Holy Spirit's work; seen most clearly in his 1746 *Hymns of Petition and Thanksgiving for the Promise of the Father*, this connection is found in all his writing.[19] Occasionally, he linked God's grace to the Spirit's "convincing role" (cf. John 16:8f.), which leads to salvation and continued growth in grace (*P.W.*, 6:374–75).

More often, however, the connection between the Spirit and grace was established in the gift connotations latent in the word *grace*. The best gift of redemption is Christ dwelling in Christians; and that visitation, Charles Wesley believed, was accomplished through the presence of the Holy Spirit.[20] This inhabitation implied both purification of the person and re-creation in the *imago Dei*.[21] Hence, it was aptly understood as a foretaste of the great heavenly feast:

> By faith we possess
>   The unspeakable peace,
> Freely justified we,
>   And rejoicing in hope our Redeemer to see:
> He gives us a taste,
>   Of that Heavenly Feast,
> His Spirit imparts,

And the earnest of glory is grace in our hearts!
(*Ms. Acts*, p. 145)

Grace, like many of Charles's basic redemption words, had many soteriological applications and connections— e.g., its association with the various terms for justification. Thus, "pardoning-grace"[22] and "reconciling-grace"[23] were prominent phrases in his hymns. Occasionally, *grace* was connected directly to the words *justification, redemption,* or *repentance.*[24]

Wesley employed colorful images to describe the role of grace in his dramatic, poetic theology. In addition to the metaphors of salt and sap (as above), the biblical allusions of light and living water became word pictures of efficacy of God's grace.[25] One of the most significant of these metaphors was "balmy grace." Grace was "balmy" in the sense of being a "healing balm," and this imagery aptly described the restorative, healing effects of God's favor (*P.W.,* 7:147, no. 123; 10:29, no. 1324; 10:32, no. 1331; 10:85, no. 1459). Charles said that sinners were made whole by grace, healed of their sins, backslidings and brokenhearts (*P.W.,* 7:147, no. 123; 6:157; 6:221, no. 4); the restoration of "health" brought perfect sanctity or "holiness" into the lives of those appropriating God's grace in Christ (*P.W.,* 10:28, no. 1322; 10:85, no. 1459). Thus, grace could be described as the "unction of His love" or "the reigning power of godliness," since both phrases related restorative grace to inward renewal.[26]

Charles's understanding and application of the word *grace* carried his theology from justification to sanctification, from "accounted righteous" toward healing and restoration of the image of Christ within. This connection was made concrete by his conception of grace as both the gift of Jesus Christ and the indwelling presence of the Holy Spirit. It is difficult to read or sing Wesley's hymns without capturing a bit of the wonder and rapture he felt in the tremendous dimensions and efficacy of God's grace:

1. O the riches of Thy grace!
    Grace surpassing all our thought,

Grace transcending all our praise,
    Finding those who sought Thee not!
Grace doth more than sin abound,
    For a world of sinners free:
Me, their guilty chief it found,
    Drew my heart to follow Thee.

2. Master of my heart and will,
    Both are in Thy gracious hand,
Seek, and call, and draw me still
    Subject to Thy mild command.
Then I after Thee shall run
    On the wings of faith and love,
Find Thee, Saviour, on Thy throne,
    Glorify Thy grace above.
                    (*P.W.*, 11:329–30, no. 1635)

LIVELY FAITH

The Old Testament conception of faith is related to etymological roots in Hebrew words of the *'AM* family; "firmness" or "stability" were their foundational connotations.[27] The Hebraic understanding of faith is basically relational; God was faithful to Israel, and His faithfulness was manifested in His actions, words, and nature (Deut. 7:19; Isa. 49:7). Israel's response to her God was "to hold Him trustworthy."[28] This trustworthiness soon extended to God's covenant and promises (1 Kings 8:26; Lam. 3:22–23). Hence, both relationship and assent were basic to the Old Testament's understanding of faith.

Much like the Old Testament used *'AM*, the New Testament used the Greek word *pisteuō* with a broad range of connotations; the basic idea was "believe," "trust," or "to give credence to."[29] In the New Testament, the classical distinctions between "faith in" (*eis*) and "faith that" (*oti*) were softened into a more relational conception, influenced no doubt by the Hebraic application, to include both trust (in) and assent (that). The distinctive aspects of faith are seen in this connection to be proclamation about Christ (as in Heb. 11:6), the content of the Christian affirmation focused on the lordship of Jesus (Rom. 10:9; 1 Cor. 15:11), and the significance of His death and resurrection (1 Cor. 15:12–19; Acts 2:36). The final distinctive element is to be gleaned from the synoptic Gospels, where faith means being in a relationship of loyalty to Jesus, being His disciple.

Faith, especially as a noun, is not a common term in Charles Wesley's writings. The idea is quite prominent, but the specific word is not. Like the author of the fourth Gospel, Wesley preferred verbs and other active forms to nouns and more static constructions; both writers used the noun *faith* rather rarely and preferred to write of "believing" or showing faith in action.

Wesley held that faith is a "gift of God" (*P.W.*, 11:393, no. 1786) "bestow'd" upon us or "bought" for us by Christ (*P.W.*, 11:393, no. 1786; 10:212, no. 181). Charles affirmed a rational content to this faith, but looked beyond sheer cognition toward a synthesis that merged trust and assent, heart and mind, through the inner reasonings of the Holy Spirit:

> 1. Faith, though rational, is founded
>   Not on man, but God alone,
>   On the great Jehovah grounded,
>   Persons three in essence one:
>   Who aright his Lord confesses,
>   Unremovable he stands,
>   Fix'd on an eternal basis,
>   'Stablished with almighty hands.
>
> 2. Not on vain imaginations
>   Do we, Lord, for proof depend;
>   Not on fancied inspirations,
>   When Thou dost Thy Spirit send:
>   Unenlighten'd reason leaves us
>   Nought to build our faith upon:
>   Evidence Thy Spirit gives us
>   Brighter than the mid-day sun.
>   (*P.W.*, 7:333, no. 34)

Charles said that this faith has its basis in the gospel witness ("the historical"):

> Faith which leads us to the skies
> In faith historical begins;
>   Faith Divine the blood applies

> That blots out all our sins.
>   (P.W., 12:431, no. 2978)

He affirmed that saving faith has its object in Christ, His death, and its saving significance ("blood"). Hence, "Obedient faith in Jesu's blood,/This is the way that leads to God" (P.W., 5:90), and John 20:31 explained how the Word and faith together achieve salvation:

> Faith comes by hearing of the Word,
>   Comes to the heart by reading too,
> While searching for our heavenly Lord,
>   Him in the sacred page we view,
> Him whom the Holy Ghost reveals,
> And pardon on our conscience seals.
>   (P.W., 12:112, no. 2306)

Examining Jesus' words in Matthew 15, Wesley drew a similar connection between faith, repentance, and the gospel (P.W., 7:383, no. 32). This saving synthesis produced not only salvation from sin but also a life of love:

> Jesus Thy record we receive,
>   And by a power from Thee believe;
> By faith Divine our seal set to
>   That Thou art God, that Thou art true,
> By faith Thy promises we gain,
>   Thy strict fidelity maintain,
> And saved from sin exult to prove
>   The truth of Thy redeeming love.
>   (P.W., 11:350, no. 1679)

While Charles believed, with the Reformers, that we are saved by faith alone, he also insisted that saving faith is not alone. Charles also followed James 2:14–26 as well as the Articles and Homilies of his church in affirming that genuine faith is expressed in loving acts of mercy:

> Our Church describes it thus: The true, lively and converting faith, the sure and substantial faith which saveth sinners, is not only a common belief of the Articles of our creed, but also a true trust and confidence of the mercy of God through our Lord Jesus Christ, and a steadfast hope of all good things to be received at God's hand. It is not in the mouth and

outward profession only, but liveth and stirreth inwardly in the heart. It is the pure conviction of the benefits which we trust to receive of God, a certifying and sure looking for Him. It is no dead, vain or unfruitful thing, but a thing of perfect virtue, or wonderful operation or working and strength, bringing forth all good motions and good works (*C.W. Ms. Sermons*, pp. 20–21).

While our deeds and virtues add nothing to acceptance before God, Wesley believed, our reconciliation with Him through faith in Christ begins a new work in us, a new work that produces holiness, not just good works.

Faith works by love. The love of God is shed abroad in all believers' hearts by the Holy Ghost which is given unto them. This love they show by keeping His commandments; which no one except believers can keep. But they are delivered not only from the guilt but also from the power of sin. The law of the Spirit of life which is in Christ Jesus hath made them free from the law of sin and death. Sin shall not have dominion over them, for they are not under the law but under grace. . . . Being then made free from sin, they become the servants of righteousness. Jesus is their Jesus for He hath saved them from their sins. He that believeth is born of God; and whosoever is born of God doth not commit sin, for His seed remaineth in him, and he cannot sin because he is born of God (*C.W. Ms. Sermons*, pp. 20–21).

Thus, in sermon and in song, justification by faith was affirmed and then included in Charles's larger concern for "full salvation," which connected pardon with purity and perfect peace:

> 1. Saving faith is not alone;
> All who savingly believe
>   Make their true affection known,
> To their dear Redeemer cleave
>   Humbly at His feet they mourn,
> All His benefits restore,
>   Never to the world return,
> Walk in Christ, and sin no more.

2. Saved by faith from sin and fear,
Bright they in His image rise,
   Meet before His face to' appear,
Sinners still in their own eyes;
   Lord on me the grace bestow,
Pardon on my heart impress;
   Saved by faith I then shall go,
Go on to God in perfect peace.
            (*P.W.*, 11:168–69, no. 1292)

His sermon "On Good Works" describes this "lively faith" as one that demonstrates itself in living: "Be sure of your faith, try it by your living; look upon the fruits that come of it; make the increase of love and charity by it towards God and your neighbor, and so shall you perceive it to be a true and lively faith" (*C.W. Ms. Sermons*, pp. 20–21). Contrariwise, Charles's hymns attack what he termed a "*Gnostic* faith," which was full of intellectual assent but devoid of deeds of love:

What doth thy *Gnostic* faith avail,
   Who seest thy brother in distress,
With ruthless heart insensible,
   And bidd'st the poor depart in peace,
Yet dost not his distress relieve,
   But words without assistance give!
            (*P.W.*, 13:168, no. 3340)

Charles Wesley preached and sang a faith "which is not idle, unfruitful, and dead, but [which] worketh by love!' (*C.W. Ms. Sermons*, p. 36). It was this sort of faith that Wesley heard echoed in the words of prophecy, "Ask for the old paths, where is the good way, and walk therein, and ye shall find rest for your souls" (Jer. 6:16):

1. *Stand* we in the good old way,
      Who Christ by faith receive,
   Heartily we must obey,
      If truly we believe:
   Other way can none declare
Than this from which we ne'er will move:
      Saved by grace through faith we are,
         Through faith that works by love.

2. Walking in this heavenly path

By saints and martyrs trod,
Freely justified by faith,
   We now have peace with God;
   Peace, unutterable peace!
The faithful *feel* in their breast,
Then the rest of holiness,
   And then the glorious rest!
      (*P.W.*, 10:15, no. 1297)

Charles's sermon "On Good Works" delineated six effects that a lively faith has upon the believer's life. The sermon paralleled the hymn above, since in each case faith touched the whole of Christian life:

(1) Reconciliation with God attested by an inward peace or conscience . . . . (2) A second effect of faith is joy. (3) A third effect of faith is liberty not only from the guilt, but likewise from the power of sin. (4) A fourth effect of true saving faith is love. The two are inseparable. (5) The Spirit itself beareth witness with our spirit, that we are the children of God. (6) This great and outward and visible mark of faith is obedience or a holy life (*C.W. Ms. Sermons*, pp. 45–50).

REDEMPTION

The foundation of the biblical conception of redemption was laid in Israel's deliverance out of bondage in Egypt. The Old Testament writers looked back upon the Exodus as a monument to God's salvation in their midst, and its significance colored their fundamental understanding of God and His salvation (Exod. 6:6; Deut. 7:8; 13:5; 2 Sam. 7:23; 1 Chron. 17:21). In the New Testament, the English words *redemption* and *redeem* represent Greek words of the *lutron* and *agorazō* families. The former term, *lutron*, carried the connotation of a ransom price that is paid to deliver a person from captivity or to repay a debt. In its ancient secular roots, *agorazō* meant "to frequent the forum," and hence by extension came to mean "to buy or purchase."[30] In each case, the basic conception was one of being delivered or "purchased" out of bondage into freedom, as in Galatians 3:13, "For Christ hath redeemed us from the curse of the law" (cf. Eph. 5:16; Col. 4:5).

Redemption and other words of that etymological family appeared frequently in Charles Wesley's hymns, over 250 times in the later corpus alone, and they also figured largely in his evangelistic sermons. Generally, he used the word *redemption* as an equivalent for *salvation*. The parallelism developed in the following hymn was typical of his application of those two terms:

> My God, Thou art in Jesus mine,
>   And early will I seek Thy face,
> A slave *redeem'd* by blood Divine,
>   A sinner *saved* by pardoning grace.
>   (*P.W.*, 7:176, no. 147, italics added)

In this verse, the linguistic connection between bondage (the status of a "slave") and redemption has been preserved; likewise, a second vital Wesleyan theme emerges— the link between redemption and blood.

The Authorized Version, which the Wesleys used alongside the Greek New Testament and the Anglican prayerbook, specifically linked redemption with blood in three places, though the connection is suggested much more frequently than that.[31] *Blood* was one of Charles's favorite terms for describing the saving effects of Jesus' death, and *redemption* was one of his many synonyms for salvation; hence, he penned many lines that said the Christian is "redeem'd through faith by blood Divine," or words to that effect.[32] The poet-preacher used this connection to expound the liberating effect of faith in Jesus' death, and (as we shall see in chapter 4) this imagery wove christology, atonement, and "full salvation" tightly together to communicate an entire Wesleyan soteriology in the phrase "the blood of Christ."

Charles's application of redemption words often reflected his understanding of the original meaning of those terms and their basis in price-paying conceptions. In some instances, Jesus' death was described in language borrowed from the world of commerce, such as *debt* and *paid*. The following verse is a characteristic example:

God over all, for ever bless'd,
  A curse and sin for sinners made,
By a whole world of guilt oppress'd,
  Who hast the general ransom paid,
Redeem'd us from the curse of God,
  And bought the grace with all thy Blood.
        (*P.W.*, 13:63, no. 3156)

Since another important connotation included in the word *redemption* is deliverance from captivity or salvation from bondage or harm, quite naturally deliverance became an important part of Wesley's application of redemption words—*liberation* from all sorts of enslaving situations. Most typically, Charles insisted that redemption is "from sin" (*P.W.*, 5:322–23, no. 130; 9:339, no. 974; 11:45, no. 1021). As he wrote, Jesus' blood "surely was spilt / To redeem us from sin, both the power and the guilt" (*P.W.*, 7:9, no. 4). Charles's poetry lists many of our enslavers, plus descriptions of *redemption* as deliverance from all such. The following verse contains his most complete list:

The peace and joy of faith
  We every moment feel,
Redeem'd from sin, and wrath,
  And death, and earth, and hell,
We do our Father's house repair,
  To meet our Elder Brother there.
        (*P.W.*, 5:387, no. 179)

Charles's standard list of oppressing tyrants was found in the phrase "Redeem'd from sin, and earth, and hell" (*P.W.*, 6:413, no. 44; 11:112–13, no. 1163); but this formula was occasionally augmented with colorful forms that communicated similar connotations: "From sin, the world, and Satan's yoke" (*P.W.*, 9:381, no. 1078).

Wesley's understanding of the redeeming power of Christ's death was not exhausted in describing deliverance or redemption *from* various situations of bondage; he stressed with equal clarity the resultant freedom (redemption *for*). As Charles wrote, "From the bottomless perdition / Redeemed, I live *for Thee*" (*P.W.*, 9:388, italics added). Just as redemption meant deliverance *from* every danger and degree of sin, so also it was redemption *for* complete devotion to God:

> Redeem'd *from* all iniquity,
> From every evil work and word,
> From every sinful temper free,
> He [the Christian] lives *devoted* to his Lord.
> (*P.W.*, 6:375, no. 5, italics added)

In Wesley's hymns and sermons, the idea of redemption always strains toward "full redemption."[33] This redemption was "full" in the sense of being complete, an idea linked to Charles's knowledge of New Testament Greek. Words of the *telos* family suggest a completeness that is a "full measure" and that possesses the quality of having attained its intended goal or purpose. Thus, New Testament terms such as *full, perfect,* and *complete* are connected to their roots in *telos* terms.[34] In the Wesleyan sense, then, this redemption was "full" not only in the extent of its influence (i.e., touching upon the whole of one's life) but more directly because it had achieved its goal (the removal of every barrier to fellowship with God):

> Their glory shall their shame exceed,
> When saved from all indwelling sin,
> Doubly redeem'd, and free indeed,
> Their conscience, and their heart is clean.
> (*P.W.*, 4:309)

"Full redemption" also spoke of the extent of one's deliverance *from* sin (its guilt and power) *for* utter consecration to God; hence, for Charles "full redemption" became a synonym for "holiness," "Christian perfection," or "sanctification":

> In our desolate estate
> We for *full redemption* wait,
> Wait the leisure of our Lord,
> Sure to be at last restored;
> We for whom our God hath died,
> We shall feel Thy blood applied,
> Perfect peace in Jesus given,
> *Finish'd holiness,* and heaven.
> (*P.W.*, 7:21, no. 15, italics added)

RECONCILED/RECONCILIATION

In its ancient biblical and secular roots, the word *reconciliation* had to do with overcoming estrangement or changing attitudes that caused a relationship to be broken.[35] The root words have a commercial foundation; they originally described a commercial exchange that is most evident in their Pauline usage, when he says that faith in Christ's death reconciles us to God (Rom. 5:9–10; 8:8–10; 2 Cor. 5:18–20; Col. 1:20–21). In passages such as Romans 5:9–10, *reconciliation* describes a renewal so pervasive that it makes one a new creature. It is so complete a summary of the New Testament teaching on salvation that *reconcilation* has become a catchword for all soteriology.

Charles's journal indicates that he asked newly "reconciled" believers to "call upon [him] after expounding." His purpose was to give them Christian instruction and to hear testimonies of their experiences of "reconciliation" (*C.W. Journal*, 1:176). The speaker in Wesley's hymns longs to "feel my sins forgiven" or to have pardon sealed upon the heart "to' assure me God is reconciled" (*P.W.*, 7:56, no. 49; 10:454, no. 802). The experiential fruits of this assurance were described as "peace," as in the lines, "My inmost soul is satisfied / With everlasting peace" (*P.W.*, 7:236, no. 112; 4:159). This peace amounted to saying, "Away with our fears!" (*P.W.*, 4:113, no. 8). The result of this peace and assurance of one's reconciliation with God was a new relationship with Him that caused Christ to be formed within the Christian:

> No evil now but pride I fear,
> For God in Christ is reconciled:
> My heart is fix'd, I find Him here,
> The witness that I am His child.
> (*P.W.*, 6:303)

Finding Christ formed within the reconciled is the same as saying that Christians have assurance of their salvation because of the witness of the Spirit:

> Thee that I may my Father know,

A grain of faith impart,
The Spirit of Thy Son bestow
  To witness in my heart;
That Thou in Christ art reconciled,
  My conscience certify,
And then Thy dear adopted child,
  I Abba Father cry.
                (*P.W.*, 7:332, no. 33; cf. 213)

Examining the theological synonyms Wesley used for *reconciliation* indicates that it ran the whole range of redemption language. Reconciliation was the same as being forgiven by grace (*P.W.*, 9:65, no. 212) or "justified" (*P.W.*, 11:502–3, no. 2047). It meant being purchased by God, generally through the agency of Christ's blood (*P.W.*, 7:92; 11:87, no. 1112) or, less graphically, "by Christ" (*P.W.*, 7:215, no. 17). This reconciliation has its basis in "astonishing grace" (*P.W.*, 4:119) or "mercy" (*P.W.*, 7:53–54; 4:406), and it results in a pardon that is not merely the Judge's decree written on a court docket but a pardon that is "written upon my heart" (*P.W.*, 7:217; 10:454; cf. *Ms. Miscellaneous Hymns*, p. 197).

Since Charles's conception of reconciliation radiated with the full spectrum of redemption hues, it touched upon sanctification. He said that reconciliation results in "The joys of holiness below, / And then the joys of heaven" (*P.W.*, 9:65, no. 212). It marks the beginning of a new relationship with God in which the heart is purified and has the image of God stamped upon it (*P.W.*, 11:502–3, no. 2047; 13:189, no. 3383).

The most characteristic emphasis of Charles Wesley's approach to reconciliation was to be found in his identification of reconciliation with the atonement of Christ— that is, the reconciliation that results between God and humanity because of Christ's death: "Thy death did once for all atone, / And God and man in Thee are one" (*P.W.*, 9:15, no. 45; 9:103, no. 329). Reconciliation was explained as drawing near to God "through the atoning blood" (*P.W.*, 10:89, no. 1468). On other occasions, Wesley wrote that God and man are reconciled, suggesting a sense of mutual estrangement between God and the human race (*P.W.*, 6:457, no. 93; 6:463, 464; 7:215; 9:15; 10:128, 143). The words not only pointed to the two-sided disruption that sin caused in the divine-human relationship, but also communicated something of the dimensions of the reconciliation Charles saw in the Christ event:

> God was in Christ, the' eternal Sire
>   Reveal'd in His eternal Son,
> Jehovah did on earth expire,
>   For every soul of man to' atone:
> The one almighty God supreme,
>   Jehovah lavish of His blood
> Pour'd out the' inestimable stream,
>   And reconciled the world to God.
>   (*P.W.*, 7:215, no. 17)

Charles's most unusual application of the word *reconciliation* was his suggestion that "God is reconciled" through the death of Christ. Numerically, this application outweighs by far all others.[36] It has a curious ideological slant to it, since typically one would say, "God and humanity are reconciled." Yet, technically speaking, two parties are "reconciled." There is, however, a theological difficulty in Charles's unusual phrase; to say that God is reconciled might suggest that there is estrangement within the Godhead or that God is passive in the reconciliation, as though something is done to Him instead of by Him to overcome our estrangement. In most instances, however, Wesley maintained the priority of God's activity in our reconciliation and looked to the Christ event as the way in which God "is reconciled in Jesus Christ."[37] Hence, he wrote:

> O God, in Christ the Saviour
>   To sinners reconciled,
> With manifested favour
>   Receive Thy suppliant child:
> On us who bow before Thee
>   Lift up Thy smiling face,
> And bid our souls adore Thee,
>   The God of pardoning grace.
>   (*P.W.*, 7:31, no. 26)

And while there are instances in which Wesley suggested that reconciliation overcomes an estrangement in God's character or attitude toward us ("His anger is turn'd into love"), the thrust of his phrase "God is reconciled in Christ" was to emphasize the unity and primacy of God's activity throughout the process of reconciliation. Hence, it is not as though sinners come before the angry God with gifts to turn aside His wrath, as suggested by the phrase, "God in Christ is reconciled." The Wesleyan thrust was formed on the pattern of Paul: "God was in Christ, reconciling the world unto himself" (2 Cor. 5:19). In other words, God takes it upon Himself to remedy and return His prodigal children to Him through His eternal Son.

PARDON

Pardon is a redemption word rarely used in the Authorized Version of the Bible; it appears only twenty-three times as a noun or verb. Even more striking, none of these occurrences is found in the New Testament! In startling contrast to the KJV, Charles Wesley used the word *pardon* over three hundred and fifty times in his later hymns alone.[38] Why this term was so popular with him is not clear, though several reasons suggest themselves.

Pardon is a picturesque word. It conjures up images of the law court or the royal hall of judgment. Its short, two-syllable construction provided Wesley with a hard-hitting synonym for *redemption, forgivenesss,* and a host of related terms. Likewise, Charles seemed to appreciate the initial *p* alliterations, since he often paired *pardon* with *peace* or other words that begin with a *p* (*P.W.*, 1:205; 9:256, no. 779; 12:158–59).[39]

Charles's use of *pardon* made it a functional equivalent for *forgiveness,* though he rarely set those two terms in direct connection. The primary focus of the word *pardon* was God's dealing with sin: "to pardon sin is Thine" (*P.W.*, 4:401; cf. 117); hence, *mercy* was a synonym for *pardon* in Wesley's soteriology.[40] His application of the word *pardon* was firmly rooted in the term's legal heritage:

O God in Christ, Thine Embassy,
    And proffer'd mercy we embrace,
And gladly reconciled to Thee,
    Thy condescending goodness praise;
Poor debtors by our Lord's request
    A full *acquittance* we receive,
And criminals with *pardon* bless'd,
    We at our Judge's instance live.
            (*P.W.*, 7:217, no. 21, italics added)

Pardon is the Judge's verdict of acquittal; it is based in Christ's "proffer'd mercy." The divine courtroom is like a debtors' court; the accused have nothing with which to purchase their release. But Christ has bought their acquittal with the price of His blood:

On us bestow the pardon
    Bought by His precious blood,
Who paid the utmost farthing
    We to Thy justice owed;
The peace and consolation
    Incomprehensible,
The knowledge of salvation,
    To all our hearts reveal.
            (*P.W.*, 10:182, no. 109; cf. 7:381)

Charles used *pardon* interchangeably with other important redemption words; it was a synonym for *mercy* (*P.W.*, 12:158–59), *ransom'd* (*P.W.*, 11:252, no. 1470), *reconciled* (*P.W.*, 8:217), and *liberation*—"loosed from every bond I feel" (*P.W.*, 9:339, no. 972). Touching upon its experiential results, *pardon* also meant "peace" (*P.W.*, 1:205; 11:256). Wesley's application of the word encompassed Wesley's treatment of justification, describing God's acceptance of penitent people because Christ canceled their sins by His death and resurrection.[41]

If one were to construct a poetical order of salvation from Charles's hymns (a challenging task indeed!), *pardon* would stand at the initiatory stage of Christian life. One of his most common poetic chains suggests this: "pardon, and holiness, and heaven" (*P.W.*, 6:374; 5:293). In the same way, *pardon* or *forgiveness* meant the canceling of our debt in sin, and both of these seem most directly connected with

justification or the beginning of the soteriological pilgrimage (*P.W.*, 9:401). Charles rarely separated justification
from sanctification. In his application, the word *pardon* or
acquittal carries with it an affirmation of inner renewal:

> I ask the gift of righteousness,
>   The sin-subduing power,
> Power to believe, and go in peace,
>   And never grieve Thee more;
> I ask the blood-bought pardon seal'd,
>   The liberty from sin,
> The grace infused, the love reveal'd,
>   The kingdom fix'd within.
>   (*P.W.*, 11:44, no. 1020)

The path to perfection lies through and beyond pardon,
which marks the beginning point from which one must
move ("liberty from sin"). But Charles's goal was continuing growth in sanctity; "grace [must be] infused, the love
reveal'd, / The kingdom [of God] fix'd within." Thus,
when one of the speakers in Wesley's hymns asked the
rhetorical question: "I have pardon—what can a poor
sinner have more?" the reply is not long in coming:

> He can have a new heart,
> So as never to start
> From Thy paths: he may be in the world as Thou art.
>   (*P.W.*, 5:26, no. 130)

Charles often termed pardon "the first gift," but sanctification he called "the best" (*P.W.*, 5:28, no. 131). Since
the Christian is both "Pardon'd, and sanctified by grace"
(*P.W.*, 9:444, no. 1215), Wesley called grace "the double
key," which opened one more door:

> Jesus, I cry for help to Thee;
>   Thou hast, Lord, the double key:
> Open the gracious door,
>   And let me live with pardon blest,
> And then obtain one blessing more,
>   And lay me down to rest.
>   (*P.W.*, 4:216, no. 7)

This quest for another gift he expressed even more clearly
in the hymn entitled "My Jesus, My Lamb":

8. Of pardon possess'd
   Yet can I not rest
In the first gift, but earnestly covet the best.

9. The best I shall prove
   When perfect in love,
I serve Thee on earth as the angels above.
                              (*P.W.*, 5:28, no. 131)

One of Charles's favorite ways of linking pardon with sanctification was to speak of "pardon sealed." The connection was sometimes set in cleansing imagery, as a way of describing the effect of "pardon sealed":

Now, even now, I yield, I yield
With all my sins to part;
   Jesus, speak my pardon seal'd,
And purify my heart,
   Purge this love of sin away,
Then I into nothing fall,
Then I see the perfect day,
   And Christ is all in all.
                              (*P.W.*, 10:24, no. 1313)

The source of this interesting phraseology is found, no doubt, in the ancient custom of sealing documents with a signet. A document that was completed was "sealed," officially marked and closed with the imprint of a royal ring. The Authorized Version reflects this application in several Old Testament passages in which the Hebrew word *chatham* (which literally means "sealed") is metaphorically translated "finished."[42] When Charles Wesley wrote of a "pardon sealed," he was contemplating a pardon that was finished or completed in personal holiness:

His bleeding love 'tis Thine to seal
   With pardon on the contrite heart:
To us, to us the grace reveal,
   The righteousness impute, impart;
Discharge Thy second function here,
   And now descend the Comforter.
                              (*P.W.*, 4:188, no. 19)

The connection made between pardon and inner renewal by referring to the coming of "the Comforter" into the "contrite heart" was typical of Charles's approach to the theology of redemption. He sought to avoid the sheer moralism (or works righteousness) that had been a part of his earlier life, and so he emphasized justification by faith alone; yet, Wesley was impatient with the sort of Christianity that stopped at a declaration of pardon, or the imputation of righteousness by faith. His theology of redemption insisted on "real substantial holiness here." Pardon reaches toward perfection; the redemption that Charles sought meant not only acceptance by faith, but holiness manifested in the believer by the renovating work of God's Spirit:

> The sinners unclean
>   Are wash'd in his blood,
> The outcasts of men
>   Accepted with God,
> Thro' Jesus his merits
>   The pardon receive,
> And fill'd with the Spirit,
>   Of holiness live.
>
> (*Ms. Acts*, pp. 202–3)[43]

ELECTION AND PREDESTINATION

Terms such as *election* and *predestination* are rather rare in Charles's soteriological hymns and sermons; he used them in the sense of one's being "chosen" or "appointed" to salvation (respectively). *Election*, in its biblical application, has to do with the selection of a whole body of people—Israel or the New Testament community of faith (Rom. 9:27; 11:5, 7, 28; 1 Thess. 1:4).[44] The idea of election is so closely connected with one's acceptance before God that in the New Testament "the elect" becomes a synonym for "Christians" or "the community of faith" (Rom. 8:33; Col. 3:12; Titus 1:1; 2 John 1:13). While the theological implications of these terms are hotly debated, Schrenk's summation of the New Testament sense of election sets an appropriate climate for understanding Charles Wesley's use of the term:

Election is fulfilled only in obedience. Hence we do not have a static doctrine of election but a dynamic theology which is oriented to the right attitude of the elect. To receive gifts is of no avail, if there is no readiness to obey. Thus the conception of election is set in living history. It is an eternal pronouncement and decision . . . . But it is not one which enslaves historical movement and decision fatalistically. On the contrary, it establishes decision.[45]

In a similar way, *predestination*, which occurred four times in Wesley's New Testament (Rom. 8:29; 11:29; Acts 2:23; 1 Pet. 1:2), had its basis in Greek words from the *proorizen* family. In their secular application, those terms carried the connotation of "to mark out beforehand" or "to decide beforehand."[46] In the New Testament, these words are rendered *predestinate*; and this predestination is usually related to being conformed to the image of Christ (Rom. 8:29, 30). It is likewise said to be an adoption based on the love and foreknowledge of God (Eph. 1:15).

In Charles Wesley's application, *election* was often said to be "free election," in the same sense that justification or grace was also described as "free" (*P.W.*, 9:390, no. 1099). He considered election to be a bestowal or gift, a blessing that was not earned or merited by the believer. Wesley identified God's love as the source of this election:

> The cause of His election
>   Unsearchable we own,
> And all our God's affection
>   Receive through Thee [Christ] alone.
>   (*P.W.*, 12:24, 2117)

This chosenness, or election, was not to become a source of pride, since it could be lost. Judas became Charles's prime example of one who fell away:

> That none of Thine elect may boast,
>   One of the chosen twelve was lost,
> He made himself perdition's son;
>   For whom Thou hadst a throne design'd,
> He sold the Saviour of mankind,
>   And forfeited his promised crown:

> Faithful he might have proved to Thee,
>   But fell from his integrity
> By no decree of Thine compell'd;
>   He cast Thy slighted grace away,
> Gave himself up, the tempter's prey,
>   And thus his own destruction seal'd.
> (P.W., 12:53, no. 2177)

Hence, Charles Wesley's conception of election was conditional; one's status before God depended upon His "proffer'd blessing" as well as an individual's ongoing response:

> The number of the call'd is great,
>   But that of the elected small,
> Invited to the gospel-treat
>   So few will answer to the call,
> So few the proffer'd blessing take,
>   And faithful to the end endure,
> Giving all diligence to make
>   *Conditional election* sure.
> (P.W., 10:335, no. 509, italics added)

This conditional concept of election had profound ethical impact. Election, for Wesley, was a call to persevere in the face of trial or adversity; and it was a call to holiness, since trials were a part of the process of purification that made "election sure":

> Thou hast into the furnace cast,
>   Yet by my griefs and sufferings pass'd
> I am not, Lord, refined:
>   I am not, but I shall be pure,
> Shall make my own election sure,
>   And leave my dross behind.
> (P.W., 9:425, no. 1172;
cf. 11:464, no. 1955)

Wesley believed the boundaries of this conditional election were not limited by the dimensions of the Atonement. Christ died for all; and the great "all" of God's acceptance was one of Charles's most persistent redemption themes. "All," used in this profound soteriological sense, occurred nearly two hundred and fifty times in his later hymns alone! As he wrote: "The universal debt to pay"; or again, "The grand and full atonement made; / God for a guilty world hath died" (*P.W.*, 12:48, no. 2166; 12:100, no. 2279).

One of Wesley's favorite ways of expressing the unlimited atonement was found in the Pauline parallelism between the first Adam and Christ, the last Adam (1 Cor. 15): "As many as in Adam died / In Christ may be restored." If this worldwide process of restoration (or recapitulation) were not complete, the failure lay not in the divine initiative or in the universal efficacy of Christ's cross, but in human recalcitrance:

> As many as in *Adam* fell,
>   And wander'd from salvation wide,
> To ransom from sin, death, and hell,
>   For them the Second *Adam* died;
> Even those unhappy souls He bought
>   Who their redeeming Lord deny,
> Will not by Him to life be brought,
>   But self-destroy'd resolve to die.
>   (*P.W.*, 10:337, no. 514)

The tension between the universal call of the gospel and the salvation of a mere remnant was keenly felt in Charles Wesley's hymns, but it did not soften his insistence upon an unlimited atonement. In the hymn verses that follow, he meditated upon John 1:29, "Behold the Lamb of God, who taketh away the sins of the world." At the beginning, Wesley strikes up a dialogue with those who believe that Christ died only for the "elect"—that is, for some people and not for others:

> 1. Did Jesus for the world atone?
>   "Yes; for the world of the elect:"
>   *Love* could not die for some alone,
>   And all the wretched rest reject:
>   For the whole helpless world that lay
>   In desperate wickedness, He died,
>   And all who dare believe it, may
>   With me be freely justified.
>
> 2. Charged with the universal load,
>   The sins of every soul, and mine,
>   By faith I see the Lamb of God,
>   The bleeding Sacrifice Divine!

> My sins, transferr'd from me to Him,
>   Shall never be by justice found,
> All carried down that purple stream,
>   All in that open fountain drown'd!
>   (*P.W.*, 11:325, no. 1625, italics added)

In Wesley's mind, the distinction between the saved and the lost lay not in God's choice of some people before the foundation of the earth; rather, it was to be found in one's belief or disbelief. Only human unbelief is able to set limits upon God's grace: "Only unbelief withstands, / Binds the gracious Saviour's hands" (*P.W.*, 10:278, no. 353). Those who are lost perish because they have "spurned" or "rejected the proffer'd grace"; thus, they are, in Charles's words, "self-destroy'd." Having "slighted" God's grace, they "justly die" (*P.W.*, 4:288; 9:376–77; 11:195). In the Wesleyan soteriology, the onus of responsibility for a person's salvation shifts from God to the individual.

Charles Wesley had both a positive and a negative thrust in discussing predestination. On the negative side, he opposed the idea that some people are lost because of a divine decision or predestinating decree made before the foundation of the earth. Wesley believed their damnation was of their own making, because of their willful rejection of the Savior:

> Their gross unfeeling heart oppose
>   And with the Saviour fight,
> Their ears against His words they close,
>   Their eyes against His light;
> By no decree of His compell'd,
>   They spurn the' incarnate God,
> Refuse to let their souls be heal'd
>   By their Redeemer's blood.
>   (*P.W.*, 10:269, no. 330)

On the positive side of the same issue, Charles emphasized that what was predestined was not an individual's salvation per se, but the fact that those who will be saved must be conformed to the image of Christ (based perhaps upon Eph. 1:1–15). In Wesley's own terms, predestination was "in Christ," hence it included the possibility of renewal in His image:

> The' unchangeable decree is past,
> The sure predestinating word,
> That I, who on my Lord am cast,
> I shall be like my sinless Lord:
> 'Twas fix'd from all eternity:
> All things are possible to me.
> (*P.W.*, 5:301, no. 112)

In a similar manner, Charles borrowed one of the images often used to illustrate particular election—the potter and the clay (Isa. 64:8; Jer. 18; Rom. 9:21)—and reapplied it to describe holiness or the "mark" of Christ as the goal for all Christians:

> My Potter from above,
> Clay in Thy hands I am,
> Mould me into the form of love,
> And stamp with Thy new name:
> Thy name is holiness;
> Now on this heart of mine
> The mark indelible impress,
> The purity Divine.
> (*P.W.*, 9:461, no. 1256)

In his doctrines of election and predestination, Charles Wesley (like his brothers and three generations of his family before them) was an Arminian; insofar as he followed the tradition established by Archibishop William Laud (1573–1645) and others within the Anglican communion, he affirmed a conditional election and a general decree of predestination. Yet, in Charles's hymns and sermons, these traditional concepts received fresh, vigorous application. In conditional election and the heightened sense of human responsibility that accompanied it, he felt a clarion call to impeccable personal piety and a strong impetus to evangelism. And Charles believed the gospel invitation was a call to "full salvation." Hence, predestination blended with his doctrine of sanctification; every believer, he thought, was predestined to be conformed to the image of Christ. To be saved was to be cast upon Christ and formed in His image; both of these vital elements were eternally fixed ("predestined") as parts of the great plan of redemption (*P.W.*, 5:301, no. 112).

Charles Wesley's proclamation that people may be "freely justified" connected him with a long line of evangelists and reformers, from the apostle Paul down through the framers of the Anglican *Articles of Religion* and *Homilies*. If Charles brought a distinctive emphasis to justification, it was that acceptance before God meant more than legal pardon; in his theology of redemption, the emphasis was upon the transforming love and joy that flow from a new relationship with God.

The action in Wesley's imaginary courtroom scene is directed away from the legal transaction and toward renewal of relationship, a renewal of heart and life. Hence, judgment and pardon move toward reconciliation and sanctification; the stern Judge melts into the Father of our Lord Jesus Christ. Even when using imagery borrowed from the law court, Charles unconsciously interprets those terms from the standpoint of family relationships.[47] The parable of the Prodigal Son became one of Wesley's favorite analogies for describing the process of reconciliation. The text was one of his favorite sermon topics (*C.W. Journal*, 1:174, 188, 319), but unfortunately none of his homilies based on that passage is extant. Yet many of his hymns based on Luke 15:20 have survived, and they give a sense of the direction his sermons must have taken:

> 1. With mercy's quickest eyes
>   His wretched son He sees,
> The prodigal far off espies,
>   And pities his distress:
>   At sight of human woe
>   His yearning bowels[48] move,
> The Father swiftly runs to show
>   His warm paternal love.
>
> 2. A late-returning child,
>   His mercy's arms embrace,
> His lips declare him reconciled,
>   His lips distilling grace;
>   The kiss dispels his fears,

With balmy words applied,
The self-condemning sinner hears,
And seals him justified.

3. Not one upbraiding word
The pardon'd sinner grieves:
In mercy rich his heavenly Lord
Forgets when He forgives:
He hears his heart's desire,
Preventing his request,
And recent from the swine and mire
Receives him to His breast.
:900 (*P.W.*, 11:236–37, no. 1141)

Juridical judgment, legal payments, debt, honor, and the Judge's wrath are not the controlling factors in Charles's law court imagery. Judgment and damnation are not to be the final words in the celestial docket, he believes, for the Judge is also the Father of our Lord Jesus Christ, and those who are related to Christ by faith are received as wayward children of God's family:

How then shall sinners meet the Lord,
Or His dread day abide,
If cast for every idle word,
Who can be justified?
The men who freely pardon'd here
On Jesu's death depend,
Shall boldly at the bar appear,
And find the Judge their Friend.
(*P.W.*, 10:264, no. 316)

But the Prodigal not only was reconciled to his waiting father, he was robed, feasted, and given costly gifts (Luke 15:22); and in the robe, ring, and shoes, Wesley found symbols of the fruits of reconciliation with God through Christ:

1. Thou hast brought forth for me
That best original dress,
That robe of spotless purity
To hide my nakedness:
The robe Thy children wear
By faith is truly mine,
The perfect heavenly character,
The righteousness Divine.

2. The ring, the Spirit's seal
   I from Thy hands receive,
Earnest of bliss ineffable
      Which only God can give:
      The signet bears His name
      Who left His throne above,
And lo, to Christ betrothed I am
      In mercy, truth, and love.

3. Shod with the gospel-peace
   I safely now go on,
Ready with all Thy messages
      In all Thy paths to run;
      I urge my way with speed,
      And strength invincible,
On serpents, and on scorpions tread,
      On sin, and death, and hell.
            (*P.W.*, 11:238–39, no. 1444)

It is not difficult to chronicle the effects of Charles's proclamation of what he termed "the two great truths of the everlasting gospel" (*C.W. Journal*, 1:286; cf. 128). Soon after his conversion, he began preaching at Newgate Prison and expounding in the religious societies of the London area the story of his newfound faith. On July 9, 1738, less than two months after his personal pentecost, Charles preached in a friend's church at Blendon and then in the vestry of St. Sepulchre church (*C.W. Journal*, 1:117). By September 3 of the same year, he was preaching regularly in the major pulpits and societies of the area; on that date his journal reports: "I preached salvation by faith at Westminster Abbey; gave the cup. In the afternoon I preached at St. Botolph's; and expounded Rom. ii. at Sims's [religious society], to above two hundred people" (*C.W. Journal*, 1:129).

That the Wesleys' "new doctrines" caused quite a stir is indicated by their frequent interviews with their ecclesiastical superiors in the fall of 1738. As early as October 21, the brothers had a tense interview with their bishop, who had been receiving complaints about their sermons. The theological focus of the interview was upon the Wesleys' doctrines of justification by faith and Christian assurance. Charles's journal gave this report of the meeting:

Sat., October 21st. I waited with my brother on the
Bishop of London, to answer the complaints he had
heard against us, that we preached an absolute
assurance of salvation. Some of his words were, "if by
'assurance' you mean an inward persuasion, whereby
a man is conscious in himself, after examining his life
by the law of God, and weighing his own sincerity,
that he is in a state of salvation, and acceptable to
God, I don't see how any good Christian can be
without such an assurance." "This," we answered,
"is what we contend for: but we have been charged as
Antinomians, for preaching justification by faith
only." "Can any one preach otherwise, who agrees to
our Church and the Scriptures?" (*C.W. Journal,*
1:133).

The interview established the fundamental validity of the
Wesleys' theology, and it ended amicably enough. Yet the
wheels of the ecclesiastical machinery were grinding against
them; by November 12, Charles's friend Rev. Piers
"refused me his pulpit through fear of man" (*C.W.
Journal,* 1:135). And two days later, Charles had another
conference with his bishop. The issue at hand had to do
with Wesley's authority to baptize, for his numerous
converts were requesting baptism or (in the case of those
who had not received the baptism of the Church of
England) rebaptism. The bishop "immediately took fire"
at Charles's request and interrupted, "I wholly disapprove:
it is irregular." Charles was not serving (and indeed had
never served) as a parish priest, and he was not a licensed
curate. As a presbyter or elder of the Church of England,
he had the ecclesiastical authority to baptize; but Wesley
and his bishop disagreed on the interpretation of the
"rubric," or church regulations, that dealt with this sort of
baptism. In Charles's mind he needed only inform the
bishop of his actions, but the bishop argued that Wesley
needed his express permission to function in that way:
"But don't you know, no man can exercise parochial duty
in London, without my leave?" A heated exchange followed, with the bishop establishing his authority over the

Methodist preacher, and yet refusing either to give Wesley his permission to perform the baptisms or to take steps to stop him. Charles's terse summary of the results of the conference suggests that charges and countercharges ran fast and furious and that the result was a stand-off:

> He railed at Lawrence on lay-baptism; blamed my brother's sermon, as inclining toward Antinomianism. I charged Archbishop Tillotson with denying the faith. He allowed it, and owned they ran into one extreme to avoid another. He concluded the conference with, "Well, Sir, you knew my judgement before, and you know it now. Good morrow to you" (*C.W. Journal*, 1:136).

In December of 1738, the officials at Oxford were also holding conversations with Charles about the Methodist doctrines: "I was with the Dean; who complained of my brother's obscurity in his sermon on salvation; and expressly denied the assurance of faith, and earnest of the Spirit" (*C.W. Journal*, 1:138).

The next year with the steady increase of the crowds attending their sermons and societies, the Wesleys also met with an increase of tensions between them and the religious establishment. In April 1739, the church wardens at Islington began to take steps to prohibit Charles from preaching there; twice they demanded his license to preach (which they knew he did not have), and by May 1 they physically barred his way to the pulpit: "The Churchwardens still kept guard on the pulpit-stairs. I was not inclined to fight my way through them" (*C.W. Journal*, 1:149). Charles's journal entry for June 23, 1739, recorded his inner conflict over taking the step that everyone around him viewed as being inevitable:

> My inward conflict continued. I perceived it was the fear of man; and that, by preaching in the field next Sunday, as George Whitefield urges me, I shall break down the bridge, and become desperate. I retired, and prayed for particular direction; offering up my friends, my liberty, my life, for Christ's sake and the

Gospel's. I was somewhat less burdened; yet could
not be quite easy, till I gave up all (*C.W. Journal*,
1:155).

The next day Charles preached on the green at Moorfields,
inviting "near ten thousand helpless sinners" in the words
of Jesus, "Come unto me, all ye that travail, and are heavy
laden, and I will give you rest." In fact, he preached three
times that day, and with such effectiveness that he
intimated in his journal: "My load was gone, and all my
doubts and scruples. God shone on my path; and I knew
His will concerning me." It was good that Wesley received
a sense of assurance and affirmation that Sunday, because
Saturday, June 30, found him back in the office of the dean
of his university, "who spoke with unusual severity against
field-preaching . . . ; explained away all inward religion,
and union with God." Charles responded by preaching his
standard message in the Oxford Univerity chapel the next
morning (July 1, 1739):

> I preached my sermon on justification before the
> University, with great boldness. All were very atten-
> tive. One could not help weeping. At night I received
> power to expound; several gownsmen were present;
> some mocked (*C.W. Journal*, 1:156).

Charles had another visit to the dean's office, who "used
his utmost address to bring me off from preaching abroad
[out of doors], from expounding in houses, from singing
psalms: denied justification by faith only, and all vital
religion." But "the bridge was broken down." Gradually
barred from the pulpits of the Church of England, Charles
and his brother became mass evangelists. Ironically, the
message which had brought their exclusion won them an
audience among the masses; Charles soon preached "justification by faith only and vital religion" to multitudes
larger than any church could hold and thereby brought the
message of God's acceptance and restorative power to the
common folk of England.

CHAPTER FOUR:

"An Interest in Jesus' Blood"

It was Charles's custom, after having preached in a town a few times, to wait upon those who were desirous of his counsel to meet with him at the house or inn where he was staying. It was a time of mutual ministry; their newfound faith must have been an encouragement to the Methodist evangelist, and his spiritual counsel marked out the path toward Christian maturity. Hence, on Wednesday, September 26, 1739, Wesley wrote: "From one to three, more came than I was able to talk with; all seeking what many have found. In particular, Anne Sparrin was filled with joy in believing, while we were at prayers last Monday. So was Mrs. Williams, in going home from church. Susanna Trapman likewise sees *her* interest in the *blood of Jesus*" (*C.W. Journal*, 1:180, italics added).

The most common word in Charles Wesley's redemption hymns is *blood*; the term appears over 800 times in his latter hymns alone—roughly twice the number of times the word appeared in Wesley's version of the Bible! *Blood* is a term that conjures up images of death, violence, and sacrifice. In the Old Testament, for example, *blood* (Heb. *dam*) appears 362 times in five basic word families.[1] The most significant and numerically predominant applications connect *blood* with death by violence (203 instances) or sacrificial offerings (103 examples).[2]

The term *blood* receives less currency in the New Testament, where it appears only ninety-eight times. These applications divide into six basic groups, and once again the usages that are most significant (both from a numerical and theological standpoint) connect *blood* (Gk. *haima*) with death by violence or the sacrifice of the new covenant— Jesus' death.[3] It is the latter connection that gives the New Testament usage its most distinctive meaning. Because of Jesus' sacramental injunctions (Matt. 26:26–28), *blood* quickly became a technical term that hearkened back to Jesus' death and yet looked beneath the historical fact to appreciate its enduring theological significance. As Behm writes, "The interest of the NT is not in the material blood of Christ, but in His blood as the life violently taken from Him. Like the cross, the 'blood of Christ' is simply another and even more graphic phrase for the death of Christ in its soteriological significance."[4]

Blood is a term that, to modern sensibilities, does not enhance the appropriateness of some of Wesley's hymns for contemporary worship. John E. Rattenbury reflected this attitude when he wrote: "Today the term 'blood,' to some minds, obscures what it symbolizes rather than illuminates it."[5] Furthermore, contemporary scholarship is divided over the exact significance of blood in the biblical doctrine of redemption. Some, like C. H. Dodd and the British Methodist Vincent Taylor, have contended that the sacrificial associations of the term emphasize the shedding of blood as a release of the life force in an animal. Linking this notion with the imagery of sacrifice, they see the sacrificial act as one of symbolic dedication of life (either one's own life or that of an animal) to the Deity. Thus, in Taylor's view, the blood of sacrifice becomes an emblem of the offering of a life and thereby an act of commitment or dedication.[6]

A second line of discussion is that which finds the primary conception of blood in its association with death. Scholars such as A. M. Stibbs and Leon Morris opt for this association; and, as Morris suggests, the second idea is inclusive of the first: "It is freely admitted that there are some passages in which it is possible to interpret the blood as signifying life, but even these yield a better sense (and one which is consistent with the wider biblical usage) if understood to mean 'life given up in death.' "[7] The question before us then is, How did Charles Wesley understand this crucial redemption word, within which he seemed to be able to include the entire story of redemption?

BLOOD AND DEATH

Charles's most basic application of *blood* seems to be in connection with the death of Christ. This usage was evident, for example, in his unpublished hymn, "For the Nation":

> Thy mercies all our thoughts transcend,
>   The worst Thou canst in Christ forgive
> O let our sins and troubles end,
>   O let our dying nation live
> Hear the loud cry of *Jesus' blood*
>   And save us by the *death of God*.
>   (*Ms. Miscellaneous Hymns*, p. 162)

In this instance and others, *blood* and *death* appear as synonymous terms.[8] This is the usage which seems to set the primary focus of Charles's understanding of blood; it is also evident in words like "the merit of faith in Jesu's blood" (*Ms. Acts*, p. 554).

Another frequent Wesleyan phrase that links blood with death is "Resisting to blood" (*P.W.*, 6:441; 7:228). Once again, the connotation of *blood* is death. The phraseology seems to have been born in Hebrews 12:4: "Ye have not resisted unto blood striving against sin." This passage sets the phrase against the background of Christ's enduring the cross, as an example of the sort of endurance and steadfastness under trial which the apostolic writer hopes to see in his readers. The implication is that the readers had not been tried unto death as their "pioneer and

perfector" had been. A similar identification is to be found
in the Wesleyan phrase, "redemption through His blood,"
which is common in Charles's journal and no doubt has its
roots in passages such as Ephesians 1:15–17 and Colossians
1:14 (*C.W. Journal*, 1:171; cf. p. 193).

In each of these instances, *blood* is a picture word for
Jesus' death. While it is laden with sacrificial overtones,
which suggest substitution and cleansing, its primary focus
is in a graphic recollection of the Lord's death and the
significance it holds for those who believe. Charles's *Hymns
on the Trinity*, No. 54, makes this identification clear in
verse three, where *blood* and *death* are presented as parallel
terms against the larger context of imparting to us the
"prevalence," or saving significance, of the sacrificial
Lamb:

> Thou its infinite desert
> Didst to Thy own *death* impart
>   Didst impart to Thy own *blood*,
> All its prevalence with God:
>   Such a Saviour us became,
> Such we worship in the Lamb!
>   (*P.W.*, 7:241, italics added)

Perhaps Charles's most succinct description of the blood of
Christ was found in a hymn in the section "For One Fallen
From Grace," where "one drop of Thy blood" is described
as "the power of Thy passion below." *Blood*, in Charles
Wesley's poetic parlance, stands for Jesus' death and its
saving significance:

> 1. How shall a lost sinner in pain
>   Recover his forfeited peace?
>   When brought into bondage again
>   What hope of a second release?
>   Will mercy itself be so kind
>   To spare such a rebel as me?
>   And O! can I possibly find
>   Such plenteous redemption in Thee?
>
> 2. O Jesus, of Thee I inquire
>   If still Thou art able to save,
>   The brand to pluck out of the fire
>   And ransom my soul from the grave?

The help of Thy Spirit restore,
  And show me the life-giving blood,
And pardon a sinner once more,
  And bring me again unto God.

3. O Jesus, in pity draw near,
    Come quickly to help a lost soul,
  To comfort a mourner appear,
    And make a poor *Lazarus* whole:
  The balm of Thy mercy apply,
    (Thou seest the sore anguish I feel,)
  Save, Lord, or I perish, I die,
    O save, or I sink into hell!

4. I sink if Thou longer delay
    Thy pardoning mercy to show;
  Come quickly, and kindly display
    The power of Thy passion below!
  By all Thou hast done for my sake
    One drop of Thy blood I implore:
  Now, now let it touch me, and make
    The sinner a sinner no more.
        (*P.W.*, 4:418–19, no. 21)

"Sacrificial Blood"

The Levitical rites explicitly linked blood with Israel's sacrifices to the Lord; and the writer of the Epistle to the Hebrews found in that older imagery a powerful analogy for describing the soteriological significance of Jesus' death (e.g., Heb. 9). Although the sacrificial image is extremely important in Charles Wesley's theology of redemption, direct references to "sacrificial blood" are few. Wesley preferred to develop what one might call a blended image: He interacted with a specific biblical text, described it by drawing in words and allusions from other passages, and then synthesized these into a new and often rather creative poetic product. For example, when Charles expounded Acts 3:22, he blended the prophetic image of the deliverer with sacrificial redemption. The prophet predicted by Moses is the sacrificial Lamb, foreshadowed in Wesley's mind by the Levitical rites and announced by the forerunner in John 1:36. Charles Wesley wove together the biblical texts and images of Acts 3:22 in this manner:

> Soon as *Moses* prophesied,
>   *Israel's* deliverance came,
> Soon as Jesus spake, and died
>   the sacrificial Lamb,
> Life, the grand effect, ensued;
>   That blood for every soul was spilt,
> Purged that all-redeeming blood
>   The universal guilt.
>
> (*P.W.*, 12:165, no. 2410)

A second phrase that carried sacrificial connotations for Charles Wesley was "the covenant blood." It occurs in three biblical passages (Exod. 24:8; Heb. 10:29; 13:20), which relate covenantal communion to sacrificial offerings. While there is some debate as to the exact nature of the connection that the Old Testament draws between covenant and sacrifice, Walter Eichrodt seems to be correct when he speaks of the "ideal of sacral communion" which, in his opinion, "throws new light on the power of sacrifice to create a bond of fellowship."[9] In this connection, the sacrifice took on the character of a sacrament: "The communion sacrifice becomes a sacrament, in which the blessing pronounced by the priest, the hymn sung to the glory of God, the casting of oracles, and the promulgation of law carried out in conjunction with the ritual, all recall men to the exalted power of their divine Lord and Judge, whose fellowship they are experiencing in the celebration."[10]

In the Hebrews passages, the phrase "blood of the covenant" becomes a part of the writer's comparison between Moses and Christ. This contrast is most explicit in Hebrews 3 and 9. In Hebrews 9:20, the "blood of the testament" (or covenant) is introduced in a comparison between the Levitical sacrifice and the death of Jesus. The "blood of the testament" is a functional equivalent for the "blood of the covenant," which is introduced in the context of Hebrews 10:29 and appears again in the benediction of Hebrews 13:20. Like the writer of Hebrews, Charles Wesley moved easily from the symbol of sacrifice and covenantal blood toward the sacrifice of Jesus and the new covenant. This sort of development is evidenced in

Wesley's comment on Jeremiah 50:5, where he tells how the triune God applies the covenant blood in a manner that both takes away our sins (a sacrificial image) and creates everlasting fellowship (a sacramental image):

> Thee, Father, Son, and Holy Ghost,
>   Let all our hearts receive,
> Present with Thy celestial host
>   The peaceful answer give;
> To each the covenant-blood apply
>   Which takes our sins away,
> And register our names on high,
>   And keep us to that day!
>   (*P.W.*, 10:46, no. 1364; cf. 10:119,
>   no. 1559)

"Atoning Blood"

In Charles Wesley's hymns and journal, the "atoning blood" was something "felt" or "applied through the ministry of the Word" (*C.W. Journal*, 1:233). Various hymns pick up the same note by attributing the application of the "atoning blood" to the renewing work of the Holy Spirit (*P.W.*, 7:33). Here one detects Wesley's emphasis on the Protestant connection of Word and Spirit, wherein the Holy Spirit applies the Word (preached, written, or sacramental) to the human heart with convicting and converting power (cf. John 15:25–26; 16:7–11).

But the phrase "atoning blood" is not, strictly speaking, a biblical one; it occurs nowhere in the Authorized Version. It is built, however, out of two crucial redemption images.[11] The first word, *atonement,* is born in the language of sacrifice and describes the way in which sin is "covered" or "washed away" through faithful observance.[12] While there is some debate about exactly how sacrifice atoned for sin—by covering it, washing it away, or turning aside God's wrath—C. L. Mitton's terse summation of the Old Testament application seems accurate and to the point: "The word [*atone*] . . . came to be used in a general sense of removing the effects of sin."[13] The second key term, *blood,* we have already identified as a graphic description of Jesus' death and its saving significance.

In the marriage of these two terms, Charles Wesley produced a redemption phrase *par excellence,* one that declared the removal of sin because of the saving death of Christ. Hence, he wrote of Jesus, "Whose blood did for their sins atone," and of believers' being "wash'd in the' atoning blood" (*P.W.,* 12:305, no. 2699). In a few instances, the washing away of sin was explicitly liked to sacrificial terms such as *expiate:*

> The Rock is smote by *Moses'* rod,
> And pours a consecrated flood:
>   I see the fountain open wide,
> I see the' inseparable tide,
>   Atoning blood and water clean,
> To expiate and wash out my sin.
>   (*P.W.,* 12:89, no. 2262)

This "atoning blood" was the source of "the true liberty of love," and it guaranteed that "we have free access to God" (*P.W.,* 13:143, no. 3297). It was likewise a description of the continuing intercession of Christ, since the Lamb still pleads this blood before the throne:

> On Thee, my Priest, I call;
> Thy blood atoned for all.
>   Still the Lamb as slain appears;
> Still Thou stand'st before the throne,
>   Ever offering up thy prayers,
> *These* presenting with Thy own.
>   (*P.W.,* 1:99)

Charles's application of the phrase "atoning blood" evidenced a clear knowledge of the etymological roots of the word *atone,* for he often linked it to the notion of "covering." His application emphasized these *sinward* connotations of the term, as in an unpublished hymn on Luke 14:16, where *covered* was synonymous with sins *forgiven* (*P.W.,* 13:235, no. 3472). A similar emphasis was maintained where "atoning blood" was used to describe "pardon and salvation" (*Ms. Luke,* p. 213), being "made clean," and "completely justified with God" (*P.W.,* 10:110, no. 1533). But a *Godward* direction was also maintained in Wesley's theology of redemption; hence, this "atoning blood" not only allows one to "know my Father reconciled" (*P.W.*, 11:502–3, no. 2047); it also is said "to quench the wrath of hostile heaven" (*P.W.*, 1:106).

The phrase "atoning blood" has its biblical heritage in the imagery of Levitical sacrifice; but, as was typical with Charles Wesley's approach to the theology of redemption, it was quickly carried forward to describe the death of Christ. Wesley maintained the basic sacrificial connotations of the phrase—the removal of sin and sin's effects. But a second biblical line was also affirmed, one that spoke of the atoning blood as "reconciling God" or "quenching" His wrath (cf. Ps. 79:5–9; 88:16–18). Each of these lines of development becomes more pronounced as we continue our examination of the role that blood played in Charles Wesley's theology of redemption.

"Sprinkled Blood"

A second Wesleyan phrase that had roots sunk deep into the Bible's sacrificial imagery was "sprinkled blood." In Bible times, the sprinkled blood signified the effects of a ritualistic cleansing from sin (Exod. 29:16, 20; Lev. 1:5, 11; 3:2, 8, 13; 6:77; 7:2; 8:19, 24; 9:12, 18). Hence, the writer of Hebrews found it a particularly apt description for the effects of Christ's sacrificial death; the sprinkling of blood is said to be "purifying" (9:13, 23), "sanctifying" (9:13), or "purging" (9:14, 22). Commentators have suggested that since this *sprinkling* described the sacrificial ceremonies (Heb. 9) and Passover (Heb. 11:28) of the old covenant, the early Christians likewise considered *sprinkling* to be baptismal language. Hence, some suggest— based on the identification of *sprinkling* with purification and a parallel between the purification rite of the old and new covenants—that texts such as Hebrews 10:22b and 1 Peter 1:2 use *sprinkling* to describe the effects of Christian baptism.[14]

Charles Wesley did not make this connection between the sprinkling of blood and baptism; High Churchman that he was, we might expect him to draw on that connection to emphasize the importance of the sacrament. But in this instance, experiential religion overwhelmed his churchmanship. For Charles, the sprinkled blood was preeminently something that was "felt."[15] This experiential dimension was further elaborated by the parallel Wesley drew between feeling and knowing, against the background of the sprinkled blood. For example, he spoke of one "Who doth not yet his Saviour *know*, / Or *feel* the sprinkled blood" (*P.W.*, 12:243, no. 2576; 12:236, no. 2560, italics added). For Wesley, "to know" was more than mental cognition; it meant to experience fully and to live in relationship with that which was known. Thus, to "feel the sprinkled blood" was to know Christ as Savior" (*P.W.*, 12:243, no. 2576) or to "know my Lord, my God!" (*P.W.*, 12:236, no. 2560). This "sprinkling" was both a revelatory and a trinitarian event:

> Of Christ the Son of Man
>   The Father doth dispose,
> And whom He raised to life again
>   He to His followers shows:
> But Jesus doth the same;
>   And sprinkling us with blood,
> To all believers in His name
>   He shows Himself as God.
>   (*P.W.*, 7:224, no. 32)

Wesley's identification of "sprinkling" and "showing" is not without its power. In point of fact, the power of the resurrection of Christ is known in this act of sprinkling:

> Thy resurrection's power make known
> Sprinkle the sinner with Thy blood,
> And show Thyself his Lord and God.
>   (*P.W.*, 12:110, no. 2301)

The power of this "sprinkling" includes redemption and cleansing from sin. The same point was made time and time again in Wesley's hymns, using slightly different terms: "Sprinkling" imparts grace (*P.W.*, 10:110, no. 1532); it comes to the hearer as Christ's "reconciling word" (*P.W.*, 10:80, no. 1449); or it is—to take all of these phrases together—the source of one's redemption:

I now in Christ redemption have,
I feel it through the sprinkled blood,
    And testify His power to save,
And claim Him for my Lord, my God!
        (*P.W.*, 6:303)

The Exodus image, which described Israel's liberation from Egyptian bondage, became an appropriate metaphor to describe the effects of the "sprinkled blood." For Wesley, Egypt became the individual's sin, a house of bondage out of which one has been delivered:

We sing as in those earliest days,
    That rapturous infancy of grace,
When first we felt the sprinkled blood,
    Exulting out of *Egypt* came,
And shouting our Redeemer's name,
    Triumphant pass'd the parted flood.
        (*P.W.*, 10:74, no. 1434)

Hence, the believer is able to feel forgiveness in Jesus' blood (*P.W.*, 4:188), and often that experiential reception was explicitly linked to ransom or reconciliation:

Jehovah's co-eternal Son
    Did in our flesh appear beneath,
He laid His life a *ransom* down,
    For every man He tasted death,
To *justify us by His blood*,
    And bring the sprinkled world to God.
        (*P.W.*, 13:3, no. 3036, italics added)

Charles Wesley's use of the imagery of sprinkled blood was heavily dependent upon the theology of the Epistle to the Hebrews. In that context, salvation is described largely in terms of having access to God; access to Him is available only to those who possess inner purity and who have found a way across the chasm sin has set between God and humanity. This sort of development is made clear by the fundamental parallel between two covenants and two priesthoods (Heb. 4–11), which forms the center pole of the book. The most common redemption term in Hebrews is *sanctify,* and the word is often used in ways that would cause us to think of the Pauline conception of justification (Heb. 2:11; 9:13; 10:10, 29; 13:12). In Hebraic Christianity, inner purity was necessary to answer the call "to draw near to God" (Heb. 7:19; James 4:8). Like the writer of Hebrews, Charles Wesley moved directly from justification (reconciliation or access language) to sanctification (cleansing, washing, or purification language).[16] This movement was central to the sacrificial understanding of the phrase "sprinkled blood." The following verse is typical of Charles's application of the sprinkling image to stress redemption and inner cleansing:

> Fain would I wash my soul from sin,
>   In Jesu's wounded side,
> From all the lusts that lodge within,
>   The spawn of self and pride.
> I would be clean, Thou know'st I would,
>   Before I hence depart,
> And feel the sprinkling of that blood
>   Which purifies the heart.[17]

Occasionally, Charles's use of this image followed quite closely the pattern of Hebrews 10:22. Compare Wesley's phrase, "that blood Divine which makes the conscience clean" (*P.W.*, 3:111), with the biblical saying, "our hearts sprinkled from an evil conscience" (Heb. 10:22). Similar effects were achieved when Wesley reported that the sprinkled blood produces "real holiness" (*P.W.*, 10:28–29), or "uttermost salvation" and "finish'd holiness" (*P.W.*, 13:91, no. 3206). The following stanza draws together several of these redemption images to form a powerful statement of Charles's hope for "holiness" in this life:

> This the fruit of Jesus' passion,
>   Peace, inviolable peace,
> Present, uttermost salvation,
>   Love, and finish'd holiness.
> Jesus paid His life to buy us
>   From all sin and guilty fear;
> Pour'd His blood to sanctify us,
>   Body, soul, and spirit here.
>   (*P.W.*, 13:91, no. 3206)

For Charles Wesley, the main image communicated in the phrase "sprinkled blood" was one of cleansing and purification. This "sprinkling" brings a person into a new, redemptive relationship with God; hence, the phrase describes the purifying quality of Christ's death ("the blood") applied to the inner life of a person through the agency of the Word and Spirit of God.

"Sacred Blood" or "Precious Blood"

Because of the transforming effects that Charles Wesley saw latent in Jesus' death, the *blood*—his short-hand expression for Christ's death and its saving significance—could appropriately be termed "sacred" or "precious."[18] When commenting on Hebrews 10:11–13, Wesley termed the blood "sacred," since it "takes the general sin away" and is "That one sufficient sacrifice" (*P.W.*, 13:142, no. 3294). Maintaining the parallel between the two covenants, Charles found the sacramental blood of the new covenant equally "precious." He moved readily from the blood sacrifice of the old covenant to the sacrifice of the Lord's Supper. Commenting on John 6:54, Wesley linked this sacramental language with future union and bliss with Christ:

> Who now His flesh and blood partake,
>   Partakes of the life Divine,
> We soon shall see our Lord come back,
>   His members all in one to join;
> And feeding on this living Bread,
>   This earnest of my glorious bliss,
> I too shall rise to meet my Head;
>   I too shall see Him as He is.
>   (*P.W.*, 11:390, no. 1777)

In commenting on a second passage crucial to our understanding of the Lord's Supper (Matt. 26:28), Wesley described the blood as a "purple fountain" which purges "the universal sin" and makes "our life and nature clean" (*P.W.*, 10:400–401, no. 673). One can only conjecture whether the purple color of the blood is a sign of royalty or the hue of the communion wine; in view of the text, perhaps the latter identification is more likely.

In John 17:24, part of what is often called the "high priestly prayer of Jesus," Charles Wesley found reference to Jesus' "testamental will," which is sealed by the Spirit and written in His own blood (*P.W.*, 12:59, no. 2291). In that case, the value of the blood was found in the connection between blood and "sharing in [Christ's] death." A rare reference, based on Acts 16:31, described Christ's blood as being "consecrating blood," which extended the heavenly kingdom to the children of the church:

> All, except the children? No:
>   Them the Lord will not accept
> Members of His church below,
>   For His heavenly kingdom kept.
> Who would helpless infants wrong?
>   Through the consecrating blood
> Infants all to Christ belong,
>   Infants all are dear to God.
>   (*P.W.*, 12:323, no. 2745)

For Charles Wesley, this blood was sacred or precious because of its source in the death of Jesus (a death that he often associated with sacrificial and sacramental images) and because of its cleansing and redemptive effects among the people of God.

"Blood Applied"

While *blood* is a soteriological epigram for Jesus' death, it is quite obvious that the effects of His death must be "applied" for new life to occur. The image of "blood applied" is loaded with sacrificial connotations, calling to mind the sacramental cleansing by sprinkling with blood. Charles Wesley demonstrated his theological versatility when he examined the way in which the saving blood was applied. Often he said that "Jesus doth His blood apply."[19] Yet it was equally valid for Wesley to write that the "Spirit of Thy Son" applied "the sprinkled blood."[20] In some instances, Wesley spoke of "The Word His blood applying / Seals forgiveness on my heart" (*P.W.*, 12:222, no. 2532). And frequently, he declared that faith applied the blood in a redemptive manner.[21]

Charles's use of the phrase "blood applied" ran the full scope of redemption categories. In almost every instance, he moved quickly from justification to sanctification language, merging those categories together as he described the effects of the "blood applied." He indicated that the application of Jesus' blood was preparatory to justification, since it convicted a person of unbelief (*P.W.*, 13:43, no. 3115). Wesley believed the conviction and call that gave birth to faith were located in the Spirit-blood nexus:

> The Spirit testifies of Him,
>   And gives us faithfully to call
> Jesus, the Lord and God supreme,
>   Whose streaming blood hath ransom'd all:
> That blood the Spirit of Christ applies,
>   That blood of God who never dies.
>   (*P.W.*, 7:279)

Since the Spirit testifies to us about Jesus (John 16:13–14), Wesley located the beginnings of faith in the historical:

> Faith which leads us to the skies
> In faith historical begins;
>   Faith Divine the blood applies
>   That blots out all our sins.
>   (*P.W.*, 12:431, no. 2978)

Virtually all of the standard redemption themes were brought into contact with "blood applied," including pardon, forgiveness, saved, and salvation. In any event, it is clear that the entire Wesleyan concept of justification could be encapsulated in the phrase:

> The blood by faith applied
>   O let it now take place,
> And speak me freely justified,
>   And fully saved by grace.
>   (*P.W.*, 6:3, no. 1)

But Charles preferred to speak of a "full salvation"; therefore, it was natural that his conception of justification by the agency of "blood applied" would merge with sanctification metaphors. Thus, he could say that the same

"blood" which justified "cleanses / Every stain" and
"Blot[s] out my offences" (*P.W.*, 7:384, no. 32). Cleansing
and washing became powerful metaphors in Wesley's
hymnology, describing the inward work begun in redemptive relationship with Christ.[22] This cleansing process is
ongoing; as Charles put it, the blood "daily purifies"
(*P.W.*, 12:299, no. 2692). Its fruits are "perfect purity and
peace" (*P.W.*, 13:173, no. 3352). Thus, in Wesley's
language, the application of the blood by the Holy Spirit
became synonymous with sanctification:

> Send us the Spirit of Thy Son,
>   To make the depths of Godhead known,
> To make us share the life Divine;
>   Send Him the sprinkled blood to' apply,
>   *Send Him, our souls to sanctify,*
>   *And show, and seal us ever Thine.*[23]

Charles testified that "Jesu's blood applies, / Absolves, and
wholly sanctifies" (*P.W.*, 13:71, no. 3170). The process of
sanctification involved both the removing of one's sin
(original and actual) and the filling with God's love:

> God of grace, vouchsafe to me
>   That Spirit of holiness,
> Sighs my heart for purity,
>   And pants for perfect peace;
> Spirit of faith, the blood apply,
>   Which only can my filth remove,
> Fill my soul, and sanctify
>   By Jesu's heavenly love.
>   (*P.W.*, 12:298, no. 2690).

Because of Charles's wonderment at the seemingly
impossible task of purifying the inward person, and his
corresponding optimism about the possibilities of God's
grace, his verse occasionally seemed to anticipate the
modern Tillichian phrase, "the impossible possibility."
What seems impossible from the standpoint of the depth of
our plight becomes possible by God's grace:

> Soon as that efficous blood
>   Applied by living faith I feel,
> I feel my heart and life renew'd

Wrought is the thing impossible;
Effaced are all my inbred stains,
And not one spot of sin remains.
(*P.W.*, 10:23, no. 1310)

A more common Wesleyan formulation of the phrase "blood applied" connected sanctification with the cleansing-filling effects of "perfect love" (*P.W.*, 7:401, no. 47).

Wesley consistently maintained an experiential dimension in his understanding of the "blood applied." Repeatedly he said that one "felt the blood applied."[24] Another experiential result of the application of the blood was what Charles termed "melting." The term described a softening of the heart hardened by sin, so that it might respond to the Word of redemption.[25] Wesley expressed much the same idea through another analogy:

Bleeding love—I long to feel it!
Let the smart Break my heart,
Break my heart and heal it.
(*P.W.*, 7:384)

The terminology of *melting* was more prominent in Charles's early hymns (*P.W.*, 3:168; 4:265) and seemed to diminish in occurrence in the material he composed after 1749, though exactly why this is so is not clear.

A third experiential focus of the application of the term *blood* was to be found in the results it brings to the soul.[26] Forgiveness is sealed on the soul or heart (*P.W.*, 12:222, no. 2532; cf. 7:397, no. 43). This was synonymous with saying that it has a calming effect (*P.W.*, 13:235, no. 3472), which "Eases all our anguish" (*P.W.*, 4:208). The result of this experience is a sense of tranquillity that stems from a cessation of the quest for inner satisfaction:

Then, then my wandering toil is o'er,
Restless I sigh and pine no more
For local happiness;
Confident in thy blood applied,
Mine inmost soul is satisfied
With everlasting peace.
(*P.W.*, 7:136)

The application of Christ's blood was a central image in Charles Wesley's soteriology. It ran the whole redemption gamut, touching upon every doctrine and rooting itself firmly in the Christ event and in Christian experience. The "blood applied" was such a complete statement of Wesley's theology of redemption that he could say the jeers of the inhabitants of Jerusalem (Matt. 27:25)—"His blood be on us, and on our children"—become the "best of prayers . . . if rightly used" (*C.W. Journal*, 1:410). In his hymnological commentary on that Bible verse, Charles wrote:

> Horrible wish! Thy murderers dare
>   The blessing to a curse pervert:
> *We* turn the curse into a prayer;
>   To cleanse our lives, and purge our heart,
> In all its hallowing, blissful powers
>   Thy blood be, Lord, on us and ours!
>   (*P.W.*, 10:423, no. 731).

"Cleansing Blood" or "Washing Blood"

The image of cleansing or washing in blood was implicit in the sacrificial and ritual purifications of the Old Testament (as we noted above); but the actual term "washing blood" does not occur in the biblical record. Several New Testament verses do, however, present this image. First John 1:7 ("and the blood of Jesus Christ his Son cleanseth us from all sin") and Revelation 1:5 ("Unto him that loved us, and washed us from our sins in his own blood") seemed formative in the development of Wesley's use of the phrase. Generally he followed the New Testament pattern by linking the cleansing effect of Jesus' death with our sin:

> The worst of the foulest slaves of sin
>   May this salvation know
> Thro' faith in Jesus' blood made clean
>   And wash'd as white as snow:
> Heathens, whene'er to Him they turn,
>   He takes their sins away,
> Exalted with us who long have borne
>   The burthen [*sic*] of the day.[27]

Occasionally, Charles used *washed* and *saved* as though they were synonymous terms (e.g., *P.W.*, 12:230, no. 2547). This connection offers an important clue to his conception of the washing image; it has its basis in justification and is an appropriate symbol for redemption and other related ideas.[28] *Washing,* in this sense, became a shorthand expression for one's entrance into a saving relationship with Christ.

But Charles's application of the washing image did not deal with justification as though it could easily or logically be separated from sanctification. Once again, the Wesleyan impulse was to hold those two distinct aspects of salvation together to form one unified mosaic:

> Fronting the throne a crystal sea,
>   Rolls on its perfect purity,
> Laver of sanctifying grace,
>   It justly holds the middle space,
> For none approach the holy God,
>   Till thoroughly wash'd in Jesu's blood.
>   (*P.W.*, 5:287, no. 1290; cf. 10:11)

The washing in Jesus' blood produced the holiness without which no one can see God.

Wesley vigorously described what unwanted aspect was washed away or cleansed in Jesus' blood. The impurity was always identified as sin, but it was described in various ways. Sometimes the "mountain sins" of "Wrath, concupiscence, and pride" were cleansed away:

> For Thine own sake I pray,
>   Take all my sins away:
> Other refuge have I none,
>   None do I desire beside;
> Thou hast died for all to' atone,
>   Thou for me, for me hast died.
>
> Hast died that I might live,
>   Might all Thy life receive;
> Hasten, Lord, my heart prepare,
>   Bring Thy death and suffering in,
> Tear away my idols, tear,
>   Save me, save me from my sin.

O bid it all depart,
  This unbelief of heart,
All my mountain sin remove;
  Wrath, concupiscence, and pride,
Cast them out by perfect love,
  Save me, who for me hast died.
          (P.W., 4:242; cf. 7:109–10, no. 91)

On other occasions, Charles stated that the "guilty load" was removed by the cleansing of one's conscience (P.W., 13:100, no. 3227). In his development of the theme, the forensic (outward) and experiential (inward) dimensions of the cleansing were welded together. Wesley consistently maintained the notion that there was also divine rejection directed against sinners or their sins; thus, those who "groan beneath the curse of God" should "plunge in the all-cleansing blood" (P.W., 13:162, no. 3327). In this and most other instances, Charles preferred to mix his metaphors to cast light on many facets of the diamond of redemption. In the following verse, which is by no means atypical, Wesley wedded the washing away of one's sins, the granting of pardon, and healing in a wholistic sense:

Come, then, his life, his strength, his peace,
  The power let Thy blood release,
Thy blood the patient heal,
  While prostrate at Thy feet we pray,
Thy blood wash all his sins away,
  And now his pardon seal.
          (P.W., 7:148, no. 123)

This all-encompassing conception of the cleansing effects of Jesus' blood had as its goal the believer's moving through justification to sanctification:

Through Jesu's blood to wash away
  My filthiness of wrath and pride;
So shalt Thou give me in that day
  A lot among the sanctified.
          (P.W., 13:200, no. 3401)

So, believers are "Wash'd in Thy sanctifying blood" (P.W., 12:379, no. 2860; cf. 6:334, no. 26). A favorite

Wesley cliché for sanctification—"saved to the utter-most"—also described the washing in the blood:

9. Now, Saviour, bring the joyful hour,
   (If pardon in Thy blood I have,)
   With all Thy sanctifying power,
   Make speed to help, make haste to save.

10. Tell me my faith hath made me whole,
    And th'roughly wash'd in Thy own blood,
    Save, to the utmost save my soul,
    And plunge me in the depths of God.
          (*P.W.*, 13:191, no. 3384)

As stated earlier, Charles's conception of Christian perfection carried with it a vision of recapturing the original righteousness lost in the Edenic Fall. This perfection was often described as a cleansing in Jesus' blood and being made pure as God is pure:

6. This, this is all my plea,
   Thy blood was shed for me,
   Shed, to wash my conscience clean,
   Shed, to purify my heart,
   Shed, to purge me from all sin,
   Shed, to make me as Thou art.

7. O that the cleansing tide
   Were now, even now applied;
   Plunge me in the crimson flood,
   Drown my sins in the *Red Sea*,
   Bring me now, even now to God,
   Swallow up my soul in Thee!
          (*P.W.*, 4:242–43, no. 24)

Charles Wesley could describe sanctification as "full redemption in the all-cleansing blood" (*C.W. Journal*, 1:307), being "Completely saved" (*P.W.*, 12:152, no. 2389), or having "perfect holiness" (*P.W.*, 12:19, no. 2105). These were synonymous terms describing the inner renovation effected as Jesus' death puts an end to inward sin.

But this process of cleansing or washing was not merely a removal of filthiness or sin; it also had the positive effects of spreading cleanliness or righteousness throughout

the person cleansed. This cleansing had as its ultimate
result Christ's entering one's life to cast out sin and to plant
His own nature in the Christian:

> I want the gospel purity,
>   Th' implanted righteousness of God:
> Jesus reveal thyself to me,
>   And wash me in thy hallowing blood;
> Enter, thyself and cast out sin,
>   Thy nature spread thro' every part,
> And nothing common or unclean,
>   Shall ever more pollute my heart.[29]

Charles often explained this work of personal
purification by linking the blood of Jesus with the work of
the Holy Spirit; hence, he wrote: "Cleansed by Jesu's
blood, / By the Spirit sanctified" (*P.W.*, 12:216, no. 2520).
In other instances, Christ's blood was said to purchase the
Comforter, and then the Comforter applies the blood to
"keep us pure in life and heart" (*P.W.*, 7:243, no. 56).

The imagery Wesley used to describe this process of
cleansing was rich and varied. As we have seen, the terms
most often depicted the removal of dirt or filthiness,
metaphorically signifying the removal of sin and unrighteousness; this exposition followed the basic pattern of New
Testament texts such as 1 John 1:7 and Revelation 1:5.
Occasionally, the blood of Christ was described as though
it were in a fountain from which we might wash (*P.W.*,
7:109–10, no. 91). Using an image drawn from Isaiah 1:18,
Charles described the process as being "wash'd white as
snow."[30] This washing resulted in the many blessings that
accompanied "full salvation":

> Liberty in Christ we have,
>   Forgiveness through His blood,
> Feel His present power to save,
>   By sin no more subdued:
> When He wash'd us white as snow,
> Clothed with righteousness and power,
>   Jesus loosed, and bade us go,
>   And yield to sin no more.
>   (*P.W.*, 13:70, no. 3168)

Charles found this same washing and renewal allegorically expressed in the crossing of the Red Sea, where "my sins were drowned" (*P.W.*, 4:242–43, no. 24).

This process of cleansing was set forth in sacrificial images, like those suggested by the word *sprinkling* (*P.W.*, 7:356). In other instances, the focus was turned from the altar to the scapegoat (Lev. 16:21) that symbolically bore away the sins of Israel (*Ms. Acts*, p. 292; *P.W.*, 6:334, no. 126). The fountain of blood was mirrored in the basin Jesus used to wash the disciples' feet in the Upper Room (John 13:4–10). Our cleansing was echoed in Peter's response to Jesus: "Unless He wash me in His blood / I have no part with Him" (*P.W.*, 7:108, no. 90). The blood likewise is found in the baptismal font, which marks the beginning of the Christian child's pilgrimage unto righteousness:

> . . . Seize the young sinner as Thy right,
> Before it good or evil know,
> And cleanse in the baptismal flood,
> And wash my babe through Jesus' blood.
>
> . . . Nor ever, Lord, Thy charge forsake,
> Nor let Thy charge depart from Thee,
> But walk in all Thy righteous ways,
> Till meet to see Thy glorious face.
> (*P.W.*, 7:62–63, no. 55)

BLOOD AND PURCHASE LANGUAGE

Charles Wesley's use of *blood* as a redemption image often placed it in conjunction with various words having a heritage in the language of commercial transactions. The Bible, of course, uses similar images to expound the doctrine of redemption; for example, the phraseology of Acts 20:28 ("purchased with his own blood") was particularly significant for Wesley, and similar ideas were suggested in various Pauline passages (cf. 1 Cor. 6:20; 7:23; Eph. 2:13; Col. 1:14).

One of the interesting innovations Charles showed in his application of the biblical purchase language appeared in his consideration of what was purchased and who the purchaser was. He began with the Pauline foundation laid in 1 Corinthians 6:20 ("Ye are bought with a price"); but in Charles's verse, the Pauline *Ye* became the more inclusive Wesleyan *We*.In this rendition of the Scripture, the singer cannot remain a spectator to the event of grace; it becomes instead a confession upon one's own lips:

> 4. Salvation to God,
>   Who bought us with blood;
>   Through Jesus's name
> Acceptance, and pardon, and heaven we claim.

> 5. By mercy alone
>   He made us His own;
>   His mercy is free;
> How else could He love such a rebel as me!
>   (*P.W.*, 5:57, no. 150)

Charles persistently personalized the biblical phraseology of redemption:

> Jesus our Shepherd great and good,
> Who dying bought us with His blood,
>   Thou hast brought us back to life again.[31]

In a similar way, Charles's songs of experiential religion blended the personal appropriation of Jesus' grace with deeds of personal discipleship:

> Long as my day of life remains,
>   My business is to work for God,
> To' employ my utmost strength and pains
>   For Him who bought me with His blood;
> No respite from the toils of love
>   I ask, till life's short season end:
> Suffice for me to rest above,
>   To rest with my eternal Friend.
>   (*P.W.*, 11:438, no. 1893)

But personalization did not narrow Wesley's redemptive focus; in fact, the focus was broadened to include "all," "the nations," or "a guilty world," in the purchase of Jesus' blood:

> 7. We feel it, and pray
>   The world might obey
>   Our Saviour and King,
> Whose mercy to all His salvation would bring.

8. O that all men would prove
   His sweetness of love,
   And come to receive
The pardon to all He so freely did give!

9. O that every knee
   Might bow unto Thee!
   Their ransom and peace,
Thee, Jesus, let every sinner confess![32]

When we consider *what* was purchased by Jesus' blood, we find once again that Wesley's pattern was rich and variegated. Often he referred to a "blood-bought pardon," "salvation," or "peace" being purchased by "the Redeemer's blood,"[33] emphasizing the lavish price paid for such wonderful gifts (as in Eph. 1:14).

Shifting imagery ever so slightly, Charles also recognized in the roots of Greek New Testament words from the *lutron* family a history in the slave trade; in fact, the primary meaning of *lutron* (ransom) in classical Greek was the sum of money that was paid to release a slave from bondage.[34] The noun was probably derived from the Greek verb *luō* (to loose, to free, or to untie).[35] The language of emancipation became a powerful tool for describing the saving effects of Christ's death. Commenting on the text of John 8:34 ("Whosoever committeth sin is the servant of sin"), Charles portrayed the human condition as a universal sin servitude:

1. Slaves we all by nature are,
   To every vice inclined,
   Foil'd and prisoners took in war,
   Our conqueror's yoke we find:
   We to sin ourselves have sold
And basely bow'd to passion's sway:
   By a thousand lusts controll'd,
   We dare not disobey.

2. By the guilt and tyranny
   Of cruel sin oppress'd,
   Lord, we will not come to Thee
   For freedom and for rest:
   Break this adamantine chain,
Who only canst the soul release,

> Change the stubborn will of man
> And bid us go in peace.
> (*P.W.*, 11:427, no. 1865)

In Wesley's parlance, a ransom was paid in Jesus' blood (*P.W.*, 6:2, no. 1; 13:63, no. 3156). Christ's death both "laid [one's] ransom down," purchasing the Christian out of the slavery of sin, and made one "free indeed," able "to sin no more":

> 1. Jesus, suffering Son of God,
>   Thy nature is to save,
>   Let me pardon in Thy blood,
>   And with Thy Spirit have:
>   Full of mercy as Thou art,
> Grant the pardon I implore,
>   Peace to keep my faithful heart,
>   And power to sin no more.
>
> 2. Liberty from my own sin,
>   Thou only canst bestow,
>   Make my guilty conscience clean,
>   And loose, and let me go.
>   If that blood Divine was shed
> The general liberty to buy,
>   Come and make me free indeed,
>   Or bought by Thee, I die.
>
> 3. Longing in my gracious Lord,
>   Redemption to obtain,
>   If I perish unrestored
>   Thyself hast died in vain:
>   Saviour, now Thy purchase seize,
> Thou hast laid my ransom down;
>   Now from all my sins release,
>   And seal me for Thine own.
>   (*P.W.*, 13:70–71, no. 3169)

Not only did the manumission imagery vividly describe deliverance from the bondage to sin, it also spoke well of the resultant state redemption implied for the believer. Charles used the phrase "redemption in His blood" as a dramatic synonym for salvation or deliverance (*C.W. Journal*, 1:177, 193; *P.W.*, 6:282; 7:370; 10:140; 12:63; 12:295); and this was quite consistent with the biblical usage. Ephesians 1:7, Colossians 1:14, and Revelation 5:9

explicitly connect blood with a redemption price; and
1 Peter 1:18–19 is especially supportive of Charles's usage,
since it identifies the "blood of Christ" as the "ransom" of
our redemption. Wesley also found *reconciliation* to be a
suitable parallel term for *redemption,* and he occasionally
employed those two terms together (*P.W.,* 10:40; 13:22).
Among the fruits of this blood-bought redemption were
reconciliation, fellowship with God, rest, and the "life of
perfect love":

> Jesus full of truth and grace,
>   To me my bondage show,
> That I gladly may embrace
>   The gift Thou wouldst bestow,
> Find redemption in Thy blood,
> The joy of Thy disciples prove,
>   Live with all the sons of God
>   The life of perfect love.
>   (*P.W.,* 11:426–27, no. 1864;
>   cf. *C.W. Journal,* 1:193)

The result of this reconciliation or blood-bought pardon is
living in the kingdom of God:

> Lord, we own the Kingdom thine,
> The Kingdom of the Dying God,
> Won by agonies Divine,
> And bought with all Thy blood.
>   (*Ms. Luke,* p. 342)

Entrance into the "Kingdom of the Dying God" meant
living in the power of His reign; justification merged and
met sanctification as Charles meditated upon the saying of
Matthew 6:10 ("Thy kingdom come"):

> 2. Our first and last desire
>   That all our God may own,
>   Thy majesty admire,
>   And worship at Thy throne;
>   That all may bow before Thee,
>   Jesus, Thy power assume,
>   And manifest Thy glory,
>   And let Thy kingdom come.
>
> 3. The virtue of Thy Spirit
>   To every soul impart,

And let us here inherit
  The kingdom in our heart,
The evangelic blessing,
  Inviolable peace,
Celestial joy increasing,
  And finish'd holiness.

4. Thy kingdom's restoration
    O might we feel within,
  Thine uttermost salvation
    Exterminating sin!
  Let sin and Satan's power
    At Thy appearing fall,
  And all on earth adore
    The glorious Lord of all.
            (*P.W.*, 10:179–80, no. 109)

One of the important Wesleyan contributions to the doctrine of redemption (which is reflected in his use of purchase language to describe the effects of Christ's death) was Charles's insistence that the Holy Spirit was purchased and bestowed upon the believer through the blood. The following verse is representative of many others:

The Comforter bestow'd
He hasten'd to declare,
  Purchased of the Redeemer's blood,
And answer of His prayer;
  Another Pentecost
That multitudes might find,
  And witness God the Holy Ghost
Pour'd out on all mankind.
            (*P.W.*, 12:370, no. 2845)

The Authorized Version offers no passage that directly links the blood of Jesus with the bestowal of the Holy Spirit. But, if we recall that blood is Wesley's epigram for the soteriological significance of Christ's death, it becomes clear that Charles's development of the connection between the purchasing blood and the coming of the Holy Spirit is consistent with the New Testament record. The Comforter would not come until Jesus "went away" (John 16:7), through His death and resurrection. The Spirit would perform the task of making the absent Christ present in the lives of His disciples (John 14:16–18, 26). Again we see that blood forms a nexus between justification and sanctification; the blood-bought pardon or forgiveness blended easily with Wesley's concept of a "taste of glorious bliss below," the gifts of the Spirit bringing a foretaste of "holiness, and heaven." This marvelous montage of biblical imagery emerges in Charles's comment on 1 Corinthians 2:12 ("We have received . . . the spirit which is of God"):

1. God on us His Spirit bestow'd
   That we His other gifts may know,
   A pardon bought with Jesu's blood,
   A taste of glorious bliss below:
   The Spirit our conscience certifies
   That God to man hath freely given
   Wine without money, without price,
   Forgiveness, holiness, and heaven.

2. The Comforter assures our hearts,
   Our Father, to His children dear;
   Fresh strength continually imparts,
   To fight, o'ercome, and persevere.
   Our Father gave to Christ alone
   Fulness of grace, and heavenly powers,
   But hath on us conferr'd His Son,
   And Christ, and all in Christ, is ours.
   (*P.W.*, 13:24–25, no. 3077)

"Pardon in Jesus' Blood"

The word *pardon* is not found in the Authorized Version of Charles Wesley's day. The closest New Testament synonym for *pardon* is found in words of the *aphiēmi* family, which are generally translated "to release," "to let go," "to hurl," "to remit," or "to forgive."[36] Charles was quite fond of expressions that linked *pardon* with the *purchase* of Jesus' blood (*P.W.*, 6:1, no. 1; 6:80; 7:114; 12:229). *Pardon* appears nearly four hundred times in his later hymns alone! Exactly why Wesley turned to this term with such frequency is not certain; perhaps Charles was simply fond of poetic alliterative effects of a two-syllable word with an initial *p* formed with *purchase*. His usage of the term made it clear that he thought of it as a synonym for *forgiveness, grace,* or *acceptance.*

One of the interesting turns that Charles gave the phrase emerged when he said that pardon was sealed by blood:

> The' atonement Thou for all hast made,
>   O that we all might now receive!
> Assure us now the debt is paid,
>   And Thou hast died that all may live,
> Thy death for all, for us reveal,
>   And let Thy blood *my* pardon seal.
>   (*P.W.*, 3:271, no. 79)

The idea behind *sealing* runs deep into antiquity, reaching back to a time when documents of any real importance were impressed with a seal. This same practice continued into the eighteenth century, and many of the Wesleys' own letters bear the imprint of having been sealed in this way. Originally, the sealing was done with clay and a signet; later, sealing wax replaced the clay. The practice was common among the Jews in the Old Testament era (1 Kings 21:8; Esth. 8:8, 10; Isa. 29:11; Dan. 9:24); but it also had a metaphorical application, in which *sealing* meant "to close up" (Dan. 6:17). This connotative use of the word was continued into the New Testament (e.g., Matt. 27:66; Rev. 20:3). Documents that were symbolically "sealed" were confirmed or attested.[37]

This extended application opened the way for *sealing* to be used as a synonym for *promise, pledge,* or *attestation.* This usage appeared occasionally in the later literature of the Old Testament (Song of Sol. 8:6; Hag. 2:23), and came into prominence in the Johannine and Pauline writings. In John 3:33 it is written: "He that hath received his testimony hath set to his seal that God is true." Here *sealed* implies attestation or confirmation. Paul's use of *sphragis* followed this same line of development.[38]

Perhaps the most interesting Pauline application of this word is found in Ephesians 1:13, in which the Ephesians are said to have been "sealed with that holy Spirit of promise." In this text, the word *sealed* does not suggest being closed but being attested or confirmed. Hence Ephesians 1:13 is probably best understood as using the imagery of the seal in the same sense that 2 Corinthians 1:22 and 5:5 say that the Holy Spirit is an "earnest" (Gk. *arrhabōn*), "pledge," or "surety" of salvation.[39] Charles Wesley's application of the phrase "pardon sealed" followed this same line of development; the forgiveness bought by the blood of Christ is sealed upon the inner person by the work and attestation of the Word and Spirit:

> 1. No outward miracles we claim,
>   Whose God and gospel are the same,
>   Yet trust our faithful Lord
>   His truth and mercy to reveal,
>   And pardon on the conscience seal
>   Through His attested word.
>
> 2. Whene'er we preach the dying God,
>   And free forgiveness through His blood,
>   The gospel-grace is given,
>   Spiritual signs are daily shown,
>   And God the Holy Ghost sends down,
>   In saving power from heaven.
>   (*P.W.*, 12:155)

Charles Wesley worked the biblical etymology to its fullest extent. When he said that the pardon was "sealed," he implied that it was closed and confirmed in Jesus' death ("blood") and that it was experientially attested by the work of the Holy Spirit.

"Healing in the Blood"

One of the main images that Charles Wesley connected with the blood of Christ was its healing aspect. Although the Authorized Version presented many examples of miraculous healing, both by Jesus and his disciples, not much is said (directly) about the healing effect of His blood. Perhaps the closest biblical parallel to Wesley's use of the term is found in 1 Peter 2:24: "Who his own self bare our sins in his own body on the tree, that we, being dead to sins, should live unto righteousness: by whose stripes ye were healed." In this passage, the word *healing* is set in structural parallel with the dying to sin and living unto righteousness—indicating a metaphorical, soteriological understanding of healing. This meaning was central to Charles's development of the image. His hymns refer to the "wounds" healed when he wished to suggest recovery from the injury that sin works upon the inner person:

> 1. Jesus, was ever love like Thine,
>   So strong, and permanent, and pure!
>   Strange mystery this of love Divine,
>   That stripes should heal, and death should cure.
>
>   . . . . .
>
> 4. Let others to the creature fly,
>   I still betake me to Thy blood,
>   I on Thy only blood rely
>   For life, for physic, and for food.
>
> 5. Thy blood did all my sorrows calm,
>   And ease the anguish of my soul,
>   And when I ask for *Gilead's* Balm,
>   It still is near to make me whole.
>   (*P.W.*, 5:66–67)

Generally, Charles Wesley's development of the healing effects of Jesus' blood took its point of departure from the prophet's rhetorical question in Jeremiah 8:22: "Is there no balm in Gilead; is there no physician there?" In Charles's allegorical exegesis, the unspoken reply to Jeremiah's question was: "Yes, Jesus' blood is the healing balm." The phrase "Gilead's balm" became a soteriological epigram for the healing effects of faith in Jesus' death; its results were peace, ease, and wholeness.

This symbol of the healing balm was often merged with other images in Wesley's hymns in order to elaborate the restorative process. The oil and wine, drawn from the parable of the Good Samaritan, was one of Wesley's standard connections:

> No peace is for the wicked found;
>   We all are wickedness within,
> Till Thou search out our spirit's wound,
>   And pour the balm of *Gilead* in,
> The joy and love, the oil and wine,
>   And heal our souls with blood Divine.
>   (*P.W.*, 10:14, no. 1295)

More often, however, Charles simply referred to *balm* without specifically identifying it with the "balm of Gilead."[40] Healing is still the major theme suggested by the shorter phrase, but Wesley seemed to prefer the broader term *wholeness* to *healing* (*P.W.*, 7:191; 10:14; 13:126, no. 3271). Occasionally, he abandoned the symbol of the balm altogether and directly described the healing properties of Jesus' blood:

> Sick of every disease that a spirit can know,
>   I out of myself for a remedy go;
> The remedy gushes from Jesus's side,
>   And my soul shall be heal'd when His blood is applied.
>
> (*P.W.*, 13:245; cf. 11:443; 12:83–84)

The soteriological effects of Jesus' death ("blood") bring *wholeness* in the fullest sense of the word. The balmy blood applied to the sinner means healing, peace, pardon, sanctification, and love:

> His precious blood both wounds and heals,
>   (When faith the balm applies,)
> My peace restores, my pardon seals,
>   My nature sanctifies;
> His precious blood the life inspires
>   Which angels live above,
> And fills my infinite desires,
>   And turns me all to love.
>
> (*P.W.*, 7:191, no. 157)

"Speaking Blood"

One of the most vivid allusions that Charles Wesley constructed out of the symbol of Christ's blood was a personification of the blood that enabled it to speak on behalf of sinners. The image is vigorous, dramatic, and mythic. Its roots are to be found, perhaps, in the only biblical passage that gives blood a voice (Gen. 4:9–10). Wesley, a master weaver of biblical texts and images, merged the accusatory "speaking blood" of Abel's death with the sacrificial blood of Leviticus and Golgotha. In his hymns, the sacrificial blood speaks, generally in intercession: "His blood that speaks and intercedes" (*P.W.*, 10:317, no. 462). This symbol of the speaking, intercessory blood reveals the mediatorial role of Christ and His death:

> O might the blood
>   Which speaks to God
> With ceaseless intercession,
>   Now remove my sinful load,
> And blot out my transgression.
>   (*P.W.*, 13:161–62)[41]

The purpose of this intercession was both the redemption and the purification of sinners; hence, the goal of the speaking blood was the restoration of Edenic perfection:

> 1. O that I could
>   Approach the blood
>   Which quench'd His indignation,
>   Satisfied a righteous God,
>   And purchased my salvation.
>
> 2. Sprinkled on me
>   Now let it be,
>   The blood that cries in heaven,
>   Loud as when it stain'd the tree,
>   And spake a world forgiven.
>
>   · · · · · ·
>
> 4. Faith lends an ear,
>   The blood to hear,
>   For sinners interceding;
>   Banishes my guilty fear,
>   And gives me back my *Eden*.
>   (*P.W.*, 13:161, no. 3326)

Wesley used three basic images to describe the intercessory role of the blood. His most common approach was simply to say that the "blood speaks."[42] He said that the blood speaks "before the throne" or in "the Father's ears."[43] In either case, however, it is clear that there is nothing magical about the blood's intercessory role. The blood is effective because it signifies Jesus' saving death.

There is a sense in which the image paints an antithesis between the Father's wrath and the sinner's plight. The "speaking blood" turns the Father's wrath to favor:

> Father, hear the blood of Jesus
>> Speaking in Thine ears above;
> From Thy wrath and curse release us,
>> Manifest Thy pardoning love;
> O receive us to Thy favour,
>> For His only sake receive,
> Give us to our bleeding Saviour,
>> Let us by Thy dying live.
>> *(P.W.,* 3:225, no. 14)

A second term that Charles used to describe the dramatic intercession of the blood was *pleading.* In this phraseology, the intercessory act was intensified.[44] The blood "pleads for all" *(Ms. John,* p. 334) or, more specifically, "pleads for me" *(P.W.,* 7:154). The goal of this pleading was generally identified as redemption, but it also included a plea for future life with God.

The third and final term that the Wesleyan hymns used to describe the intercessory role of the blood emerged in connecting it with *prayer.*[45] Prayer is in itself an intercessory act; but its mediatory power is emphasized when the idea of prayer is linked to the blood of Christ's intercession through phrases such as "praying blood." Wesley used this phrase to refer to prayer for mercy on behalf of sinners *(P.W.,* 4:158; 7:370), though in some instances it referred to a prayer for the sending of the Comforter:

> 4. The Spirit of their God,
>> Doth in the saints abide,
> He is, He is by Thee bestow'd,
>> For Thou *art* glorified;
>> Thy blood's unceasing prayer,
>> And strong prevailing plea,
> Hath now obtain'd the Comforter
>> For all mankind, and me.
>> *(P.W.,* 4:171–72; cf. 4:203–4)

Charles's hymns also gave the blood a voice of declaration; occasionally the blood pronounced the sinner forgiven, pardoned, or justified.[46] There was a transforming element involved in this declaratory work of the blood. Wesley said that the blood "speaks within" to "blot out my offenses," or it "speaks my spirit whole" (*Ms. Miscellaneous Hymns*, p. 83). Because of the inner changes wrought by the blood of Christ, Wesley could say that it "speaks me to paradise" or "speaks Thy rebels up to heaven" (*P.W.*, 7:398, no. 6). The blood's declarations justified the sinner and brought inward renewal; the individual's inner transformation and future destination were cemented together in Charles's poetic presentation of the "speaking blood."

The "speaking blood" stood at the hub of Charles Wesley's christology and his theology of redemption. It linked the saving death of Jesus with the effectiveness of His heavenly intercession and the coming of the Comforter into the lives of Christians. The following unpublished verse shows how the blood, which convicts of "sin and righteousness" and seals one's pardon, has further effects in heaven and on earth. It pleads on high and sends the Spirit to "impute impart righteousness" to the faithful:

1. Come then to those who want thine aid,
    Who now beneath their burthen [*sic*] groan,
    Bind up the wound Thyself hast made,
    The righteousness of faith make known,
    Offer'd to all of Adam's lair,
    The perfect righteousness Divine.

2. Convince the sons who feel their sin
    There is, there is a ransom found
    A bitter righteousness brought in,
    And grace doth more than sin abound;
    Pardon to all is freely given,
    For Jesus is return'd to heaven.

3. He died to purge our guilty stain,
    He rose the world to justify,
    And while the heavens our Lord contain,
    No longer seen by mortal eye,
    He reigns our Advocate above,
    And pleads for all his bleeding love.

4. His bleeding love is Thine to seal
    With pardon the contrite heart;
    To us, to us the grace reveal
    The righteousness impute impart,
    Discharge thy second function here,
    And now descend the Comforter.

5. The righteousness of Christ our Lord
   For pardon of our sins, declare,
Inspeak the everlasting word,
   That freely justified we are,
By grace receiv'd and brought to God,
And sav'd thro' faith in Jesu's blood.[47]

Although it had its inception in Jesus' once-for-all sacrifice in the historical past, the blood shed on Calvary's hill has a voice as long as it has saving effectiveness. Jesus' blood continues to intercede for us before the Father's throne:

Thy blood which pleaded on the cross,
   Prevalent still for sinners cries;
It speaks; and it hath gain'd my cause
   And bought my mansion in the skies.[48]

Charles's poetic personification of Jesus' blood moved back to Golgotha and forth again to touch the life experience of contemporary Christians. He believed that history, though a medium of divine revelation, was no barrier to the "prevalence" or ongoing significance of Jesus' death:

Save me, through faith in Jesu's blood,
   That blood which He for all did shed;
For me, for me, Thou know'st it flow'd,
   For me, for me, Thou hear'st it plead;
Assure me *now* my soul is Thine,
   And all Thou art in Christ is mine!
        (*P.W.*, 4:228, no. 14)

Charles knew that the atonement of Christ extended into the life of Christians; it had a voice or a "prevalence" so long as Jesus' death has saving significance. The Atonement, though complete as an act of history, continues metaphorically in the effectiveness of Jesus' intercession and the application of His blood through the work of the Holy Spirit.

"Quenching Blood"

One of the most picturesque poetic images found in Charles Wesley's hymns was formed when Wesley linked the blood of Jesus' death with divine wrath.[49] Generally, the blood was said to have "quenched the wrath of hostile Heaven" or "quench'd the righteous wrath of God" (*P.W.*, 3:242, no. 36; 13:161, no. 3326; 13:191–92, no. 3387). This symbolism, suggested perhaps by the phraseology of Ezekiel the prophet (Ezek. 21:31–32), saw God's wrath as a raging fire which was extinguished by the blood of Christ. This divine wrath is said to be "just" or "righteous," indicating its propriety by drawing legal images into the motif (*P.W.*, 3:243; 13:192, 3387).

Both John and Charles Wesley were fond of a phrase gleaned from Zechariah 3:2, referring to "a brand plucked out of the fire burning." For John Wesley, the text became a memorial of his being saved out of an inferno at the Epworth rectory when he was a small boy (Feb. 9, 1709). Furthermore, scholars have suggested that his description of the "strangely warmed heart" of his Aldersgate experience (1738) was based in the purifying flames of Zechariah 3:2. In November 1753, when John Wesley believed himself to be on the verge of death, he composed his epitaph: "Here lieth the body of John Wesley, a brand plucked out of the burning: Who died of a consumption in the fifty-first year of his age, not leaving, after his debts are paid, ten pounds behind him: praying, God be merciful to me, an unprofitable servant!" (*J.W. Journal*, 2:90).

The first line of that epitaph is of particular interest, since it indicates that John Wesley continued to think of himself as one "taken out of the fire." Charles's journal carried an emended version of the same epitaph which changed the first sentence ever so slightly: "Here lieth the body of John Wesley, a brand *not once only*, plucked out of the fire" (*C.W. Journal*, 2:97, italics added). The younger brother likened John's deliverance from the flames of the Epworth home to a spiritual metaphor of the Aldersgate experience. It is quite likely that John's understanding of the phrase "a brand plucked out of the burning" followed similar lines.[50]

Charles's frequent application of the image of a "brand plucked out of the fire" should be seen against this background. The phrase was not a common one in the Wesleyan hymns. But when he wrote the odd-sounding lines, "And pluck'd the brand out of the fire, / And quench'd it in Thy blood" (*P.W.*, 7:392, no. 39), Charles was telling the story of redemption. Often the fire that torments the lost soul is both the flame of perdition and the wrath of God:

> Who would not dread the frown of Him
>   Whose anger burns unquenchable,
> Whose breath like a sulphureous stream,
>   Kindles, and blows the flames of hell!
> Our God is a consuming fire,
>   And fastening on the sinful soul,
> Destroys what never can expire
>   Long as eternal ages roll.
>   (*P.W.*, 10:239, no. 255)

The hymnological comment on Zechariah 3:2 made it clear that deliverance from the flames of torment came through the death of Jesus:

> By a miracle of grace
>   My soul redeem'd hath been,
> In the furnace of distress,
>   And in the fire of sin:
> Rescued every day I am,
>   I prove the God of *Israel* mine
> Pluck'd out of the hellish flame,
>   And quench'd with blood Divine!
>   (*P.W.*, 10:113, no. 1540)

Blood was Charles Wesley's dramatic expression for Jesus' death and its saving significance. It is a word loaded with sacrificial, legal, and commercial connotations. Wesley skillfully wove the separate biblical phrases and allusions into one harmonious, interpretive fabric. His point of departure was generally a passage from the Authorized Version; but Charles was able to weave, paraphrase, and extend the biblical passages far beyond their usual connotations. This use of the term *blood* in Wesley's lyrics emphasized not only that it was redemptive, pardoning, and full of cleansing power; Wesley suggested that the blood of Christ also continued to intercede for the believer and quench the fiery consequences of sin. No-where is his poetic development of the theology of redemption more familiar than in his famous hymn, "Arise, My Soul Arise":

1. Arise, my soul, arise;
       Shake off thy guilty fears;
   The bleeding Sacrifice
       In my behalf appears;
   Before the throne my Surety stands,
   My name is written on His hands.

2. He ever lives above
       For me to intercede,
   His all-redeeming love,
       His precious blood, to plead;
   His blood atoned for all our race,
   And sprinkles now the throne of grace.

3. Five bleeding wounds He bears,
       Received on *Calvary*;
   They pour effectual prayers,
       They strongly speak for me;
   Forgive him, O forgive! they cry,
   Nor let that ransom'd sinner die!

4. The Father hears Him pray,
       His dear Anointed One,
   He cannot turn away
       The presence of His Son;
   His Spirit answers to the blood,
   And tells me I am born of God.

5. My God is reconciled,
       His pardoning voice I hear,
   He owns me for His child;
       I can no longer fear,
   With confidence I now draw nigh,
   And Father, Abba, Father, cry!
           (*P.W.*, 2:323–24)

John Rattenbury observed that Wesley's use of *blood* as a redemption word obscures what it symbolizes rather than illuminates it. If that is so, not a small part of this failure of communication lies on our own side of the historical chasm that separates us from Charles Wesley. His development of this theme was grounded in a close examination and application of biblical terms and passages; and while he enjoyed extending the images to make them more graphic or dramatic, the redemptive center of Wesley's imagery was always clear, and his departure from that center was always measured and well defined.

Some have suggested that the word *love* will serve as an appropriate substitute for *blood* in many of the Wesleyan hymns, signifying "love made vivid and effective by the death of Christ."[50] But *love* will not replace *blood* as the starting point for Charles Wesley's theology of redemption; the two terms are clearly complementary, but they are not synonymous. Charles even occasionally joined them to create his own term, "bleeding love"; but while *love* is a rather abstract term, *blood* takes the reader or singer of Wesleyan hymns to stand at the foot of the cross on Calvary's hill. *Love* certainly describes the motive and power of the Christ event; but it does not propel us with the same graphic intensity back to the historical foundation of our redemption. Nor does it describe, with a sense of drama worthy of Wesley, the cleansing effects of Jesus' death for those who believe. The Wesleyan phrase "bleeding love" aptly characterizes the relationship of the two terms; the former is a response to the latter and a gift flowing from it:

> Thy bleeding love declare,
>   Too strong for life to bear;
> Let it purge, and break my heart,
>   Then my heart's desire I prove,
> Bowing on Thy cross depart,
>   Pay Thee back Thy bleeding love.
>   (*P.W.*, 7:362, no. 10)

The last line of the verse is worthy of note. *Love*, in the Wesleyan vocabulary, is never self-centered; it is other-directed. The love emblemed in the cross of Christ must be mirrored back to Him out of the depths of a faithful heart.

CHAPTER FIVE:

"Love Perfected"

No one word is more characteristic of Charles Wesley's soteriology than *love*. It is a term that resounds with religious experience, and Wesley found *love* to be an apt description of his search for Christ and for his eventual conversion. On May 21, 1738 he described his conversion in this fashion: "I now found myself at peace with God, and rejoiced in hope of loving Christ."[1] *Love* was the personal dimension of his acceptance before God; it ratified God's decree of justification in the inner man. Three days after his conversion, the journal again finds Charles praying for *love*: "At eight I prayed by myself for love; with some feeling, and assurance of feeling more."[2] Constancy in love and an accompanying sense of assurance became a sort of spiritual barometer for the younger Wesley. He expected his new life in Christ to be increasingly filled with the love of Christ and of his neighbor. Charles's reliance on this attitude of love became apparent four days after his conversion as Wesley prepared himself to receive the sacrament of the Lord's Supper:

> I commended myself to Christ, my Prophet, Priest and King . . . . I left it to Christ, whether, or in what measure, he would please to manifest himself to me,

> in this breaking of bread. I had no particular
> attention to the prayers: but in the prayer of
> consecration I saw, by the eye of faith, or rather, had
> a glimpse of, Christ's broken, mangled body, as
> taking [*sic*] down from the cross. Still I could not
> observe the prayer, but only repeat with tears, 'O
> love, love!' At the same time, I felt great peace and
> joy; and assurance of feeling more, when it is best.[3]

Similar sentiments were voiced in Charles's hymn, composed that same week, "Amazing love! how can it be / That Thou, my God, shouldst die for me?"[4] Love then connected the cross of Christ with Charles's conversion or his reception of forgiveness by faith in Christ's death; and Charles's journal is replete with records of the testimonies of those who met "inexpressible love" when they received Christ by faith.[5] This same love connected assurance and sanctification, since the initial glow of conversion must enlarge into purification of heart and life:

> I spoke plainly to the women-bands of their unadvisableness, want [lack] of love, and bearing one another's burdens. We found an immediate effect in the enlargement of our hearts. Some were convinced that they had thought too highly of themselves; and that their first love, like their first joy, was only a foretaste of that temper which continually rules in a new heart.[6]

Love, in Charles's application of the term, became an apt summation of the Christian gospel. The word appears nearly fifteen hundred times in Wesley's later published hymns, a frequency of more than one occurrence per hymn! Charles's journal shows that the "love of God," expounded from John 3:16, was one of Wesley's favorite sermons; unfortunately, no written copy of that homily has survived.[7]

The symmetry and the pervasive power that Charles found in Christian love were certainly based in the New Testament understanding of the Greek word *agape* (love). *Agape* is preeminently a Johannine term; in the Fourth

Gospel and in the First Epistle of John, *love* is a foundational truth about God: "God is love" (1 John 4:8). This *agape* is the motive of Jesus' saving mission (John 3:16), as well as both the norm and the power for Christian living (1 John 3–4). Paul celebrated *agape* as the "more excellent way" (1 Cor. 12:31) and "greatest" of the qualities of Christian life in his memorable love-hymn of 1 Corinthians 13. *Agape* is the New Testament description of that other-directed, selfless love that was in Christ and in His new commandment for Christians (Matt. 5:43–48; Mark 12:30–33; John 15:10–13).[8]

Charles Wesley's conception of love was well informed by the New Testament *agape*. He looked to the Christ event to find the essence of the word; the Advent and the Cross formed two great parentheses around this idea of love, marking it off from any common connotations. Love was the motive of Christ's coming and the reason for His sacrificial death.[9] Charles's reading of Philippians 2:7 caused him to place love and "self-emptying" (Gk. *kenosis*) side-by-side as explanations of the Incarnation:

> The' eternal God from heaven came down,
>   The King of Glory dropp'd His crown,
> And veil'd His majesty;
>   Emptied of all but love He came;
> Jesus, I call Thee by the name
>   Thy pity bore for me.
>   (*P.W.*, 4:120)

Not even the terror caused by the earthquakes that shook England on March 8, 1750, which seemed to foreshadow the end of the world and gave occasion to several Wesleyan hymns, could shake the believer out of the security of Jesus' love:

> If earth its mouth *must* open wide,
>   To swallow up its prey,
> Jesu, Thy faithful people hide
>   In that vindictive day:
> Firm in the universal shock
>   We shall not then remove,

Safe in the clefts of *Israel's* rock
Our Lord's expiring love.
(*P.W.*, 6:22–23)

The wonder and joy that Wesley felt in this love was due to not merely its stability ("the clefts of *Israel's* Rock"); more directly, it found its source in Jesus' death ("Our Lord's expiring love"). This combination of wonder and celebration emerged in Charles's famous hymn "Wrestling Jacob":

9. 'Tis Love! 'tis Love! Thou diedst for me;
   I hear Thy whisper in my heart:
      The morning breaks, the shadows flee:
   Pure *UNIVERSAL LOVE* Thou art;
      To me, to all Thy bowels move
   Thy nature, and Thy name is Love.
         (*P.W.*, 2:175, italics added)

Following the New Testament record, Charles moved easily from the revelation of God's love in Jesus to the affirmation that love describes the divine nature: "Thy nature, and Thy name is Love." Hence, Wesley declared that the impartation of love in Christian redemption is both "incompatible with sin" and synonymous with the formation of a "heavenly principle within":

9. Love incompatible with sin
      If Thou dost in Thyself bestow,
   The heavenly principle within
      In streams of purest life shall flow.
         (*P.W.*, 13:255; cf. 4:350; 5:95)

Charles was also fond of describing the bestowal of love in the language of 2 Peter 1:4, which refers to Christians as "partakers of the divine nature." The following verse, from an unpublished hymn based on Acts 19:5 that Charles left in manuscript, is typical of this connection:

Truly baptized into the name
   Of Jesus I have been,
Who partaker of His nature am
   And sav'd indeed from sin;
Thy nature, Lord, thro' faith I feel

> Thy love reveal'd in me:
> In me, thy full salvation, dwell
> To all eternity.[10]

Following the Johannine dictum that "God is love," Charles Wesley expected to find God—the indwelling Christ—formed within the believer as love. This love was straining toward "full salvation" and "eternity," as the last two lines of the hymn above indicate. The gift of love was synonymous with the imparting of Christ, and both visitations brought the same cleansing effects:

> God in thee, O Christ, is love,
> To me Thyself impart,
> All my evil to remove,
> And fill my hallow'd heart.[11]

Another important Wesleyan description of the effects of love was based on the phraseology of Romans 8:29: "to be conformed to the image of his Son." Thus, Charles wrote, "His image in thy soul impress, / His love that fill'd thy faithful breast!" (*P.W.*, 6:331, no. 31). His hope of conformity to the image of Christ was to be realized through the reception of "spotless love" and through the work of the Holy Spirit:

> O might we put Thine image on,
> That robe of spotless love receive!
> Clothed with the Spirit of Thy Son
> We could not then our Father leave,
> Nor couldst Thou from our mind depart,
> For ever dwelling in our heart.
> (*P.W.*, 10:5–6, no. 1277)

Occasionally turning to a second Pauline image, Wesley used "the mind of Christ" (1 Cor. 2:16) to identify the christological character of "meek and benevolent love" (*Ms. John*, p. 80).

Divine love comes into the believer's life as power; "to save and His power to prove / His whole omnipotence of love" (*Ms. Luke*, p. 18). Since "love is incompatible with sin" (*P.W.*, 10:5–6), just as self-giving is irreconcilable with selfishness (sin as concupiscence), Christ's love enables the Christian to overcome sin in the inward person:

> 4. Love excludes the selfish passion,
>   Love destroys the carnal mind;
>   Love be here my full salvation,
>   Love for Thee and all mankind:
>   Let Thine own compassion move Thee
>   Thy own nature to impart,
>   Force me now to cry—I love Thee,
>   Love Thee, Lord, with all my heart.
>   (*P.W.*, 7:390, no. 37)

In a similar way, Wesley wrote of "the liberty of love," which enabled the Christians to "free from sin their lives commend" (*Ms. Luke,* p. 101). Commenting on Jeremiah 31:33 ("I will put my law in their inward parts, and write it in their hearts; and will be their God and they shall be my people"), Charles understood Jeremiah's new law as being "The law of liberty from sin, / The perfect law of love" (*P.W.*, 10:41, no. 1354). Yet, love has its vertical (God-ward) and horizontal (societal) trajectories; and Wesley's *love* was love in action, which blended inner rectitude with outward obedience, since "Obedient love is present heaven" (*Ms. Luke,* p. 174).

Renewal is a powerful New Testament term describing salvation as the restoration of the image of God within, rehabilitating a person's inner life, even as creation itself will experience eschatological restoration.[12] Charles's hymns celebrated these transforming effects of love.[13] In Wesley's words, renewal effected by love "conquers this rebellious heart" and allows a Christian to "live in the image of my Lord" (*P.W.*, 12:235; cf. 12:355). One of his rhymes "For Children" succinctly described the nature and source of this renewal:

> Love, that makes us creatures new,
>   Only love can keep us true,
> Perfect love that casts out sin,
>   Perfect love is God within.
>   (*P.W.*, 6:404, no. 37)

Following the text of Titus 3:5, Charles described the renewal in love as a work of the Holy Spirit that was not gained by exerting "our best endeavours vain" nor earned by fulfilling God's "righteous law." By having received salvation as a gift, the Christian is enabled to keep God's "utmost counsel" and live a life "Unblamable in spotless love":

> Not by our best endeavours vain,
>   Not by the strength of nature's will,
> Shall we that great salvation gain,
>   And all Thy righteous law fulfil:
> But strengthen'd by Thy Spirit's might,
>   We shall Thine utmost counsel prove,
> And humbly walk with Christ in white,
>   Unblamable in spotless love.
>   (*P.W.*, 10:114, no. 1543)

Charles Wesley's vision of love was all-encompassing. He believed that gospel love (*agape*) was both the foundation and the summation of the entire Christian life. Personified as a word for the Godhead in one of his "Hymns and Prayers to the Trinity," *love* literally expressed Wesley's "all in all":

> Love our real holiness,
>   Love our spotless character,
> Love is liberty and peace,
>   Pardon, and perfection here;
> Less than this cannot suffice;
>   Love be Thou our all in all;
> Then we in Thine image rise,
>   Then we into nothing fall.
>   (*P.W.*, 7:346, no. 50)

PERFECT LOVE

One of the Wesley brothers' most complicated doctrines, yet one absolutely crucial to their conception of the Christian faith, was Christian perfection as perfect love. The theological language they employed was thoroughly biblical, but it was not based in Pauline Christianity. Therefore, it sounds somewhat foreign to the ears of modern Protestants. While they appreciated Paul's formulation of justification by faith, the Wesleys included in their understanding of redemption a vision of Christian wholeness that was more characteristic of non-Pauline Christianity (John 17:23f.; 1 John 2:22f.; 4:17; Heb. 6:1). To the Pauline conception of justification (e.g., Rom. 3:23–25; Gal. 3:10, 11) they added a concern for inner renewal that sought to break through the double-mindedness (*dipsuchē*) of James 1:8, go on to the perfection (*teleiotēs*) of Hebrews 6:1, and be filled with the perfect (*teleioō*) love of 1 John 4:17–18. No small part of difficulty of the Wesleyan doctrine of Christian perfection lies in a misunderstanding of the meaning of the basic terms employed to describe this perfection.

To our modern minds, the word *perfection* seems appropriate to describe a grade of a hundred percent on an exam, full attendance, a flawless job, or an unsurpassable standard of performance. But for one to aspire to "perfection in love" seems to suggest either arrogance or an impossibility; and while Charles Wesley was fond of calling Christian perfection the "grand impossibility," it is clear he anticipated a real restoration of inner purity through the "omnipotence of grace":

1. Live without sin! It cannot be!
     This the enormous mountain stands,
   The grand impossibility,
     The hindrance to our Lord's commands!
   But when the God of perfect love,
     To build His church, appears again,
   The' enormous mountain shall remove,
     And sink, and flow into a plain.

2. By faith we see our Lord descend,
     And every obstacle give place:
   He comes, He comes, our sin to end,
     With all the' omnipotence of grace!
   He comes, He comes, His house to build,
     He bids the inbred bar depart:
   And tempted then, we cannot yield,
     We cannot sin, when pure in heart.
             (*P.W.*, 10:114, no. 1544)

Charles was not content to hold out perfection as an empty ideal; rather, he saw Christian perfection as the logical fulfillment of the gospel of Love, a fulfillment that Wesley expected here:

Love our real holiness,
  Love our spotless character,
Love is liberty and peace,
  Pardon, and perfection *here.* . . .
      (*P.W.*, 7:346, no. 50, italics added)

As to the arrogance of the claim, this criticism must be evaluated against the background of the meaning of the biblical terms employed. Therefore, we must consider the biblical description of the nature of this perfection and the means whereby perfect love was to be achieved.

The New Testament term for "perfection" is *teleios* or a related term from the *telos* family of words. The basic meaning of *teleios* has to do with enjoying the full benefits the end, goal, or outcome of something.[14] The Greeks used *teleios* differently from the way the Romans used the word *finis* (from which we get the English word *finish*). *Teleios* implies a sense of continuing growth or progress toward completeness; it can be rendered, "attaining the end or purpose, complete, perfect." *Finis* carries the more static connotation of an "ended" state. The qualitative distinction between *teleios* and *finis* is particularly important for discerning Wesley's conception of Christian perfection; a *finis* concept of perfection would make it a final attainment, not subject to further improvement, while *teleios* (the New Testament concept of perfection) makes continued growth an aspect of perfection. For the Wesleys to speak of perfection in the New Testament sense was not to claim perfect performance or "having arrived" as spotless believers (as the fanatical "angelic perfectionists" of London would later contend). They referred to a perfection that was *complete* in the extent of one's yieldedness before God and the dimensions of God's love in the life of the inner person.[15] "Completeness" in the sense of *teleios* is not a static conception; it is "completeness" with reference to a specific goal (e.g., restitution of the *imago Dei* or being filled with *agape*). The New Testament application of *teleios* words does not suggest a perfection in which a certain level of moral virtue is attained; rather, perfection in this sense is an ongoing life of totality or wholeness.[16] *Teleios* describes not so much an absolute moral infallibility as it does a moral restoration that overcomes human brokenness, unifying person and life through God's saving work.

Although the Wesleyan teaching of perfection (*teleios*) describes a complete change of the believer's life principle, we must recall that the change is a process of maturation and purification, not a *finalized* realization. Blurring the boundary between *teleios* ("perfection" as inner renewal and growth in grace) and *finis* ("perfection" as a static, absolute state) makes the language of the Wesleyan doctrine problematic. The Wesleys preached, sang, and longed for a renewal of the inner person that was complete, unmixed in motives, undivided in intentions, without making arrogant-sounding claims about their perfect deeds or outward, finished performance.

Charles Wesley's perfectionist language was clearly not based in moral achievement, as though perfection amounted to a perfect score in all one's deeds. "Perfection" was preeminently the language of inner renewal, a renewal so powerful and pervasive that it touched the totality of one's existence. The etymology of *teleios* reminds us that this perfection is with reference to a certain end or goal; and the goal, as Wesley saw it, was quite simply to be as God would have one to be. Often Charles called this renewal "perfection in love" or "perfect love," since God is love and God's love within the believer was deemed to be the source and power of this inner renovation.

His terminology for describing Christian perfection was rich and variegated. He said that "Perfect love which God supplies," for example, is "perfect holiness":

> Can it never be fulfill'd?
>   Then we can never love:
> But by Thy good Spirit seal'd,
>   We all the truth shall prove;
> Thou our hearts shalt circumcise,
>   And give us meekly to confess
> Perfect love which God supplies
>   Is perfect holiness.
>   (*P.W.*, 13:20, no. 3067)

Charles Wesley was a master of the mixed metaphor. Note that in the preceding lyric he said love is sealed (i.e., attested or impressed) upon the Christian's heart by the Holy Spirit in a way that is metaphorically connected to the utter consecration of circumcision and its redemptive cleansing (Lev. 19:23; Isa. 52:1; Rom. 4:11).[17] In Scripture, the heart figuratively circumcised was opened, yielded and obedient to God's command, as opposed to being closed or stubborn (Deut. 10:16; Jer. 4:4; Rom. 2:28f.; Col. 2:11). The resultant effect, as suggested in Deuteronomy 30:6, was an all-encompassing love of God that produced renewed life: "The LORD thy God will circumcise thine heart . . . to love the LORD thy God with all thine heart, and with all thy soul, that thou mayest live." Similar themes emerged in Charles Wesley's poetic rendition; he declared that the work of the Spirit produces a yieldedness of heart ("meekly"), which results in perfect love or perfect holiness.

Perfect love and *perfect holiness* were synonymous terms in Charles's theological-poetical parlance; this love, which was perfect (i.e., complete with regard to its redemptive purpose), produced holiness in a double sense. Terms such as *sanctification* and *holiness* (as we shall see below) have their roots in ritual consecrations, suggesting a sort of setting apart from ordinary or secular usage for the service of God. Because this consecration is unto God and establishes relationship with Him, it pours moral power and purity (holiness, sanctity) into the life of believer. Perfect love produces perfect holiness because of its consecrating impact upon the heart (circumcision), and moral power is produced as love fills and unifies the inner person. Likewise, Charles believed, being "perfected in love" was the same as being "completely sanctified" (*P.W.*, 13:69, no. 3165). *Perfect* is synonymous with *complete* in the sense of the *teleios* root word; it suggests the total restoration that redemption has as its goal. Often it was Wesley's practice to stack his various synonyms for *perfection* on top of one another so that the reader or singer could not miss the import of the message:

> 5. I trust in Thee alone
>   Who never canst deceive,
>   (After I have Thy pleasure done)
>   The promised grace to give,
>   The *holiness complete,*
>   The *spotless purity,*
>   The *perfect love,* which makes me meet
>   To share a throne with Thee.
>   (*P.W.,* 13:83, no. 3192, italics added)

The results of this perfect love are that faith is purified like gold in the refiner's fire and all the dross of sin is removed (*P.W.,* 10:31–32, no. 1329). This purification swallows up the believers' fear and sin:

> Our fear and sin at once remove,
>   Sin by purity Divine,
>   And fear by perfect love.
>   (*P.W.,* 10:34, no. 1336; cf. 4:293)

Hence, the life of perfect love is nothing else than a "life of holiness" (*P.W.,* 10:111–12, no. 1535). The latter term had many nuances in Charles Wesley's application, but the following verse offers an apt summation of what he meant by *holiness*:

> Meanest [i.e., least] vessel of Thy grace,
>   Jesus, unto me impart
>   True substantial holiness;
>   Come, and make me pure in heart,
>   Witness of Thy hallowing word,
>   Full of purity Divine,
>   All devoted to the Lord,
>   Body, soul, and spirit Thine.
>   (*P.W.,* 10:127, no. 1584)

In this verse, several important factors coalesce: "grace" is imparted; "holiness," "pure in heart," and "All devoted" emerge as parallel descriptions of an utter consecration to God; and this consecration opens a person to a "hallowing" by "word" or "grace" and an infilling with purity that unifies the person ("Body, soul, and spirit") in complete, restorative fellowship with God.

One of Charles Wesley's favorite ways of describing perfect love was to link it with the restoration of the image

of Christ.[18] Central to his development of this conception
were 2 Peter 1:4 (where Christians are said to be "partakers of the divine nature") and Romans 8:29 (where we are
said to be "conformed to the image of his Son"). The
connection between perfect love and conformity to Christ
was a logical extension of Wesley's use of the word *love* to
describe both the nature of God and the empowering work
of the Holy Spirit. Holiness or perfect love was considered
to be a work of the Holy Spirit:

> 2. Father, send into our hearts
>   His Spirit from above,
>   Write it in our inward parts,
>   The law of perfect love.
>   Hence let all our works proceed,
>   All our words and tempers pure,
>   Then in Jesus' steps we tread,
>   And then our heaven is sure.
>   (*P.W.*, 13:42–43, no. 3113; cf. 13:45, no.
>   3117)

Two critical questions emerge in any discussion of
Charles Wesley's conception of perfect love or Christian
perfection. The first question deals with the matter of its
attainability: Did Charles expect perfection in this life?
And the second has to do with its manner of reception:
Does it come as an experience of crisis or as a pilgrimage
and process of maturation? Since these issues were elements in the disputes among the early Methodists and in
the dialogue between the Wesley brothers on sanctification,
they are treated extensively under the heading "A Brother-
ly Debate" (chapter 7); but they bear mention at this
juncture as well.

First of all, it is clear that Charles Wesley was not
interested in perfection as a lofty, unattainable ideal. The
man and his task were far too practical for empty idealism;
rather, he sought "True substantial holiness" or "real
holiness" (*P.W.*, 10:127, no. 1584; cf. 12:58, no. 2189).
Charles was equally insistent that Christian perfection is
"perfection here." There was no pie-in-the-skyism in his
conception; while Wesley longed to live blamelessly in his

heavenly Father's presence, he understood that his transla-
tion into the other realm at death would be a continuation
of the perfection begun here and not a substitute for it:

> Faithful I account Thee, Lord,
> To Thy sanctifying word;
> I shall soon be as Thou art,
> Holy both in life and heart;
> Perfect holiness attain,
> All Thine image *here* regain,
> Love my God entirely *here*,
> Blameless *then* in heaven appear.[19]

He found himself criticizing those who cried, "There's no
perfection here below."[20] In a passage penned late in his
career (when Charles was chiding those Methodists who
claimed perfection in such a simplistic and strident manner
that more pious souls were tempted to remain silent on
sanctification rather than associate themselves with the
fanatical perfectionists), Charles refused to give up on the
hope of having "perfection here":

> 1. Why were they left to disagree?
>   Not to encourage sin,
>   Or prove the' impossibility
>   Of constant peace within;
>   Not to confirm the daring lie
>   'Gainst Christ the Finisher,
>   Or countenance the men who cry
>   "There's no perfection here."
>   (*P.W.*, 12:310, no. 2712)

In the earliest Charles Wesley hymns—those written
in the beginning of the Methodist revival and published
jointly with his brother John—Charles seemed to prefer to
speak of Christian perfection as a crisis experience, which
in some sense paralleled and completed the experience of
conversion. Since crisis seemed to remain John Wesley's
characteristic emphasis in expounding the doctrine, and
since so few of Charles's handwritten manuscripts from this
earliest period of joint authorship have survived, we are left
to wonder whether the published hymns reflect the
younger brother's authorship or the elder brother's editori-

al corrections.[21] In the hymns that Charles wrote and published after 1749, he seemed more prone to picture Christian perfection as a process of growth and maturation. For example:

> Make our earthly souls a field
>   Which God delights to bless,
> Let us in due season yield
>   The fruits of righteousness;
> Make us trees of paradise
>   Which more and more Thy praise may show,
> Deeper sink, and higher rise,
>   And to perfection grow.
>   (*P.W.*, 10:55, no. 1386)

This shift in emphasis (if not in the conception of the doctrine) that occurred in Charles's later hymns did not mark a complete departure from his brother's point of view; but it does reveal that Charles adjusted his hymns to a historical and theological dispute that touched him more directly than it did John. Though Charles adjusted his form for expressing the doctrine of Christian perfection, he did not abandon the doctrine! Perfection or "perfect love" remained one of the center poles and unifying themes of his theology. It meant receiving the "treasure of celestial grace, / The riches of true holiness," since "Jesus in our hearts doth live" (*P.W.*, 13:45–46, no. 3118). It manifests the Lord's glory within so that "the veil of unbelief is removed"[22] and hence brings a sense of assurance or God's acceptance, since "the sense of pardon'd sins" is communicated (*P.W.*, 10:115, no. 1546) as the bentness of fallen human nature (Rom. 1:18–25) is straightened and the root of original sin is removed:

> Jesus, the first and last,
> On Thee my soul is cast:
> Thou didst Thy work begin
> By blotting out my sin;
> Thou wilt the *root* remove,
> And *perfect me in love*.
>   (*P.W.*, 13:221, no. 3445, italics added)

The renewal that Christ works within the Christian through love is so complete or perfect that the renovation makes sinless living possible (*P.W.*, 10:114, no. 1544). But Charles would have no part of a purely moralistic conception of perfection. He believed that perfection is synonymous with perfect love; it is a divine work in the motivational center of a person, not a matter of moral achievement. True to his theological symmetry, Wesley saw each person of the Trinity active at work in this process of re-creation through love:

> 1. Jesus, with Thy Father come,
>   And bring our inward Guide,
> Make our hearts Thy humble home,
>   And in Thine house abide,
> Show us with Thy presence fill'd,
>   Fill'd with glory from Thy throne,
> And *perfected in one*.
>
>   (*P.W.*, 12:58–59, no. 2190, italics added)

HOLINESS, PERFECTION, AND SANCTIFICATION

Sanctification is a biblical term that has come to stand for an entire cluster of related religious ideas. It is derived from the same family of words that are used to connote *holiness*; hence, in Scripture as in popular usage, those two terms are closely intertwined. In its Old Testament roots, *sanctification* comes from QDH (to cut, to divide); hence, it implies separation.[23] The Hebrew word suggests an absolute distinction between the sacred (*qodesh*) and the secular or profane (*cheled*). Because it implied this separation from potential defilement, *qodesh* became a rough equivalent for "purity." The primary picture in the Old Testament understanding of holiness is one of separation; since it is a profoundly religious concept, *holiness* implied both a separation from defilement and unto God, symbolized in rituals of consecration and cleansing (Lev. 20:26; 6:8–18, 19–30; Num. 6:1–7).

Old Testament scholar Edmund Jacob observes "a marvelous flexibility" in the terms employed, since *holiness* came to signify both a state of being and moral actions; it thereby became an apt description for the power of God.[24] In a similar fashion, Walter Eichrodt links the Old Testament concept of holiness with God's sovereign power, since the ancient Jews understood separation as being either by or unto the Lord.[25] The correlation between Israel's worship, ethical life, and God's very nature was well established in the divine injunction: "Be holy: for I the LORD your God am holy" (Lev. 11:44–45; 19:2; cf. 20:7, 26). The unparalleled holiness of Israel's God (Deut. 6:4, 5; Josh. 24:19; 1 Sam. 2:2) demanded unmixed devotion of His people: "Thou shalt have no other gods before me" (Exod. 20:3). The nation's dedication to the Lord was manifested through a special day (Exod. 31:14, 15), through liturgy and priestly garments (Exod. 35:19f.), through consecrated vessels (Jer. 27:16–18), and through consecrated oils (Exod. 30:31), all of which were dedicated to Him through service. But Israel's ability to connect *holiness* with the very character and actions of God moved the Old Testament conception beyond mere ritualistic tabu; holiness implied godlikeness in one's moral and inward life.[26] Even as Israel moved beyond the rituals of tabernacle and temple to link *holiness* more directly with an elevated ethical standard (Heb. *Torah*, "the Law"), *holiness* was not merely an ethical standard; it was understood to be the moral perfection that inheres in God's commandments and will.[27] This holiness, so characteristic of Israel's ethical monotheism, was based in an utter consecration toward God that manifested itself in a desire to replicate His character (as revealed in His law) as a concrete sign of belonging to the Lord.

The New Testament application of the term *holiness* maintained echoes of the Hebraic emphasis on separateness and ritual language; but the personal and moral implications of the New Testament term (Gk. *hagiazō*) are kept in the forefront.[28] *Holiness* or *sanctification* became synonymous for purity of heart and other related conceptions.[29] But it was not a new law or legalism, since the early Christians understood that holiness is a work of the Holy

Spirit (Rom. 15:16; 1 Thess. 4:7; 2 Thess. 2:13; 1 Pet. 1:2), who produces both inward renewal and sinlessness in believers (Rom. 6).

Perfection has its roots in several biblical words. Generally, the Old Testament connotation was one of wholeness (*shalem*) or completion (*kalil; tamim*). In its New Testament usage, *perfection* was almost always represented by terms of the *telos* family.[30] These terms can be alternately translated "whole, complete, finished, mature, or up to standard."[31] Although *sanctification* and *perfection* are rough equivalents throughout the New Testament usage, there is an obvious distinction in their application; the terms *sanctification* and *sanctified* were generally the choice of Paul, whereas *perfection* was more typically the language of non-Pauline writers.[32]

The New Testament refers to *sanctification* in a double sense. On the one hand, it applies to something already complete; on the other hand, it is something that still remains to be completed.[33] Christ loved the church and gave Himself "that he might sanctify and cleanse it" (Eph. 5:26f.). The people of the Corinthian church, certainly among the most morally deficient Christians whom Paul pastored, were ironically said to be sanctified already: "Ye are washed, but ye are sanctified" (1 Cor. 6:11). Clearly, this sanctification does not pertain merely to the moral persistence of those people; it is primarily a work of God, who has "from the beginning chosen you to salvation through sanctification of the Spirit" (2 Thess. 2:13). It was grounded in the sacrifice of Jesus: "Wherefore Jesus . . . that he might sanctify the people with his own blood, suffered without the gate" (Heb. 13:12), and those who belong to Him by faith in His death are one with Jesus in sanctification: "Both he that sanctifieth and they who are sanctified are all of one; for which cause he is not ashamed to call them brethren" (Heb. 2:11).

On the other hand, *sanctification* is also spoken of as a goal yet to be reached or an end still to be accomplished. Thus, the same Corinthians who are said to be "sanctified" are also urged to rid themselves of uncleanness, "perfecting

holiness [Gk. *hagiōsunē*] in the fear of God" (2 Cor. 7:1).
In a similar way, the Thessalonians are exhorted to
"abstain from fornication" and "the lust of concupiscence," so that "every one of you should know how to
possess his vessel [body] in sanctification and honor"
(1 Thess. 4:3–6). The Romans are told to cease serving
uncleanness and "yield your members servants to righteousness unto holiness" (Rom. 6:19). Timothy is told to
"purge himself" from iniquity and "youthful lusts," "but
follow righteousness, faith, charity, peace, with them that
call on the Lord out of a pure heart" (2 Tim. 2:19–22).

This tension in the New Testament presentation of
sanctification is probably best understood as referring to
two ends of the same line of thought. *Sanctification*,
particularly in the Epistle to the Hebrews but elsewhere as
well, is almost a synonym for *justification*; it describes
salvation from the perspective of the renewing effects of
Christ's saving death (Heb. 2:11) which allow us to draw
near to God. *Sanctification*, when used in this sense, refers
to the new status that salvation establishes for Christians
and the inward effects that begin to emerge in their lives. It
is certainly in this same positional or potential sense that
the New Testament calls believers "holy ones" or "saints"
(*hagios*), irrespective of their moral or spiritual qualities
(Acts 9:13; Rom. 8:27; 12:13; 1 Cor. 6:1f.). At the other
end of the same train of thought, *sanctification* describes the
moral perfection that is created in Christians as Christ's
love abounds in their midst, "To the end that he may
stablish your hearts unblameable in holiness before God,
even our Father, at the coming of our Lord Jesus Christ
with all his saints" (1 Thess. 3:13). In Wesleyan theological language, the double usage has been described as the
difference between initial and "full" salvation.

A similar tension between potential and actual sanctification is present in the Johannine application of the
word *perfection*. The writer characterizes the Christian life
as one of sinlessness: "Whosoever abideth in [Christ]
sinneth not: whosoever sinneth hath not seen him, neither
known him" (1 John 3:6). John says that those who

confess Christ as their Lord know and love God, and they are known and loved by Him: "God is love; and he that dwelleth in love dwelleth in God, and God in him" (1 John 4:15–16). He says that the love within the Christians is "made perfect [*teleioō*], that we may have boldness in the day of judgment: because as he is, so are we in this world" (1 John 4:17). Yet the apostolic exhortation for sinlessness is also softened by a proviso: "If any man sin, we have an advocate with the Father, Jesus Christ the righteous: and he is the propitiation for our sins: and not for our's only, but also for the sins of the whole world" (1 John 2:1b–2). Sinlessness through perfect love is the teleological goal behind the gospel of redemption, and as such, it is as apt a summation of Christianity as the other Johannine mark of a Christian—*agape* (cf. 1 John 2:2–7; 3:5–11; 4:6–13). By the power of Jesus' propitiation and the gift of His Spirit, perfection in love becomes the goal and potential for all who belong to Him (1 John 4:8–21); yet the reconciliation with God has been established, and if they sin, the Advocate of their salvation will plead their case.

Charles Wesley showed an obvious preference for the terms *perfection* and *holiness* instead of *sanctification* when it came to expressing this doctrine so essential to his theology. In the early sermons, he used *sanctification* and related terms 7 times; *perfection* and related terms appeared 45 times. In Charles's later hymns, this pattern became even more pronounced; *sanctification* words appeared in 128 instances, and *perfection* words were used nearly 5 times more often. This clear preference for *perfection* was probably more poetic than theological, since for Charles *perfection* and *sanctification* were synonyms. His picture-painting methodology lent itself to the more dramatic, colorful terms and probably moved Wesley away from more staid, static words. A characteristic description of sanctification as perfection is found in the following verses:

> 2. But what Thou didst for sinners shed,
>   Thou only canst apply,
> And purge whom Thy own hands have made,
>   From crimes of deepest dye,

Thou wilt blot out the' engrafted stain,
  My nature's filthiness;
Nor let one evil thought remain,
  To violate my peace.

3. Enabled by Thy word, I rise
   And wash my sins away;
   Strong in the life Thy death supplies
   I for salvation pray.
   I pray, believing that Thy blood
   Its full effect may have,
   And bring me *sanctified* to God,
   And to *perfection* save.
               (*P.W.*, 10:12, no. 1291, italics added;
               cf. 12:58–59, no. 2190)

Charles's prayer for perfection in the preceding hymn included some rather typical elements: blotting out the stain of original sin, removing evil thoughts, and granting inner peace. In these characteristic concerns, the Wesleyan hymns paralleled the Minutes of the Methodist Conference of 1759:

> *Question:* 'What is Christian perfection?' *Answer:* The loving God with all our heart, mind, soul, and strength. This implies, that no wrong temper, none contrary to love, remains in the soul; and that all the thoughts, words, and actions, are governed by pure love (*J.W. Works*, 11:394).

In his prose writings, the closest that Charles Wesley came to a formal definition of Christian perfection occurred in his journal entry for Monday, September 26, 1740: "utter dominion over sin, constant peace, and love and joy in the Holy Ghost; the full assurance of faith, righteousness, and true holiness" (*C.W. Journal*, 1:250).

One of his favorite descriptions of sanctification was "wholly sanctified" (e.g., *P.W.*, 4:169; 10:35, 101). The lone biblical occurrence of that exact phrase is found in 1 Thessalonians 5:23: "And the very God of peace sanctify you wholly; and I pray God your whole spirit and soul and body be preserved blameless unto the coming of our Lord Jesus Christ." For Charles, being "wholly sanctified" meant being "from every spot and wrinkle clean" (*P.W.*, 10:101, no. 1507). It paralleled a second phrase, "perfect [complete] righteousness"; in each case, the wholeness of this sanctification is "complete" or "entire" (*P.W.*, 10:46–47, no. 1550). That the perfection of which Wesley wrote had its primary focus in a sense of "completeness" (Heb. *shalom*; Gk. *teleios*) came out clearly in the following verse:

> Master, at Thy feet I wait,
>   Thy reviving voice to hear;
> Raise me to my first estate,
>   Show Thyself the Finisher,
> *Perfect* what Thou hast begun,
>   And when all my griefs are past,
> And when all my work is done,
>   Glorify my soul at last.
>   (*P.W.*, 13:222, no. 3446)

In this case, *perfect* is used as a replacement word for *complete*, without further theological explanation; the usage was quite in keeping with the Greek root of both terms involved (*telos*). Thus Wesley also paralleled *perfect* with *wholeness* and the phrase "all complete"; likewise, *perfect* and *whole* appear as functional equivalents in Wesley's hymns.[34] Being wholly sanctified was often described through metaphors of being washed or cleansed in Jesus' blood. Occasionally, Wesley said that this purification was accomplished as the Holy Spirit applied the saving significance of Jesus' death ("blood"):

> The cleansing blood to' apply,
>   The heavenly life display,
> And *wholly sanctify*,
>   And seal us to that day,
> The Holy Ghost to man is given;
>   Rejoice in God sent down from heaven.
>   (*P.W.*, 4:169, italics added)[35]

Charles Wesley emphasized that perfection or sanctification was "full salvation" because it was the completion of the saving work and purpose of God. Hence, "full salvation" became one of his favorite phrases for the doctrine of sanctification. It meant an undoing of the effects of the Edenic Fall and its corruption of human nature, through an invasion of divine love that healed a divided mind (Gk. *dipsuchos*) and mixed intentions. The Holy Spirit accomplished this transformation by unifying one's inner life through an infilling of God's love (*agape*). This love was the "one thing needful" that completed God's saving intention and brought wholeness to the Christian's life by casting out fear, selfishness, and sin as the Holy Spirit indwelt the Christian's heart and the mind of Christ was formed within.

CHAPTER SIX:

"The Life of God in the Soul"

England of the late seventeenth and early eighteenth centuries was a land of marked religious contrasts. Although popular recollection has left us a picture of widespread moral decay among the common folk and a Deist erosion of classical Christian doctrines among the educated and elite, the age was also marked by a resurgent interest in personal piety and holiness. This pious counterpoint to the gin mills and the notion of a Watchmaker God found expression in religious societies of the Restoration era that predated the Wesleyan revival.[1] As we observed elsewhere, the existing literature of practical and devotional piety was influential in the Wesleys' spiritual formation. John Wesley's tract *Christian Perfection* chronicled his spiritual formation at Oxford by the books he was reading: "In the year 1725, being in the twenty-third year of my age, I met with Bishop Taylor's *Rule and Exercises of Holy Living and Dying*" (*J.W. Works*, 11:360). The next year he "met with Kempis's *Christian's Pattern*. The nature and extent of inward religion, the religion of the heart, now appeared to me in a stronger light than it had done before." Soon thereafter ("a year or two"), he read William Law's *Practical Treatise on Christian Perfection* and *A Serious Call to a Devout and Holy Life*, and these solidified John's resolve to "be all-devoted to God, to give him all my soul, my body, and my substance." Law was especially formative for the brothers Wesley. His *Christian Perfection* introduced them to a redemptive vision of holy living that captured their hearts and minds and never let them go; the *Serious Call* supplied specific patterns and prescriptions for holy living. But one book, the one that was probably the most important to Charles Wesley's Oxford piety, was absent from his older brother's list: *The Life of God in the Soul of Man*, by Henry Scougal.

The Life of God was one of the most frequently printed books in the eighteenth century. First appearing in 1677, it was reprinted on the average of once every three years for the next hundred.[2] It was a favorite in the Epworth manse, and in one of her letters from 1732, Susanna Wesley recommended it to her sons as "an excellent good book, and was an acquaintance of mine years ago; but I have unfortunately lost it."[3] Charles was reading Scougal not long after he began the Holy Club, and he managed to part with his copy too; he loaned it to nineteen-year-old George Whitefield, who later recalled: "He let me have another book, entitled, *The Life of God in the Soul of Man*; and though I had fasted, watched and prayed, and received the Sacrament so long, yet I never knew what true religion was, till God sent me that excellent treatise by the hands of my never-to-be-forgotten friend."[4] Whitefield's full description of the impact of "that excellent treatise" vibrates with exhilaration:

> God soon showed me [the nature of true religion]; for in reading a few lines further, that 'true religion was union of the soul with God, and Christ formed within us,' a ray of Divine light was instantaneously darted in upon my soul, and from that moment, but not till then, did I know that I must be a new creature.
>
> Upon this, like the woman of Samaria, when Christ revealed Himself to her at the well, I had no rest in my soul till I wrote letters to my relations, telling

them there was such a thing as the new birth. I imagined they would have gladly received it. But alas! My words seemed to them as idle tales.[5]

A Scottish Anglican, Scougal distinguished vital, living religion from "all those shadows and false imitations of it" in the same passage that held so much significance for Whitefield:

> They who are acquainted with [religion] will . . . disdain all those shadows and fake imitations of it. They know by experience that true religion is an union of the soul with God, a real participation in the Divine nature, the very image of God drawn upon the soul, or, in the Apostle's phrase, *it is Christ formed within us*. Briefly, I know not how the nature of religion can be more fully expressed than by calling it a *Divine Life*.[6]

While Scougal's phrasing is a bit foreign to Charles Wesley's explanation of the essence of true Christianity, the author's emphasis on the formation of Christ within the Christian as the manifestation of "true religion" has a Wesleyan (as well as apostolic) ring to it. As the Scottish mystic defined the phrase "Divine Life," one begins to sense the influence this book had on the Methodists. *Life* signified religion as a "vital principle"—living, inward religion as distinguished from "that obedience which is constrained and depends on external causes."[7] To term it "*Divine* Life" described religion with regard to its source and its nature:

> I come next to give an account of why I defined it by the name of *Divine Life*; and so it may be called, not only in regard to its fountain and original [*sic*], having God for its author and being wrought in the souls of men by the power of his Holy Spirit, but also in regard of its nature, religion being a resemblance of the divine perfections, the image of the Almighty shining in the soul of man: nay, it is a real participation of his nature; it is a beam of the eternal life, a drop of that infinite ocean of goodness; and

they who are endued with it may be said to have *God dwelling in their souls and Christ formed within them*.[8]

Not only did Henry Scougal's *Life of God in the Soul of Man* anticipate Methodism's concern for practical piety and disciplines of spiritual formation, the book seemed to provide the central themes of Charles's exposition of its grand depositum and most distinctive doctrine—Christian perfection. Scougal considered sanctification to be an indwelling of God, described as a visitation of the Holy Spirit or the formation of Christ within, which produced a "resemblance of the Divine perfections."

John Wesley also picked up the book his mother recommended so highly. He began reading it on February 24, 1736, just a few days after arriving in Savannah, Georgia, at the beginning of his missionary service there (*J.W. Journal*, 1:167). By July 24 of the same year, Scougal's *Divine Life* became a focal point of John's pastoral supervision for "Miss Sophy" and a few of his parishioners (*J.W. Journal*, 1:247–48). The book seemed to possess lasting value for the elder Wesley, since he abridged and published *Life of God* in 1742, and that edition was reprinted at least six times. Several of Scougal's sermons appeared in John's *Christian Library*, and they elaborated the same themes established in *Life of God*.[9]

It is difficult to ascertain precisely how much influence Scougal's little book had upon Charles Wesley; but its emphases on inward religion, spiritual disciplines, and identification of love as the theological center of vital Christianity were certainly concerns that continued in Wesley's works. For example, Scougal described love as "that powerful and prevalent passion by which all the faculties and inclinations of the soul are determined and on which both its perfection and happiness depend."[10] Love is basic to human happiness and holiness, and it transforms the loving soul into the image of the One loved:

> The worth and excellency of a soul is to be measured by the object of its love. He who loveth mean and sordid things doth thereby become base and vile, but

a noble and well-placed affection doth advance and improve the spirit into a conformity with the perfections which it loves. The images of these do frequently present themselves unto the mind, and, by a secret force and energy, insinuate into the very constitution of the soul and mould and fashion it unto their own likeness.[11]

How much more is the soul transformed and conformed to the likeness of its beloved when God and His nature become the object of one's contemplation and love: "The true way to improve and ennoble our souls is by fixing our love on the Divine perfections that we may have them always before us and derive an impression of them on ourselves, and beholding with open face, as in a glass, the glory of the Lord, we may be changed into the same image, from glory to glory."[12] Scougal identified charity (Gk. *agape*), purity, and humility as the characteristics ("excellences") of divine love.[13] The path of love is marked out by contemplation of God's love, participation in Christian disciplines, and avoidance of those affections that are contrary to the establishment of the the love of God in the human soul (e.g., pride, selfishness, and worldliness). In the nexus of grace, worship, and discipleship, God's love is insinuated into the life of the Christian "to inflame our souls with the Love of God."[14] By defining vital religion as the life of God in the human soul, both Scougal and Charles Wesley emphasized that divine love is a force for renewal, a force that produces conformity to God's perfections; and in Scougal's combination of the means of God's grace (Word and sacrament), personal prayer and adoration, with concrete deeds of Christian love, the pattern for Wesley's conception of Christian perfection seemed to be established.

Charles Wesley was very much concerned with personal purity and perfection. Several important elements emerge in his early discussions of Christian perfection. First, Charles strongly declared his concern for holiness at the very outset of his public ministry. Second, he described holiness as the restoration of the image of God within a person, a restoration that was often described in healing metaphors. And third, Charles connected the new birth with the restoration of the *imago Dei*.

Charles's earliest hymns are full of phraseology that describes sanctification as being "filled with God." In a manner not unlike the *theosis* doctrine of the Eastern Fathers, Wesley came to describe holiness as the result of an infusion of God or His love into the life of the Christian. The focal point of this approach was exemplified in the contrast found in two of Charles's hymns from the 1740 edition of *Hymns and Sacred Poems*. The first hymn, entitled "The Resignation," is a long lament (twenty-two verses!) that bewails the singer's divided heart, "'Tis worse than death, my God to love, / And not my God *alone*" (*P.W.*, 1:267, italics added). The title itself evidences Charles's proclivity for double meaning. "The resignation" refers to the singer's giving up self-will in order to achieve harmony with God's will, the surrender of worldly affections in favor of the love of God. Resignation also describes one's willingness to die in order to purge one's heart from earthbound hindrances to the love of God. First the singer decries the tempest of the divided nature of his soul:

> 5. My peevish passions chide,
>   Who only canst control,
>   Canst turn the stream of nature's tide,
>   And calm my troubled soul.
>
> 6. O my offended Lord,
>   Restore my inward peace:
>   I know Thou canst: pronounce the word,
>   And bid the tempest cease.
>   (*P.W.*, 1:267)

The cure for the singer's "tortured breast" (v. 3) was found in being sprinkled with blood (v. 7), a visitation of the Holy Spirit who bestows "The living water of Thy grace, / That I may thirst no more" (v. 8). The lure of Christ's love, revealed in His "suffering life below" (v. 13), "calls me still to seek Thy face, / And stoops to ask my love" (v. 11). In view of the great love and sacrifice of Christ, the singer of Charles's hymn finds the courage of self-resignation: "To tear my soul from earth away, / For Jesus to receive" (v. 15):

> 16. Nay, but I yield, I yield!
>   I can hold out no more;
>   I sink, by dying love compell'd,
>   And own Thee conqueror.
>
> 17. Though late, I all forsake,
>   My friends, my life resign:
>   Gracious Redeemer, take, O, take
>   And seal me ever Thine.
>
> 18. Come, and possess me whole,
>   Nor hence again remove;
>   Settle, and fix my wavering soul,
>   With all Thy weight of love.
>
> 19. My one desire is this,
>   Thy only love to know,
>   To seek and taste no other bliss,
>   No other good below.
>
> 20. My Life, my Portion Thou,
>   Thou all-sufficient art;
>   My Hope, my heavenly Treasure, now
>   Enter and keep my heart.
>   (*P.W.*, 1:268–69)

A second selection from the same hymnal described Charles's message of sanctification as the life of God in the human soul, but from the opposite perspective. In "The Resignation," the emphasis was upon the resignation of a person's will as a prerequisite for the unification of life and faith by a divine visitation in love (Spirit and Christ). But in "Christ Our Sanctification," a hymn based on 1 Corinthians 1:30, Charles approached the question from the opposite point of view. He described holiness not so much as a product of the resignation to the lure of love, but as a dimension of the liberation and lordship of a victorious Christ. The former hymn expounded sanctification by beginning with theological anthropology—discussing the Fall, the divided nature of humanity, and the need to respond to God's overtures of grace. But the latter hymn was ordered christologically, emphasizing the victory of Christ's death and resurrection:

1. Jesu! my Life, Thyself apply,
     Thy Holy Spirit breathe,
   My vile affections crucify,
     Conform me to Thy death.

2. Conqueror of hell, and earth, and sin,
     Still with Thy rebel strive;
   Enter my soul, and work within,
     And kill, and make alive.

3. More of Thy life, and more I have,
     As the old *Adam* dies:
   Bury me, Saviour, in Thy grave,
     That I with Thee may rise.

4. Reign in me, Lord, Thy foes control,
     Who would not own Thy sway;
   Diffuse Thy image through my soul;
     Shine to the perfect day.

5. Scatter the last remains of sin,
     And seal me Thine abode;
   O, make me glorious all within,
     A temple built by God.

6. My inward holiness Thou art,
     For faith hath made Thee mine:
   With all Thy fulness fill my heart,
     Till all I am is Thine!
               (*P.W.*, 1:284)

Beyond the opposite points of departure (i.e., from below, beginning with humanity, and from above, beginning with Christ), these two hymns present several elements that became theological constants in Charles's conception of Christian perfection. (1) In each case, sin causes division in the inner person that is overcome through a renovation of the fallen nature. (2) The renewal produces wholeness in all of one's affections and unity of one's life through the love and lordship of Christ. (3) The process of restoration is realized through a visitation of divine love, the Holy Spirit, or Christ. (4) Perfection could be described either as purity of intention or as a corresponding sinlessness. (5) Perfection involves a unification of will and deed in a life-faith synthesis.

This pattern of expression continued through the Wesleyan hymnals of the 1740s. *Moral and Sacred Poems*, issued jointly by the brothers in 1744, carried six lengthy expositions of various chapters of the Book of Isaiah which were replete with *theosis* language. These hymns often described sanctification as being "Immeasurably fill'd with God," filled by "love," or filled by the Holy Spirit (*P.W.*, 3:137, 140, 141, 144). In each case, the result was roughly the same: unification of the sin-divided heart or mind, and renewal effected by the establishment of righteousness, love, or the Kingdom of God within:

> 15. He will the steadfast mind impart,
>   The power that never shall remove,
>   And fix in every sinless heart
>   His throne of everlasting love.
>
> 16. The zeal of our Almighty Lord
>   His great redeeming work shall do,
>   Perform His sanctifying word,
>   And every waiting soul renew;
>
> 17. Bring in the kingdom of His peace,
>   Fill all our souls with joy unknown,
>   And 'stablish us in righteousness,
>   And perfect all His saints in one.
>   (*P.W.*, 3:139–40)

This same phraseology was quite prominent in Charles's later (post-1749) hymns. It continued to point to Christian perfection as a result of the life of God in the soul of an individual, "By perfect purity possess'd / For ever fill'd with God."[15] While Wesley's expressions and descriptions often sound a bit startling and unguarded—especially when describing the relationship between suffering and perfection ("the cross and the crown") or the dimensions of the perfection he anticipated—the fundamental thrust of Charles's application of this conception is clear. He equated an infusion of the divine life with the restoration or re-creation of the *imago Dei* within the Christian. In this way, Greek *theosis* phraseology played a crucial role in Wesley's doctrine of sanctification, since it described both the process toward and the goal of Christian perfection. The key to Charles's conception of Christian perfection was its christocentricity. His application was formed, no doubt, on the pattern of the various Pauline metaphors for describing sanctification as Christ being formed within the Christian (Rom. 8:10, 29; 1 Cor. 2:16; Gal. 4:19; Col. 1:27).

Wesley could describe this process of renewal from either Testament. For example, the "garment" of Isaiah 61 became his vehicle for explaining the blessed exchange in which Christ's righteousness is exchanged for our unrighteousness. In Charles's exposition of the passage, he says that Christ put on human "garments," a veiled reference to His incarnation and substitutionary death in order to clothe us in His image:

> 13. Jesus my garments hath put on,
>   Hath clothed me with the milk-white vest,
> And sanctified through faith alone,
>   And in His glorious image dress'd.
>   (*P.W.*, 4:311)

Similar connotations could be found in Wesley's hymn on the Beatitudes (*P.W.*, 4:320–21) or in a poetic prayer "For A Sick Friend" (*P.W.*, 5:75, no. 165). In each instance, the central theme was restoration or renewal of Christians' inner lives because Christ's image is formed in them:

> 10. Thou hast heal'd me in part,
>   And ready Thou art
> To fill up my faith, and possess my whole heart.

> 11. Thou art just to Thy word,
>   And I shall be restored,
> And holy, and perfect, and pure as my Lord.

> 12. In patience I wait,
>   For my God to create,
> And raise me on earth to my former estate.

> 13. My faith is not vain,
>   I am sure to regain
> His image, and lord of His creatures to reign.
>   (*P.W.*, 5:30, no. 133)[16]

In this typical exposition of the theme, Christ's image is identified as the "former estate" or original righteousness which was lost in the primordial Fall. The restoration of this image Charles described in perfectionist terminology: "holy, and perfect, and pure." The image of God which was both lost and regained was often described as love:

> Thine image is love,
> And I surely shall prove
> That holy delight of the angels above.
> (*P.W.*, 5:26–27, no. 130)

And as noted above (chapter 5), Charles's application of the word *love* extended into the phrase "perfect love" as he developed his doctrine of sanctification:

> Thou, Lord, its Finisher shalt be;
> The second house begun by Thee
> Shall soon to full perfection rise:
> Thou wilt fulfil Thy people's hope,
> And build Thy living temples up,
> By holiest love to reach the skies.
> (*P.W.*, 10:115, no. 1548)

Hence, the divine image restored through love was synonymous with being filled with God, which Wesley described as "paradise" and "finish'd holiness" here:

> Then the whole earth again shall rest,
> And see its paradise restored;
> Then every soul in Jesus bless'd
> Shall bear the image of its Lord,
> In finish'd holiness renew'd,
> Immeasurably fill'd with God.
> (*P.W.*, 4:190, no. 22)

Wesley's identification of the *imago Dei* comes full circle again. Since "God is love," His image established within the believer could alternately be termed "finish'd holiness" or "perfect love."

THE PROMISE OF THE FATHER

One of the ways in which Charles Wesley's conception of sanctification (as being filled with God) went beyond the boundaries marked out in Scougal's *Life of God in the Soul of Man* emerged in Wesley's development of Scougal's *theosis* doctrine by describing the indwelling of God as the presence of the Holy Spirit. Oddly enough, Scougal seemed not to develop a pneumatology as a parallel to his theology of divine love. His concept of the indwelling life of God was based on the Christian's adoration, imitation, and infusion by divine love, but it did not assume an invasion by the Spirit of God. Charles, on the other hand, had a robust pneumatology, and he consistently connected inner renovation with the work of the Holy Spirit.

This connection was established in his early hymn, "Groaning for the Spirit of Adoption," which appeared in *Hymns and Sacred Poems*, 1740 edition. It named the "Spirit of power" as the bringer of love, health, pardon, peace, comfort, and righteousness, and it said simply, "all with Christ is mine":

> 2. I want the Spirit of power within,
>   Of love, and of an healthful mind;
>   Of power to conquer inbred sin,
>   Of love to Thee and all mankind;
>   Of health, that pain and death defies,
>   Most vigorous when the body dies.

> 3. When shall I hear the inward voice,
>   Which only faithful souls can hear!
>   Pardon, and peace, and heavenly joys
>   Attend the promised Comforter:
>   He comes! And righteousness Divine,
>   And Christ, and all with Christ is mine!
>   (*P.W.*, 1:307–8)

Charles's imagery for the presence of the Holy Spirit in the life of the Christian likened it to the way in which the presence of God filled the Old Testament temple (2 Chron. 5:14; 1 Cor. 3:16):

> 4. O that the Comforter would come,
>   Nor visit as a transient guest,
>   But fix in me His constant home,
>   And take possession of my breast,
>   And make my soul His loved abode,

The temple of indwelling God!
(*P.W.*, 1:308)

The gifts of the Spirit that Wesley included in his description of Christian perfection included forgiveness as well as assurance of sin forgiven. His description encompassed purity (baptized with fire) and inward renewal that "cannot rest in sin forgiven" but presses on for a "Fulness of love," an "earnest" of heaven:

5. Come, Holy Ghost, my heart inspire,
   Attest that I am born again!
   Come, and baptize me now with fire,
   Or all Thy former gifts are vain.
   I cannot rest in sin forgiven;
   Where is the earnest of *my* heaven?

6. Where the Indubitable Seal
   That ascertains the kingdom mine?
   The powerful stamp I long to feel,
   The signature of Love Divine:
   O, shed it in my heart abroad,
   Fulness of love, of heaven, of God!
   (*P.W.*, 1:308)

The single most important contribution that the Wesleyan hymns made to pneumatology was the hymnal entitled *Hymns of Petition and Thanksgiving for the Promise of the Father*, which the brothers published jointly in 1746.[17] It was a collection of hymns for the celebration of Pentecost Sunday. Perhaps what is most startling about the thirty-two songs is that, when a biblical text is identified as the focal point of the poem, the hymns invariably look to the Johannine record; and with one exception, they focus upon chapters 14–16 of the Fourth Gospel. Only the title of the collection is drawn from the narrative of the first Pentecost (Acts 1:4), and even that connection seems to have the chief purpose of describing the coming of the Holy Spirit ("the promise of the Father") as an event that binds both Father and Son in covenantal promise with those who receive Christ. So the hymns do not merely recount the story of Pentecost, they re-create the event in the lives of contemporary Christians. The singers of these hymns pray for their own Pentecost. The Johannine passages which these hymns expound identify the Spirit as One who makes the ascended Christ and the power of His resurrection life present in the lives of Christians.

Although we face the "vexed problem of joint authorship" in these compositions, Charles certainly had a hand in them. The first hymn in the collection serves as a theological prologue to the rest; it establishes the agenda (restoration from the fall of Adam) and the agent whereby it is to be fulfilled (the Comforter who imparts God's grace):

> 2. Thou hast THE PROPHECY fulfill'd,
>   The grand original compact seal'd,
>   For which Thy word and oath were join'd:
>   THE PROMISE to our fallen head,
>   To every child of *Adam* made,
>   Is now pour'd out on all mankind.
>
> 3. The purchased Comforter *is* given,
>   For Jesus is return'd to heaven,
>   To claim, and then THE GRACE impart:
>   Our day of Pentecost is come,
>   And God vouchsafes to fix His home
>   In every poor expecting heart.
>   (*P.W.*, 4:165)

Although Timothy Smith was correct to note that many of these hymns utilized Pentecostal imagery to describe sanctification "unambiguously as a second moment," the main thrust of the Wesleys' pneumatology lay in a different direction.[18] It was the connection between the ascended (absent) Christ and the presence of the Spirit ("of Thy Son") that each of these hymns made most emphatic:

> 6. Send us the Spirit of Thy Son,
>   To make the depths of Godhead known,
>   To make us share the life Divine;
>   Send Him the sprinkled blood to' apply,
>   Send Him, our souls to sanctify,
>   And show, and seal us ever Thine.
>   (*P.W.*, 4:166)

This hymn established the pattern of virtually every hymn in the collection. (1) It begins with a plea for the sending of the Holy Spirit. (2) It associates grace (v. 3) or cleansing (v. 6) with the coming of the Spirit, since the Spirit applies the "blood" or saving effects of Christ's death. (3) The visitation of the Holy Spirit is synonymous with being filled with God, with holiness, or with love. These developments were consonant with the Johannine foundations of the "Hymns for Whitsunday" (as Charles called them). John records that, anticipating His physical absence (John 14:16), Jesus prayed to the Father to give His disciples "another Comforter"—that is to say, One who would be to them the sort of Comforter Jesus was. Jesus promised that the Father would send the Comforter in Jesus' name so that he might "teach you all things, and bring all things to your remembrance whatsoever I have said unto you" (John 14:26). Thus, Jesus stood before His disciples in the Upper Room, hours before His death and resurrection, and told them that it was better ("expedient") that He should leave them since His leaving meant that the Spirit would come. The expediency of the coming of the Comforter lay in the Spirit's ability to convict of sin, righteousness, and judgment, and to guide Jesus' disciples into all truth. The Holy Spirit is the Spirit of Christ, who takes the things of Christ and shows them to the disciples (John 16:7–15). Sanctification thus could be described as the "life" or (to use Scougal's terms) the "perfections" of God filling the human soul as the Holy Spirit makes the human heart its "constant shrine":

1. Eternal Spirit, come
     Into Thy meanest home,
From Thine high and holy place
     Where Thou dost in glory reign,
Stoop in condescending grace,
     Stoop to the poor heart of man.

2. For Thee our hearts we lift,
     And wait the heavenly Gift:
Giver, Lord, of life Divine,
     To our dying souls appear,

Grant the grace for which we pine,
Give Thyself THE COMFORTER.

3. No gift or comfort we
Would have distinct from Thee,
Spirit, principle of grace,
Sum of our desires Thou art,
Fill us with Thy holiness,
Breathe Thyself into our heart.

4. Our ruin'd souls repair,
And fix Thy mansion there,
Claim us for Thy constant shrine,
All Thy glorious Self reveal,
Life, and power, and love Divine,
God in us for ever dwell.
(*P.W.*, 4:167–68)

The imagery or typology of Pentecost, however important
it is for describing being "filled with God," was not the
center of Charles Wesley's understanding of sanctification.
Although he used Pentecostal imagery with great effect to
describe sanctification, and although being filled with God
(which we have termed *theosis*) certainly lends itself to the
language and imagery of Pentecost, Charles's doctrine of
sanctification was not based on the third Person of the
Trinity. Christ was the foundation upon which Wesley's
Pentecostal imagery stood. Charles affirmed that the Holy
Spirit is the infilling, vivifying presence of God and the
Creator of life divine in the Christian; but he first affirmed
that the work of the Spirit is defined by its connection with
Christ. In his christological grasp of sanctification, Charles
followed classical Christianity rather than the "enthusiastic" Spirit-centered conceptions of his own day and of some
revivalists who came after him.[19] The phraseology of "the
Promise" continued into Charles's later hymns, but it was
never univocally Holy Spirit terminology (*Ms. Acts*, p. 5;
P.W., 12:40, no. 2152). Whitsunday was the anniversary
of Charles's conversion, and it was a vantage point from
which he considered justification as well as its logical and
theological consummation, sanctification.

Hymns on the Trinity, published in 1768 under
Charles's name alone, continued the theme of God's being

formed within the Christian: "And *in* us when the Spirit dwells, / We all are fill'd with God" (*P.W.*, 7:248, no. 62). Again the sanctifying work of the Spirit is affirmed, but generally in the larger context of the entire work of the Godhead:

> 4. The merciful God, The hallowing three
> Himself hath bestow'd On sinners like me:
> Our full Sanctifier He perfects in one,
> And raises us higher, And seats on His throne.
> (*P.W.*, 7:297, no. 135)

Charles knew that the believer's inner renovation is the work of the whole Trinity: "The Sender and the Sent are One" (*P.W.*, 7:227, no. 35). The interconnection of Jesus and the Spirit forms the basis of "the hallowing" of the believer, but sanctification is a Triune work:

> Jehovah who in Jesus dwells
> His whole Divinity imparts,
> To souls prepared His Son reveals,
> And sends His Spirit into our hearts.
> (*P.W.*, 7:211, no. 9)

The formation of Christ within an individual produces "perfection" and recovers one's status with God before the Fall, as the Christian is "fill'd with God":

> 2. Soon as in Christ we truly are,
> We see the Father in the Son,
> His pure unsinning nature share;
> And know that God and Christ are one,
> Till faith's perfection we receive,
> And fill'd with God for ever live.
> (*P.W.*, 7:218, no. 21)

This same emphasis was firmly established in Charles's *Short Hymns on Select Passages of Scripture* (1762), both in its published and unpublished versions. Wesley's *Short Hymns* based on John 14–16 were especially significant, since those passages had played such a prominent role in the jointly published volume of 1746 (*The Promise of the Father*). The *Short Hymns* escaped John Wesley's editorial pen, so the views expressed in these nearly five thousand compositions are the mature and unvarnished ideas of the younger Wesley brother. Once again we find Charles affirming that sanctification or Christian perfection, described as the restoration of the image of God (or Christ) within the Christian, is a Trinitarian event. He said that the Holy Spirit completes the redemptive work of Christ by overcoming sin and planting the "life Divine" within the faithful, as in this unpublished hymn based on John 16:11:

> 1. Again, Thou Spirit of burning come,
>   Thy last great office to fulfill,
> To show the hellish tyrant's doom,
>   The hellish tyrant's doom to seal,
> To drive him from Thy sacred shrine
> And fill our souls with life Divine.
>
> 2. Of judgement now the world convince,
>   The end of Jesus' coming show,
> To sentence their usurping prince,
>   Him and his works destroy below.
> To finish and abolish sin
> And bring the heavenly nature in.
>
> . . . . . .
>
> 5. Then the whole earth again shall rest,
>   And see its paradise restor'd
> Then every soul in Jesus blest
>   Shall bear the Image of its Lord,
> In finish'd holiness renew'd,
> Immeasurably fill'd with God.[20]

IN CHRIST

As in his earlier hymns, Charles's *Short Hymns* describe indwelling of God (or *theosis*) christologically: "And Christ Himself inhabit there, / And every saint be fill'd with God" (*P.W.*, 9:440, no. 1207). In these hymns framed on the Pauline concept of mystical union—being "in Christ" and having "Christ in" us (Rom. 8:10–35; 2 Cor. 5:17–21; Gal. 2:20, 21; Eph. 1:11)—Charles joined the sending of the Son and the coming of the Spirit in one grand movement of redemption, righteousness, and perfect love:

1. Father, Thy most benign intent
      With warmest gratitude we own,
   Thou hast in human likeness sent
      Thy Son, for all our sins to' atone,
   Sinless, yet like His brethren made,
   He died a victim in our stead.

2. He died, that sin in us might die,
      Condemn'd, when Jesus breathed His last:
   Sin in the flesh we now defy;
      Its guilt and tyranny are past;
   And dying of its mortal wound,
   It soon shall be no longer found.

3. The righteousness Thy law requires
      Shall then be all in us fulfill'd,
   Who now renounce our own desires,
      And to Thy Spirit's motions yield;
   And following our celestial Guide,
   Go on, till wholly sanctified.

4. In us the full obedience true,
      Which Jesus for His people wrought,
   Shall be by Him perform'd anew,
      While saints in deed, and word, and thought,
   Fill'd with the triune God, we prove
   The righteousness of perfect love.
            (*P.W.*, 13:10–11, no. 3046; cf. 13:76–77)

Applying his typological exegesis to Joshua 20:7, Wesley identified the theme of fellowship with the Old Testament site of Hebron, and he developed that theme in a manner reminiscent of the Pauline idea of union with Christ:

Thee, Saviour, I my refuge make;
And when Thy nature I partake,
   And all Thy fulness feel,
From fear, and sin, and sorrow free,
   In perfect fellowship with Thee
I shall for ever dwell.
            (*P.W.*, 9:129, no. 396)

In an unpublished hymn based on Luke 9:14–16 (the feeding of the multitude), Charles blended Luke's account of the feeding with the Johannine identification of Jesus as the "bread of life" (John 6) to describe the Christian's fellowship with Christ in metaphors borrowed from the eucharistic rite: We feed on Jesus in our hearts, / And filled with God forever live."[21] The remedy for humanity's fallen nature ("an evil heart") was prescribed in Charles's prayerful response to Jehu's question, "Is thine heart right?" (2 Kings 10:15):

> It must remain an evil heart,
> Till Thou Thy hallowing grace impart,
>   And Christ is form'd within.
>   (P.W., 9:196, no. 618)

This was synonymous with saying that the old Adam, "the rebel man within," was crucified with Christ (Gal. 5:24):

> 1. We that are Christ's, have crucified
>   The flesh, the rebel man within,
>   Passion, and appetite, and pride,
>   And all the brood of inbred sin;
>   The *Adam* old (the selfish love)
>   By faith we nail'd him to the tree,
>   From whence he never shall remove,
>   But bleed to death, O Lord, with Thee.
>   (P.W., 13:66–67, no. 3163)

Contrariwise, a new Adam has come in Christ to bring holiness to the inner person:

> Who shall that holiness explain?
>   *Adam*, descended from above,
> Answer by forming me again,
>   By perfecting my soul in love.
>   (P.W., 13:82, no. 3191; cf. 13:83–89)

Charles depicted the results of Christ's indwelling presence with the terms *full perfection, whole salvation, purity, love,* and similar synonyms for *sanctification.*[22] Christ's indwelling was understood to be nothing less than the end of sin's grip upon a person's life and a corresponding inclusion in the resurrection life of Christ:

> 3. Whether by slow or swift degrees,
>   The selfish and the proud desire,
>   The *Adam* old shall surely cease,
>   And the last breath of sin expire;
>   My actions, words, and thoughts impure,
>   Sin's members, all destroy'd shall be,

And then of full salvation sure,
  I dwell in Christ, and Christ in me.
      (*P.W.*, 13:7, no. 3041)

Occasionally, Charles explained the restoration of purity or of the *imago Dei* as the coming of the kingdom of God, which Jesus announced and brought as a reign of righteousness and peace. Wesley's unpublished poem based on Luke 17:21, "The Kingdom of God Is Within You," identified re-creation in love as the kingdom or reign of God in the life of the Christian:

Love, the power of humble love
  Constitutes Thy Kingdom here:
Never, never to remove
  Let it, Lord, in me appear,
Let the pure, internal grace
  Fill my new-created soul,
Peace, and joy, and righteousness,
  While eternal ages roll.[23]

In a similar way, he said the kingdom is "present heaven" established in the heart where Christ rules to "Set up Thy kingdom in [the believer's] heart":

Thyself in him and his reveal,
Thyself in every bosom dwell,
  Our everlasting Guest.
      (*P.W.*, 10:235, no. 242)

Just as Wesley's hymns emphasized that faith in Christ brings the eschatological kingdom into the present life of the Christian, so also perfection was connected with a future expectation. The hymns declared that salvation could be consummated either in Christ's return to earth or in the Christian's passage through the veil to be within Him, passing through death to perfect life eternal:

1. With longing eyes and restless heart
     I await His full return,
   Who kindly promises to' impart
     Himself to all that mourn.
   The word His Blessed lips hath pass'd
     The soul-renewing word
   And I shall surely find at last
     Perfection in my Lord.

2. I now my consolation see,
    But through a darkening veil;
Come, Jesus, come and comfort me,
    Nor let Thy promise fail;
Come Thou Thyself, for all Thy grace—
    Thy gifts cannot suffice,
And make the brightness of Thy face
    My constant paradise.[24]

Charles Wesley's language to describe his longing for complete renewal occasionally came close to sounding as though he desired to be absorbed into God's essence: "Sweetly set the prisoner free, / Swallow up my soul in Thee."[25] In such sentiments, often expressed in illness or the contemplation of death, Wesley seemed to follow Hellenistic or Eastern thought more directly than the biblical record, since the New Testament vision of afterlife is resurrection of the body and not absorption into God. Charles's correspondence to such mystical ideologies in this respect may be attributed to poetic license; but the heart of the matter, irrespective of the imagery employed, was the Wesleyan emphasis upon self-resignation as being vital to Christian perfection. John Wesley also used rather unguarded language to describe sanctification as a process of laying one's self aside to follow Christ more and more completely: "True humility is a kind of self-annihilation, and this is the centre of all virtues" (*J.W. Works*, 11:437).

A helpful clue to Charles's application of the annihilation theme is found in his unpublished hymn based on Luke 17:33 ("Whoever shall lose his life shall preserve it"):

That happy loss I long to know,
    To lose myself, a man of woe,
A man of life and heart unclean,
    A wretched man of inbred sin;
O could I gasp my parting breath,
    And find myself redeemed from death,
Impassive, omniscient above,
    Fill'd with glorious God of love.[26]

The loss or resignation of self was another of the Wesleys' double-sided doctrines. On the one hand, it meant a purging of self-will or self-love as one is filled with God's selfless love (*agape*); on the other hand, the same phraseology described the loss of the former, unregenerate person as one is re-created by being filled with God or love. Such statements of self-resignation were common in the dying testimonies that Charles recorded in his journal. Charles was present at the passing of a Mrs. Hooper on May 5, 1741, and her dying testimony caused him to consider the resignation of self-will as a part of the process of perfection:

> My soul was tenderly affected for [Hooper's] sufferings, yet the joy swallowed up the sorrow. How much more then did her consolations abound! The servants of Christ suffer nothing. I asked her whether she was not in great pain. 'Yes,' she answered, 'but in greater joy. I would not be without either.' 'But do you not prefer life to death' [Wesley asked]; she replied, 'I have no will of my own.' This is *that holiness* or *absolute resignation,* or *Christian Perfection!* (*C.W. Journal*, 1:272, italics added).

Wesley's connection of Christian perfection with resignation or utter self-commitment has some basis in the etymology of biblical sanctification words, stemming from rites of consecration and dedication (*qodesh,* for example).[27] But Charles's development of this theme also took a few turns uncharacteristic of Scripture. We notice in his record of Hooper's death several echoes of two themes that would eventually cause controversy between the Wesleys. The first was Charles's willingness to connect sanctification and human suffering, and the second was his growing conviction that Christian perfection (while realizable in this life) was received only in the moments before death. As we shall see in chapter 7, each of these issues brought disagreement into early Methodism.

Again note that the center of Charles Wesley's doctrine of sanctification is to be found in his Trinitarian emphasis. Perfection meant simultaneously being "fill'd with God," having the "mind" or "image" of Christ, or having "the promise of the Father." A similar symmetry could be seen in his use of the word *love*; it is the essence of the Deity, emblematized in the coming of Christ and endued upon the inner life of the faithful as the Spirit applies the "blood" of Christ. Charles expounded sanctification through a panoply of biblical images, phrases, and allusions that powerfully describe it as an indwelling of Christ by the power of His Spirit. His hymn based on the prediction of Jesus' birth (Matt. 1:23) was typical of the cohesion and theological symmetry Charles found in the divine life:

> 1. Celebrate *Immanuel's* name,
>   The Prince of life and peace;
>   God with us, our lips proclaim,
>   Our faithful hearts confess:
>   God is in our flesh reveal'd;
> Heaven and earth in Jesus join;
>   Mortal with immortal fill'd,
>   And human with Divine.
>
> 2. Fullness of the Deity
>   In Jesu's body dwells,
>   Dwells in all His saints and me,
>   When God His Son reveals:
>   Father, manifest Thy Son,
> And, conscious of the' incarnate Word,
>   In our inmost souls make known
>   The presence of the Lord.
>
> 3. Let the Spirit of our Head
>   Through every member flow;
>   By our Lord inhabited,
>   We then *Immanuel* know:
>   Then He doth His name express,
> And God in us we truly prove,
>   Fill'd with all the life of grace,
>   And all the power of love.
>   (*P.W.*, 10:141–42, no. 8)

Immanuel—"God with us"—seems to be an apt summation of Charles's understanding of Christian perfection; it is as though the incarnation of Christ continues in all those who are filled by His Spirit. Christ who took flesh among us also takes flesh as "God in us," dwelling in "all His saints and me," reforming us by His image, by His Spirit, and by His love.

THE VIRTUE OF CHRIST

Virtue is a rather common word in Charles Wesley's writings. It occurs more frequently in his hymns than in his sermons or journal. *Virtue* is a biblical term, though it appeared a bare ten times in the Authorized Version of Charles's day. Of those, six suggest strictly moral connotations, as with "a virtuous woman" (Prov. 12:4; 31:10). This ethical connotation also predominated in Wesley's application of *virtue* in his published sermons, where he proclaimed "Christian virtues" (*C.W. Sermons*, p. 203).

But three of the New Testament uses of *virtue* (Mark 5:30; Luke 6:19; 8:46) suggest more than mere moral qualities. In each instance, *virtue* translates the Greek word *dunamis*; the Greek term has the basic meaning of "power, might, strength, or force."[28] In a secondary or derived sense, it came to mean "ability, resources, meaning," or "that which gives power." Thus, the "mighty deeds" of Jesus (Matt. 11:20–23; 13:54) were literally *dunamati*, "works" or "deeds" of "power." The *Oxford Dictionary* suggests that in Wesley's day the word *virtue* was more directly connected with the supernatural than it is in most applications today; hence, the lexicographer might define the term as "power, or operative influence inherent in a supernatural or divine being."[29] When used to describe a quality, *virtue* meant something's "power or efficacy."

In most instances, Charles Wesley's use of the word *virtue* suggested that *power* was a synonym for what he had in mind; thus he wrote: "That virtue doth from Christ proceed,/ That power which animates the dead" (*P.W.*, 7:324, no. 28). An invigorating element was found in Charles's use of the term. Hence, *virtue* is occasionally described as an "animating power" (*P.W.*, 9:191, no. 600). It is nothing less than the power of Christ's resurrection; "He did through His own virtue rise" (*P.W.*, 11:490, no. 2016). "The energy Divine" was another important Wesleyan phrase for *virtue* (*P.W.*, 10:59, no. 1395). The moral connotations of the term were not lost on Charles; in fact, he found a delightful double meaning in the word *virtue*

that allowed him to speak both of moral deeds and of the
power that actuated them. But his most typical usage of
virtue indicated that he had in mind the animating,
invigorating life force that the Spirit of Christ implants in
the believer. *Virtue*, as Charles Wesley most often used the
term, was another name for the transforming power of
redemption:

> 2. That virtue doth from Christ proceed,
>   That power which animates the dead
>   The Spirit of life exerts;
>   The Father His own Son reveals,
>   The Triune God His image seals
>   With pardon on our hearts.
>   (*P.W.*, 7:324–25, no. 28)

Charles most often connected the word *virtue* with the
blood of Christ.[30] As we have noted, *blood* was Charles's
picture-word for the death of Christ and its saving
significance; so it was quite naturally considered the locus
of the power or *virtue* for Christian living. In fact, the
connection between *virtue* and *blood* was a constant theme
across the whole Wesleyan hymnological corpus. It described the Son, "Omnipotent [all-powerful] to save" by
the "virtue of His blood":

> Trusting in our Lord alone,
>   A great High-priest we have!
> Jesus, God's eternal Son,
>   Omnipotent to save,
> With the virtue of His blood,
>   Ascending to the holiest place,
> Pass'd the heavenly courts, and stood
>   Before His Father's face.
>   (*P.W.*, 13:126, no. 3270)

Occasionally, Charles picked up the healing imagery
suggested in the three New Testament passages where
virtue is used, and he connected *virtue* with the restorative
effects of Jesus' blood:

> 3. Invited and urged to draw nigh,
>   We trust in a merciful God,
>   To Thee, the Physician, apply,

> And wait for a drop of Thy blood:
> Thy blood can all sicknesses heal;
>   Its virtue, O Jesus, impart,
> Our pardon infallibly seal,
>   And heaven implant in our heart.
>   (*P.W.*, 7:27–28, no. 22)

In a corresponding way, the elements of capacity or ability, which were latent in the etymology of the term, emerged most emphatically when Charles drew *virtue* and *blood* together to describe the reality of sanctification, and it was sanctification that he considered to be the supreme enabling:

> 2. What is that preparation
>   For fellowship with Thee,
> For final full salvation,
>   But faith and purity,
> The dire handwriting blotted,
>   The peace and life of God,
> The holiness unspotted
>   Which comes with Jesus' blood!
>
> 3. Its virtue sanctifying
>   O might I throughly know,
> And on His death relying
>   To life eternal go!
> Father, send forth His Spirit
>   Into my hallow'd heart,
> And meet [i.e., fit] Thy throne to' inherit,
>   Meet am I to depart.
>   (*P.W.*, 7:114–15, no. 96)

On numerous occasions, Wesley wrote more directly of the virtue of Jesus' death, simply laying aside the imagery of redemptive blood.[31]

Another important point of contact for the virtue that Charles found in the redemptive work of Christ was in connection with His *name*.[32] Scripture attests that the divine name, or Jesus' name, is a locus of power, and hence His name can be identified as an appropriate source of virtue (Ps. 25:11; Luke 9:49; John 16:23). This biblical (and Wesleyan) fascination with the name of Jesus was not a magical conception; it was not a notion that one can manipulate the Deity by invoking Christ's name. Rather, the virtue of the name is its close identification with the person named. In Hebraic culture, the association between a person's nature and name was so close that Walter Eichrodt describes it as a "reciprocal relationship,"[33] and Scripture abounds with instances in which a change of character necessitated or was signaled by a change in name (Gen. 17:5, 15; 35:10; Matt. 16:18). Wesley's use of the phrase "Jesus' name" recognized that in the biblical sense of the term, *name* stood for the nature of a person; hence, Jesus' name represents His power to restore "inward peace" and "perfect holiness":

> 5. Yes, O Thou all-redeeming Lamb,
>   The virtue of Thy balmy name
>   Restores my inward peace;
>   Thy death doth all my guilt remove,
>   Thy life shall fill my heart with love
>   And perfect holiness.
>   (*P.W.*, 7:100, no. 84)

Love plays such a prominent role in Charles Wesley's soteriology that one might anticipate that love is said to have virtue or power, and this is certainly the case:

> I tremble at what I have done,
>   But look for my help from above,
>   The *power* that I never have known,
>   The *virtue* of Jesus's love.[34]

The connection between *virtue* and *love* created an interesting play on words, since love is an important Christian virtue and love exerts virtue (power) in the inner life of a Christian. Thus, the singer in Wesley's hymns longs for "A flame of reciprocal love" which both renovates and produces moral qualities in its aspirant (*P.W.*, 4:478).

During Wesley's polemical struggles (1740–42) with the "Moravianized Methodists," who elevated the inward voice over outward means of spiritual improvement and discipline, Charles used the term *virtue* in his defense and explication of the Lord's Supper. The "still brethren" believed that the most appropriate form of worship and discipleship was to wait for the still, small voice of God. Prayer, Scripture reading, public worship, and the Lord's Supper fell into disuse among them, since they believed each of these practices signaled an immature faith that must rely on externals. Both Wesleys had a high regard for the Eucharist (and other "means of grace"), and they eventually broke with the Fetter Lane Society and several of their close friends who had been "swallowed up in an ocean of stillness." Charles, however, held that there was no "virtue" in the Lord's Supper apart from Christ Himself: "What e'er the instrument of means / Tis Jesus makes the sinner whole."[35] But, Charles concluded, because Christ's effective presence was mediated through the sacraments, they could be described as instruments that have a saving purpose:

> 2. The weakest instrument Divine,
>   Water, or earth, or bread or wine,
>   Can work upon the soul:
>   Thou giv'st the means their saving use,
>   And then Thy virtue they transfuse,
>   And make the sinner whole.
>   (*P.W.*, 11:440, no. 1898)

Charles's 1749 hymn, "The Bloody Issue" (based on the Gospel pericope describing the woman healed of a hemorrhage—Mark 5:29–30; Luke 8:42–46), linked virtue with the "means" of Jesus' garment, which was an instrument for curing her malady. In Wesley's poetic extension, this passage became a metaphor for describing the sacrament of the altar:

> 7. His body doth the cure dispense,
>   His garment is the ordinance
>   In which He deigns to' appear;
>   The word, the prayer, the broken bread,
>   Virtue from Him doth here proceed,
>   And I shall find Him here.
>   (*P.W.*, 4:452)

Similar imagery reappeared thirteen years later when Charles's *Short Hymns* commented on the same passage, though working with Matthew's version (Matt. 9:20f.) on that occasion:

> 2. The smallest things, the weakest means,
>   The mournful fast, the plaintive prayer,
>   His sanctifying power dispense,
>   His efficacious grace confer,
>   And through His sacramental clothes
>   The healing emanation flows.
>
> 3. Yet not in outward veils of grace,
>   But in Himself the virtue lies,
>   The' infusion of His righteousness
>   This fountain of corruption dries;
>   And sure as I in Christ believe,
>   I shall a perfect cure receive.
>   (*P.W.*, 10:225, no. 216)

Thus, according to Wesley, there is virtue in the sacrament. It is the power of Christ's righteousness; but this virtue is not communicated mechanically, "And sure as I in Christ believe, / I shall a perfect cure receive." The sacraments are aptly described as "outward veils of grace," suggesting that God's grace is operative in them; yet the locus of their virtue is not in the sacraments per se, but in Christ—the One with whom a believer has communicated. While Charles consistently considered the sacraments to be means of grace, he insisted that their virtue was found in the sacramental presence of Christ, not localized specifically in the elements:

> 1. Come, Holy Ghost, Thine influence shed,
> And realize [i.e., make real] the sign;
>   Thy life infuse into the bread,
> Thy power into the wine.
>
> 2. Effectual let the token prove,
> And made, by heavenly art,
>   Fit channels to convey Thy love
> To every faithful heart.[36]

Healing images became Charles's main method for describing the effects of Christ's virtue; this development was certainly in keeping with the biblical usage, since the woman with a hemorrhage (Mark 5:29–30) and the multitude that pressed upon Jesus (Luke 6:19) experienced healing, "for there went virtue out of him, and healed them all." In Wesley's poetical exegesis, the biblical healings became metaphors for redemption, wholeness, and sanctification (*C.W. Journal*, 1:194). Because of its images of healing, virtue was sometimes termed "balmy," in the sense of being a "healing balm" (*P.W.*, 7:100; 9:47, no. 151; 9:329, no. 946). This healing meant not only forgiveness of sins but also union with Christ by faith:

> Giver of life, and strength renew'd,
>   I bless Thy balmy name,
> Heal'd by the virtue of Thy blood
>   My Healer I proclaim,
> Jesus, Thou canst with equal ease
>   Pronounce my sins forgiven,
> And bid me rise, and go in peace,
>   And bear my cross to heaven.
>   (*P.W.*, 5:377–78, no. 171)

Such healing by the virtue of Christ's blood not only effected justification ("sins forgiven"), but also brought the renewal of the inner person in sanctification or Christian perfection:

> 1. Jesus full of holiness,
>   Holiness proceeds from Thee,
>   Virtue pure and gospel-grace
>   Cures our souls' infirmity:
>   Thee who touch by faith and prayer
>   Shall the balmy effluence feel,
>   Throughly heal'd to all declare
>   Love is inexhaustible.
>
> 2. Now I seek to touch my Lord,
>   Now as yesterday the same,
>   Hear the evangelic word,
>   Trust the virtue of Thy name:
>   Lord, in me Thy grace reveal,
>   (Grace which every soul may prove,)
>   All my sicknesses to heal
>   Now infuse Thy sovereign love.[37]

In a similar way, Charles Wesley moved from the healing "virtue" imagery of the Gospels to the life-quickening power exercised in Ezekiel's valley of dry bones (Ezek. 37:3–4):

Can these dry bones perceive
  The quickening power of grace,
Or Christian infidels retrieve
  The life of righteousness?
All-good, almighty Lord,
  Thou know'st Thine own design,
The *virtue* of Thine own great word,
  The *energy Divine.*
                    (*P.W.*, 10:59, no. 1395, italics added)

"Healing virtue" became one of Wesley's vivid word pictures for ultimate healing or renovation, for redemption out of death and into new life in Christ:

Thy virtue, Lord, if Thou exert,
The merits of Thy death impart,
  Though dead in trespasses
My soul shall suddenly revive
Obedient to thy touch and live
  The sinless life of grace.
                    (*P.W.*, 10:224, no. 321)

Hence, commenting on the man with a withered hand (Mark 3:5), Wesley found a metaphor of the way Christ's virtue flows through our broken efforts to touch Him by "faith and prayer" to the end that in reaching forth our hands in love we, like the man of the narrative, are healed:

2. But Thou, my Saviour, must confer
    The energy of faith and prayer,
  The life of charity [love],
    Whoe'er exerts his wither'd hand,
  Transmitted through Thy sole command
    The virtue comes from Thee.

3. Thy hand, O Lord, o'er us extend,
    To bless and strengthen and defend,
  To heal and sanctify,
    To fit for every righteous deed,
  To mold after Thy will, and lead
    And lift us to the sky.[38]

In much the same way, Charles connected the healing virtue with spiritual wholeness. The physical wholeness anticipated in the Gospel accounts pointed the way to a washing away of the old carnal spirit and re-creating it anew, hallowing and perfecting "the penitent soul":

5. By the blood of the Lamb
    The martyrs o'ercame;
And its virtue is now, and for ever the same.

6. It washes the foul,
    It makes the sick whole,
And hallows, and perfects the penitent soul.

7. I felt it applied,
    The life-giving tide
Hath brought me to God, and in God I abide.

8. I shall feel it again
    Washing out the old stain:
Then away with your spots, for not one shall remain!

9. My Lord from above
    Shall the mountain remove,
And I then shall be spotless, and perfect in love.
          (*P.W.*, 5:28–29, no. 132)

The virtue of Christ's blood or name, with its healing effects—one of Wesley's chief themes for expounding "full salvation"[39]—connected his soteriology with ethics, because of the moral connotations of the term *virtue*; and it described the sacraments as life-giving signs that set Christ before the church. *Virtue* also described the process of Christ's being formed within Christians:

4. O that the world might know
    The great atoning Lamb!
Spirit of Faith, descend, and show
    The virtue of His name:
    The grace which all may find,
    The saving power impart,
And testify to all mankind,
    And speak in every heart.

5. Inspire the living faith,
    (Which whosoe'er receives
The witness in himself he hath,
    And consciously believes;)
    The faith that conquers all,
    And doth the mountain move,
And saves whoe'er on Jesus call,
    And perfects them in love.
          (*P.W.*, 4:197)

THE NEW BIRTH

Few phrases have become more closely linked with evangelistic preaching than the saying, "Ye must be born again." The biblical imagery of new birth is most exclusively that of Johannine Christianity (John 3:3–8; 1 John 2:29; 3:9; 4:7; 5:1, 4, 18). Its most quoted form, "born again," is phrased in the form of a wonderful theological double entendre which can be translated either "born again" (that is, a second time) or "born from above" (by the power or Spirit of God). Nicodemus's response to Jesus (John 3:4) suggests that he was inclined to understand the phrase as meaning twice born, whereas Jesus' injunctions regarding the Spirit, the kingdom of God, and "heavenly things" suggest that He thought of "born again" as being from above, by the power of the Spirit. The theme receives further elaboration in 1 John where being "born of God" is explained in terms of being sinless, being filled with love, believing that Jesus is the Christ, and overcoming the world (1 John 3:9; 4:7; 5:1, 4, 18).

Based on the recent popularity of this phrase to describe conversion or renewed life in Christ, one might expect that it was also prominent during the Wesleyan revival. This, however, does not seem to have been the case! According to Charles's journal, these Johannine texts did not appear among his sermons. Only two of John Wesley's sermons, "Salvation by Faith" and "The New Birth," turned to this theme with the insistency we might expect from a Methodist evangelist (*J.W. Works*, 5:7–17; 6:65–77). Yet, Harald Lindström was correct to see "new birth" as a crucial component of John Wesley's postconversion conception of Christianity, since John used the term to describe the change within the Christian who is saved from both the guilt and the power of sin.[40] Although Charles's early proclamations of the new birth (if there were any) are not extant, John's sermon by that title gives a clear exposition of his views on the matter.

The older brother described the new birth by considering the how, what, and why of salvation with characteristic thoroughness. John began his homily by naming justification and new birth as the "fundamental" doctrines of Christianity, "the former relating to that great work God does for us, in forgiving our sins; the latter, the great work which God does in us—, renewing our fallen nature" (*J.W. Works*, 6:65). These occur simultaneously, John wrote, "in order of time"; but in the "order of thinking," justification precedes new birth, since "we first conceive [God's] wrath to be turned away, and then His Spirit to work in our hearts" (*J.W. Works*, 6:66).

As to the "why" of the new birth, Wesley insisted that humanity, though created in God's image, had fallen into sin "and became unholy and unhappy":

> The natural consequence of this is, that every one descended from [Adam] comes into the world spiritually dead, dead to God, wholly dead in sin; entirely void of the life of God; void of the image of God, of all the righteousness and holiness where in Adam was created. . . . Hence it is, that, being born in sin, we must be 'born again.' Hence every one that is born of a woman must be born of the Spirit of God (*J.W. Works*, 6:67–68).

When considering the "how" of this rebirth, John turned more directly to the biblical analogy:

> It is only then when a man is born, that we say he begins to live. . . . Now [in new birth] he may be properly said to live: God having quickened him by his Spirit, he is alive to God through Jesus Christ. He lives a life which the world knoweth not of, a 'life which is hid with Christ in God.' God is continually breathing, as it were, upon the soul; and his soul is breathing unto God (*J.W. Works*, 6:70–71).

Thus, by the analogy of birth, be it natural or supernatural, the nature of the doctrine was clarified:

> It is that great change which God works in the soul when he brings it into life; when he raises it from the death of sin to the life of righteousness. It is the change wrought in the whole soul by the almighty

Spirit of God when it is 'created anew in Christ
Jesus;' when it is 'renewed after the image of God, in
righteousness and true holiness;' . . . In a word, it is
that change whereby the earthly, sensual, devilish
mind is turned into the 'mind which was in Christ
Jesus' (*J.W. Works*, 6:71).

In his closing section of the sermon, treating the
inferences that one may draw from this doctrine, John
distinguished between new birth and sanctification. New
birth "is a part of sanctification, but not the whole; it is the
gate to it, the entrance into it. When we are born again,
then our sanctification, our inward and outward holiness,
begins; and thenceforward we are gradually to 'grow up in
Him who is our Head' " (*J.W. Works*, 6:74). Returning to
the analogy of birth (natural and supernatural), John
Wesley concluded that new birth, while being the beginning of sanctification, differed from it as an event of "a
short time, if not in a moment," differs from a maturation
"by slow degrees" by which a person "grows up to the
measure of the full stature of Christ" (*J.W. Works*,
6:74–75).[41]

At present it does not seem possible to date the
composition of John Wesley's standard sermon "The New
Birth"; but as early as October 1, 1738, he was using
language roughly parallel to that contained in the sermon.
He described the new birth as producing both "happiness
and holiness," since it "is the life of God in the soul; the
image of God fresh stayed on the heart; an entire renewal of
the mind in every temper and thought, after the likeness of
Him that created it" (*J.W. Journal*, 2:88–91). The
Wesleyan hymnals of this same period (1738–39) were
joint publications, and the hymns therein followed a line of
development similar to that of John's sermon. Commenting
on Hebrews 4:9 ("There remaineth therefore a rest to the
people of God"), the Wesleys described the new birth as an
inclusion in Christ, an inclusion that both cleanses and
renews fallen human nature, so that "We *strive* with sin no
more":

4. Our life is hid with Christ in God;
   The agony is o'er,
We wrestle not with flesh and blood,
   We *strive* with sin no more.

5. Our spirit is right, our heart is clean,
   Our nature is renew'd;
We cannot now, we cannot sin,
   For we are born of God.
                    (*P.W.*, 1:370–71; cf. 1:275–76)

Interestingly enough, these two descriptive (and perhaps extravagant) verses were omitted in all editions of this hymn beginning with *Hymns and Sacred Poems* (1740).

The earliest Wesleyan hymns also connected the new birth with the indwelling of the Holy Spirit, who brought not only forgiveness but also the "fulness of love, of heaven, [and] of God":

5. Come, Holy Ghost, my heart inspire,
   Attest that I am born again!
Come, and baptize me now with fire,
   Or all Thy former gifts are vain.
I cannot rest in sin forgiven;
Where is the earnest of *my* heaven?

6. Where the Indubitable Seal
   That ascertains the kingdom mine?
The powerful stamp I long to feel,
   The signature of Love Divine:
O, shed it in my heart abroad,
Fulness of love, of heaven, of God!
                    (*P.W.*, 1:308; cf. 1:95)

The Wesleys' experience of new birth in 1738 had a marked impact upon their appreciation of their former mentor, William Law; neither found much of their own conception of the new birth in Law's *Treatise on Regeneration* (1739). John's journal entry for Tuesday, October 23, noted that "riding to Bradford, I read over Mr. Law's book on the New Birth: philosophical, speculative, precarious; Behemenish, void, and vain!" (*J.W. Journal*, 2:297).[42] The elder brother's standard sermon "On God's Vineyard," which was a short history on the beginnings of Methodism, pointed to a confusion about proper understanding of justification and sanctification that emerged in the early years of the movement: "At the same time a man is justified, sanctification properly begins. For when he is justified, he is 'born again,' 'born from above,' 'born of the Spirit'; which although it is not (as some suppose) the whole process of sanctification, is doubtless the gate of it" (*J.W. Works*, 7:205).

Later in the same sermon, John pointed to William Law's *Treatise On Regeneration* as one of the culprits in this confusion: "A late very eminent author, in his strange 'Treatise on Regeneration,' proceeds entirely on the supposition, that it is the whole gradual process of sanctification. No; it is only the threshold of sanctification, the first entrance upon it" (*J.W. Works*, 7:205).[43] Wesley returned to this same complaint in his "Open Letter to William Law" of 1756, which carried a point-by-point refutation of his former mentor's doctrine of the new birth (*J.W. Letters*, 3:357–61).

Charles Wesley read Law's *Treatise on Regeneration* the week before his brother saw it. Charles's journal entry for October 19, 1739, suggests both the level of his anticipation and the depths of his disappointment in reading Law's discussion of the new birth: "I read part of Mr. Law on Regeneration to our Society. How promising the beginning! how lame the conclusion!" (*C.W. Journal*, 1:191). The younger Wesley agreed with Law's basic conception of the nature of the new birth: "Christianity, [William Law] rightly tells us, is a recovery of the divine image; and a Christian is a fallen spirit restored and reinstated in paradise; a living mirror of Father, Son, and Holy Ghost." Thusfar, Charles Wesley and William Law were in agreement; then Charles registered his complaint that Law had no theology of Christian experience connected with his conception of the new birth: "He supposes it is possible for him to be insensible of such a change; to be happy and holy, translated into Eden, renewed in the likeness of God, one with Father, Son and Holy Ghost, and yet not know it." From "this wretched inconsistency" in Law's doctrine, Charles felt forced to conclude "that his

knowledge of the New Birth is mostly in theory." John
Wesley reacted strongly against William Law's tendency to
expand the category of "new birth" to include the entire
process of sanctification; whereas Charles—apparently not
fastening on that point—questioned the validity of Law's
teaching, since it failed the test of reason and experience.
In these differing reactions to William Law's conception of
the new birth, we detect a foreshadowing of the brothers'
differing emphases regarding Christian perfection.

John Wesley's primary focus in his conception of the
new birth was justification.[44] As Charles moved out from
under John Wesley's editorial umbrella, it became clear
that the younger Wesley more typically thought of the
phrase "new birth" as describing the result of sanctification
or Christian perfection. John placed the new birth at the
beginning of the process of sanctification, but Charles
located it at the end, at the realization of faith's goal.
Charles's two-volume *Hymns and Sacred Poems* of 1749,
which escaped his brother's editorial examination, is
replete with examples of Charles's distinctive emphasis
regarding the new birth. One of his birthday hymns from
that collection provided Charles ample opportunity to
describe the second birth as "the life of heaven," or
"spotless love":

4. Long as I live beneath,
        To Thee O let me live,
    To Thee my every breath
        In thanks, and blessings give;
    Me to Thine image now restore,
    And I shall praise Thee evermore.

5. Thy former gift is vain,
        Unless Thou lift me up,
    Begetting me again
        Unto a lively hope;
    O let me know that *second birth*,
    And live the life of heaven on earth.

6. I wait Thy will to do
        As angels do in heaven,
    In Christ a creature new,
        Eternally forgiven;

> I wait Thy perfect will to prove,
> When sanctified by spotless love.
> (*P.W.*, 5:16, italics added; cf. 5:232, no. 3;
> 5:312, no. 20)

Charles's birthday hymn also serves as a fine example of the way in which John Wesley, editor of the pre-1749 hymnals, conformed Charles's theological expressions to his own. An examination of its structure is particularly instructive in this regard. The hymn begins by praising God for "my natal hour." The second verse continues this theme, reflecting on the grace of God which sustained the singer to the anniversary of his birth:

> From whom alone my birth,
>   And all my blessings came;
> Creating and preserving grace
> Let all that is within me praise.

Verse three offers a vow of consecration and stewardship of all the singer's "happy hours" to God. The fourth verse, cited above, makes an important transition as the singer's attention turns from the past toward the present and future: "to Thine image now restore, / And I shall praise Thee evermore." The fifth stanza despairs of the first birth if it was not followed and completed by the "second birth," a phrase that was synonymous with the restoration of the *imago Dei*.

Verses six and seven are recapitulations of verse five, though now expressed in the language of longing: "I wait Thy perfect will to prove, / When sanctified by spotless love." And in verse seven:

> O might I soon attain
>   My holy calling's prize!
> And grow, when born again,
>   And to Thy stature rise.

In both verses, Charles aspired to have the image of God restored within, being "sanctified by spotless love," which he termed "the second birth," or acquiring the "stature of Christ." Wesley's concluding verse eight indicated when he anticipated that this work of restoration would be completed:

8. Then, when the work is done,
    The work of faith with power,
Call home Thy favour'd son
    At death's triumphant hour,
Like *Moses* to Thyself convey,
And kiss my raptured soul away.
        (*P.W.*, 5:17)

John Wesley republished this birthday hymn in *A Collection of Hymns for the Use of the People Called Methodists* (1780). His version of "God of My Life, To Thee" had six verses, omitting two of Charles's original stanzas. Although the question of whether Christian perfection occurred at the instant of death had become controversial issue among the Methodists, John allowed verse eight to stand just as Charles had originally written it. But verse three, with its language of consecration, and verse four, which described the restoration of the *imago Dei* as the "second birth," were both expunged. Having removed Charles's distinctive ideas about the new birth implying utter self-surrender and the formation of the life of God within, John Wesley made the version of the hymn in the 1780 hymnal conform to his own ideas about being "born again."[45]

Charles's *Hymns and Sacred Poems* of 1749 contradicted another of John Wesley's favorite images for describing the new birth. Where John drew the analogy between natural and supernatural birth to describe the immediacy of being born again (in "a short time, if not in a moment"), Charles used the same analogy to depict the long struggle in prayer and suffering involved in the two birthings. He believed that only after the travail is past are we "pure and perfect," in possession of "our calling's prize":

12. O! satisfy their soul in drought;
    Give them Thy saving health to see,
And let Thy mercy find them out;
    And let Thy mercy reach to me.

13. Hast Thou the work of grace begun,
    And brought them to the birth in vain?
O let Thy children see the sun!
    Let all their souls be born again.

14. Relieve the souls whose cross we bear,
    For whom Thy suffering members mourn;
Answer our faith's effectual prayer:
    Bid every struggling child be born.

. . . . . .

18. Then, when our sufferings all are past,
    O! let us pure and perfect be,
And gain our calling's prize at last,
    For ever sanctified in Thee.
            (*P.W.*, 5:232–33, no. 3)

Charles's distinctive emphasis on the new birth continued into his *Short Hymns on Select Passages of Scripture* of 1762 and the literally thousands of "short hymns" which have survived in manuscript. His comments on John 3:2–3 suggest that the matter of discernible signs, tokens, and marks of the new birth had become an issue among the Methodists. Charles turned from outward fruits to the inner work of the Spirit and its accompanying sinlessness as the truest "witness":

The truth, and blessedness, and need
    Of this great change I know:
But can I witness it indeed,
    Can I the tokens show?
Marks of this birth, they all are vain
    Without the Spirit's power:
Then only am I born again,
    When I can sin no more.
            (*P.W.*, 11:340, no. 1656;
            cf. 11:343, no. 1661)

In addition to sinlessness, the new birth was described by Charles as a "heavenly birth," in which one is "restored / To all the image of my Lord" and begins to live all "the life of love" (*P.W.*, 11:340–41, no. 1657). Restoration of the paradisaical image of God became Charles's response to Jesus' injunction: "Marvel not that I said unto thee, Ye must be born again":

1. Adam descended from above
    Thou only canst that Spirit impart,
That principle of heavenly love
    Regenerating the sinful heart:

> O might He now from Thee proceed,
>   Fountain of life and purity,
> Implant the nature of our Head,
>   And work the mighty change in me.
>
> 2. The seed infused, the good desire,
>   Into a tree immortal raise,
>   With all Thy sanctity inspire,
>   With all Thy plenitude of grace;
>   Spotless, and spiritual, and good,
>   My heart and life shall then be Thine,
>   And in my Lord's similitude
>   Renew'd I shall for ever shine.
>   (*P.W.*, 11:341–42, no. 1659)

The Johannine attestation to the sovereignty of the Holy Spirit (John 3:8) became Wesley's platform for presenting the new birth as renewal by a work of the Spirit, while leaving open the matter of how or when:

> 1. Strangers to nature's mystery,
>   We hear its sound, but cannot see
>   The vague impetuous wind:
>   The Spirit's course we cannot trace,
>   The secret motions of that grace
>   Whose sure effects we find.
>
> 2. The ways of God are dark to man,
>   In vain we would describe, explain,
>   Delineate, or define:
>   The manner still remains unknown,
>   The sure reality we own,
>   And feel that birth Divine.
>
> 3. Just as He lists, the Spirit blows,
>   But whence He comes, and whither goes,
>   No mortal comprehends;
>   How He begins His power to' exert,
>   By what degrees renews the heart,
>   Or when His progress ends.
>   (*P.W.*, 11:342–43, no. 1660)

John Wesley's sermon "The New Birth" distinguished between baptism and new birth, "the one is an external, the other an internal work; that the one is a visible, the other an invisible thing, and therefore wholly different from each other" (*J.W. Works*, 6:73–74). Hence

John concluded, "As the new birth is not the same thing with baptism, so it does not always accompany baptism: They do not constantly go together" (p. 74). But Charles's unpublished hymn based on John 3:5 found the inward and outward dimensions of the sacrament joined so that those "Who the baptismal rite receive" are born again:

> 1. The water and the Spirit join
>   The inward grace and the outward sign
>   In that great mystery
>   Thro' which our souls are born again
>   Thy kingdom first on earth obtain;
>   And then Thy glory see.
>
> 2. Who the baptismal rite receive,
>   And by and in Thy Spirit live,
>   The sinless life unknown,[46]
>   Children of God they reign in love,
>   Joint-heirs with Thee, O Christ, remove
>   To share Thy heavenly throne.[47]

Charles seemed more willing than John to link the sacrament directly with the new birth because of the operative influence of the Holy Spirit, both in baptism and in regeneration.

This same corpus of late "short hymns" showed Charles connecting new birth with the progressive dimension of sanctification, the very emphasis his brother decried in the writings of William Law! Charles's poetic comment on John 3:4 seized on the biblical phrase, "How can a man be born when he is old," in a way that seemed autobiographical:

> I ask no more, how can it be?
> But leave the manner now to Thee,
>   And wait in *age* to prove
> That *heavenly birth*, by faith restored
> To all the image of my Lord,
>   To all the life of love.
>   (*P.W.*, 11:340–41, no. 1657, italics added)

Charles's rendition of 1 John 3:6, characteristically emphasizing the new birth and using the language of progress or pilgrimage, provides an appropriate summation of his understanding of this vital doctrine:

3. I would be of Thy Spirit born,
   And find that I can sin no more;
My soul into Thy likeness turn,
   Wisdom of God, and Truth, and Power,
Fulness of the Divinity,
Jesus, appear and dwell in me.

4. Then, only then my God I know,
   Divinely taught, divinely pure:
Yet onward to perfection go,
   And happy to the end endure,
Till faith is swallowed up in sight,
In glorious, full, eternal light.
                    (*P.W.*, 13:203–4, no. 3407, italics added)

It seems quite appropriate for Charles Wesley to describe sanctification as the life of God in a person's soul. Although he probably borrowed the phraseology from Henry Scougal, Charles filled it with biblical significance and connected it with the central themes of a Wesleyan soteriology. Under the tutelage of Scougal's book, Charles made this fundamental conception the basic thrust of his theology of redemption. For Charles, being filled with God implied both a resignation of self-will and an invasion by the liberating and restorative power of divine love. The believer's participation in the life of God could be described as a visitation of the Holy Spirit or of love, as Christ being formed within, as restoration of the *imago Dei*, or as an engrafting of the believer into Christ. Terms such as *virtue* and *balm* in Wesley's hymns described the medicinal effects of God's love, and they connected Charles's conception of Christian perfection with the means of grace and the life of disciplined discipleship. Charles believed that the renovation God works within the faithful is so radical that it could be termed a "new birth"; but his soteriological optimism gradually turned that phrase into a statement of the completion of sanctification, whereas John had placed "new birth" at the beginning of the process.

In this latter development, the younger Wesley began to step out from his older brother's shadow and establish his own theological formulas for describing Christian perfection. This departure is well attested in Charles's later hymns, as well as in John's editorial revisions of them.

CHAPTER SEVEN:

"A Brotherly Debate"

The most complete chronicle of the Wesley brothers' developing doctrines of sanctification is John's treatise entitled *A Plain Account of Christian Perfection*. It is arguably the definitive statement of the Wesleyan doctrine that its title names, and it is one of the most succinct statements of Christian perfection available throughout the brothers' writings.

The treatise approaches its task chronologically, tracing the Wesleys' understanding of sanctification from its earliest beginnings at Oxford through the mid-1760s. Since it was written around 1765 and reissued in 1777, there is a sense in which John's little book should be read against the backdrop of the turmoil that shook Methodism in the mid-1760s when a group of fanatics ("enthusiasts" in the eighteenth-century idiom) in the London society claimed to be as "perfect as angels." They were so obnoxious and hypocritical that the Methodists outside of London virtually ceased preaching perfection in any fashion, for fear of being associated with the pretenders of London. With characteristic directness, John Wesley described the long-term effects of the London debacle by writing, "They made the very name of Perfection stink in

the nostrils even of those who loved and honoured it
before" (*J.W. Letters*, 5:38).

Written in a climate of controversy and division, at a
time when rival factions were each claiming to be genuinely
Wesleyan on the doctrine of Christian perfection, John's
treatise emphasized both the continuity of the Wesleys'
conception of sanctification and the unanimity of John and
Charles on that same issue. John's account of the early
years of the revival (1738–44) was particularly full of
expressions of the mutual agreement: "In the same senti-
ment did *my brother and I* remain" (*J.W. Works*, 11:369,
italics added). Or again, "In 1739 *my brother and I*
published a volume of 'Hymns and Sacred Poems.' In
many of these we declared our sentiments [on Christian
perfection] strongly and explicitly" (*J.W. Works*, 5:370,
italics added). In a similar way, the 1741 edition of *Hymns
and Sacred Poems* was a joint venture at delineating the
doctrine under consideration: "*We* published a second
volume of Hymns. As the doctrine was still much misun-
derstood, and consequently misrepresented, I judged it
needful to explain yet farther upon the head; which was
done in the preface" (*J.W. Works*, 5:378, italics added).

John's preface to the 1740 hymnal is vintage Wesley;
biblical words and phrases were woven into a tapestry of
eleven succinct paragraphs that present his entire soteriology. Paragraph four began his explanation of full salvation
with the classical themes of recapitulation and liberation; it
is the "great gift of God," "which is begun on earth, but
perfected in heaven, is no other than the image of God
fresh stamped upon our hearts. It is a renewal in the spirit
of our minds after the likeness of Him that created us. It is
salvation from sin, and doubt, and fear" (*J.W. Works*,
14:323). Seizing upon John the Baptist's phrase (Matt.
3:10), John Wesley showed how God defeated inward sin,
having "laid the axe to the root of the tree" in "purifying
[the Christians'] hearts by faith, and cleansing all the
thoughts of their hearts by the inspiration of the Holy
Spirit" (*J.W. Works*, 14:323). Thus, Christians are positionally pure because of their inclusion in Christ ("holy as

he which hath called them is holy"), and they possess wholeness of heart and purity of intention as God works renewal within them ("Not that they have 'already attained' all they shall attain").

Wesley's tone was vibrantly victorious. Employing the familiar Johannine texts in part six of his preface, John identified sinlessness as the freedom depicted in John 8: "A first principle among true believers, 'We know that whosoever is born of God sinneth not" (*J.W. Works*, 14:324). Thus, Christians experience ever-increasing victories over sin and evil as they are conformed to the image of Christ by through the work of the Holy Spirit: "They daily go on 'from strength to strength: Beholding now as in a glass the glory of the Lord, they are changed into the same image, from glory to glory, as by the Spirit of the Lord.'" This victory over sin through Christ and the restorative power of His Spirit brought tangible effects into the lives of Christians; it meant freedom "from that great root of sin and bitterness, pride," and a corresponding sense of absolute dependence upon God: "They feel that all their sufficiency is of God; that it is he alone who is in all their thoughts, and 'worketh in them both to will and to do his good pleasure.'" It means "they are freed from self-will," since believers desire "nothing no, not for one moment, (for perfect love casteth out all desire), but the holy and perfect will of God." And this full salvation is liberation "from evil thoughts," since evil "does not now come in; there being no room for this in a soul which is full of God" (*J.W. Works*, 5:326). As a corollary effect, Christians are "free from wanderings in prayer," "from all darkness," since they have unity of intention ("their eye being single") and "their whole body is full of light."

This preface, though written by John, certainly reflected theological concerns and phraseology that were also characteristic of Charles, including themes such as the restitution of the *imago Dei*, "singleness of eye," and being filled with God. The hymnal—preface and hymns together—was intended to clarify the Wesleys' doctrine of sanctification, and it seemed largely successful, although in retrospect John's *Christian Perfection* hinted that the 1740 statement went too far in at least a few points: "This [hymnal] is the strongest account we ever gave of Christian perfection, indeed too strong in more than one particular" (*J.W. Works*, 11:378). The preface was "too strong" in its claims for the practical or experiential effects of Christian perfection. John Wesley would later disassociate sanctification and matters such as freedom from pain, wandering thoughts, anxiety as to what to speak, and freedom from temptation.

A second important point emerged in John's evaluation of the 1740 *Hymns and Sacred Poems*, with its preface on perfection: "There is nothing which we have since advanced upon the subject either in verse or prose which is not either directly or indirectly contained in this preface" (*J.W. Works*, 11:381). The unity ("we" emphasized above) and the constancy of the Wesleys' teaching on Christian perfection come to the forefront again. In point of fact, neither of John's claims was completely true. Despite their essential theological unity, which touched all the major doctrines—including sanctification—it became clear by the time John wrote his treatise on Christian perfection that there was no complete consensus between them or among the Methodists.

As to the constancy of the Wesleys' view of Christian perfection, again the claim is partially true since the theological center of the doctrine remained constant; but it is also clear that Charles Wesley's views underwent a series of developments as he adapted his teaching to the immediate problems Methodism faced at various points of its formative pilgrimage. Thus, while John's *Christian Perfection* was substantially accurate as a chronological survey of the development of the brothers' doctrine and the essential unity they had in their vision of holiness as the logical and theological completion of redemption, it had an apologetic agenda. It tells its history from the perspective of *John* Wesley and from the context of the acrimony caused by those who claimed angelic perfection.

During the 1740s, the Wesleys had continuing

difficulties in presenting their views on Christian perfection in ways that were readily understood by the uninitiated. This concern surfaced in the preface to their 1742 edition of *Hymns and Sacred Poems,* where John wrote: "The dispute being now at the height, we spoke upon the head more largely than ever before. . . . Perhaps the general prejudice against Christian perfection may chiefly arise from a misapprehension of the nature of it" (*J.W. Works,* 11:383). While John spoke "more largely" on the topic, the preface was streamlined to six points; it applied less Wesleyan theological jargon than usual—probably in an attempt to speak more directly to those who disputed the doctrine "from a misapprehension." Composed in the heat of the Wesleys' controversy with the "still brethren" (whom Charles called "Moravianized Methodists"), the preface began by stating clearly and extensively what perfection was *not*: "We willingly allow . . . there is no such perfection in this life, as implies either a dispensation from doing good, and attending all the ordinances of God; or a freedom from ignorance, mistake, temptation, and a thousand infirmities necessarily connected with flesh and blood" (*J.W. Works,* 14:328).

The first section of the disclaimer is designed to distance the Methodists from the elitism and inactivity of their "still" opponents. The "ordinances" mentioned in paragraphs one and two of John's statement of the true nature of perfection could be taken as having a double meaning—implying either "God's laws" or "God's sacraments." Both meanings seem to have been embraced as the term was clarified at the close of John's second point; he described those who seek "the measure and stature of Christ" as those who do not eschew the means of grace, but rather apply themselves "as oft as they have opportunity . . . to eat bread and drink wine in remembrance of Him; to search the Scriptures; by fasting, as well as temperance, to keep their bodies under . . . subjection; and above all to pour out their souls in prayer, both secretly, and in the great congregation." The Wesleyan concept of Christian perfection describes it as a Christ-life that is both a gift of

God's grace and an inner dynamic that is cultivated and nurtured through spiritual disciplines such as reading or hearing the Word, partaking of the sacraments, and engaging in prayer and deeds of Christian service.

The second clause of the 1742 disclaimer attacked a few of the popular misconceptions about Christian perfection, several of which can be traced directly to the "too strong" preface of the earlier edition of *Hymns and Sacred Poems*. Where the earlier preface had been too extravagant in stating the liberty and victories of Christian perfection, the 1742 preface attempted to defuse the explosive issues causing controversy. When the doctrine was stated constructively (as opposed to saying what it was not) in the closing paragraphs, John's emphasis was upon the restorative power of love, unity of intention ("singleness of eye"), and life under the power of God: "This it is to be a perfect man, to be sanctified throughout, created anew in Jesus Christ; even 'to have a heart all flaming with the love of God,' . . . 'so as continually offer up every thought, word and work, as a spiritual sacrifice, acceptable unto God through Christ'" (*J.W. Works*, 14:330).

Having repeated this solid summation of his theology of sanctification from his 1742 preface, John returned his *Christian Perfection* to the apologetic task: "This is the doctrine which we preached from the beginning, and which we preach at this day." According to the older Wesley, the trials and pilgrimage of the years had only solidified the brothers' convictions and unanimity about Christian perfection: "Viewing it by every point of light, and comparing it again and again with the word of God . . . the experience of the children of God . . . we saw farther into the nature and properties of Christian perfection. *But still there is no controversy at all between our first and our last sentiments*" (*J.W. Works*, 14:328, italics added).

The controversy among the Methodists and the general misapprehensions regarding the Wesleyan approach to sanctification made Christian perfection a standing topic at the Annual Conferences of the Methodist preachers. It was directly addressed, for example, on June

25, 1744, the second day of the very first Methodist assembly. Using a question-and-answer format, the Minutes of the conference defined its "doctrine of sanctification or Christian perfection" in the following fashion: "Question: 'What is it to be sanctified?' Answer: 'To be renewed in the image of God, in righteousness and true holiness.' Question: 'What is implied in being a perfect Christian?' Answer: 'The loving [of] God with all our heart, mind and soul'" (*J.W. Works*, 11:387). The formulation of sanctification given at the 1744 Conference was one that Charles Wesley could have easily affirmed, and he must have had a hand in framing it; in fact, this earliest confessional statement is phrased in precisely the terms Charles himself preferred (restitution of the image of God and of divine love).

The Wesleyan hymns of this period fall under the shadow of "the vexed problem of joint authorship," and it does not seem to be possible to extricate the work of one Wesley from the other.[1] Methodist tradition has assigned almost all of the original compositions to Charles, since John Wesley made most of the translations; but this generalization, for the most part true, does not represent a hard and fast rule, since John also composed and Charles also translated hymns.[2] It does not seem possible in these earliest hymns to distinguish Charles's original compositions from John's editorial emendations. These earliest hymnals are inextricably the work of both Wesleys—as John Wesley preferred to phrase it, "my brother and I."

The earliest Wesleyan hymnbooks drew their inspiration from classical and contemporary Christian authors, as well as from the Scriptures, to expound the doctrine of sanctification. Drawing upon Clement of Alexandria for a "Description of a Perfect Christian," the Wesleys sought "the simple life Divine" or "A peace beneath [here] appears" so that

> . . . in that peace we see and act
>   By instincts from above;
> With finer taste of wisdom fraught,
>   And mystic powers of love.[3]

Influenced by a biography of the French mystic De Renty, they composed a hymn "On Reading M. De Renty's Life," which longed for

> . . . that second birth:
> By change of place dull bodies may improve,
> But spirits to their bliss advance by love.
>   (*P.W.*, 1:15)

From the German J. A. Freylinghausen they borrowed the hymn "Christ Protecting and Sanctifying."[4] And biblical passages such as Hebrews 12:2 described a redemption "that speaks me whole":

> 6. Speak, gracious Lord, my sickness cure,
>   Make my infected nature pure;
>   Peace, righteousness, and joy impart,
>   And pour Thyself into my heart.
>   (*P.W.*, 1:83).

The Wesleyan hymns of the early 1740s were insistent in their longing for sanctification or Christian perfection. These (almost exclusively) original compositions were full of the language of pilgrimage or the imagery of one's quest after holiness. The tone of *Hymns and Sacred Poems* (1742) was set by the inclusion of several series of hymns such as "Desiring to Love," "Groaning for Redemption," and "Waiting for the Promise" (*P.W.*, 2:72–75; 126–33; 159–66; 293–99; 299–303). They are full of ardent expectancy and aspiration after perfect love, full salvation, Christian perfection, or fixing the image of God within the human heart by a work of His Spirit.

This pattern was perpetuated in the Wesleys' *Moral and Sacred Poems* (1744), through hymn series such as "Desiring to Be Dissolved" (*P.W.*, 3:161–65), and in *Hymns of Petition and Thanksgiving for the Promise of the Father* (1746), with its Johannine explanation of the work of the Spirit and formation of Christ within:

> Sinners, lift up your hearts,
>   THE PROMISE to receive!
> Jesus Himself imparts,
>   He comes in man to live;

The Holy Ghost to man is given;
Rejoice in God sent down from heaven.
(*P.W.*, 4:168, no. 4)

Hymns For Those That Seek and Those That Have Redemption in the Blood of Jesus Christ (1747) was a collection of occasional hymns that took the quest for holiness into the daily life of the singer. The hymn "For a Minister of Christ," for example, describes the effectiveness of "the saving power of God":

Saved from the guilt and power of sin
By instantaneous grace,
They trust to have *Thy life brought in*,
And *always* see Thy face.
(*P.W.*, 4:232–33)

This line of development reached its climax in Charles's two-volume *Hymns and Sacred Poems* of 1749. The hymnal was hastily built out of Charles's manuscripts and published without John's approval or emendations, as Charles tried to raise his "bride price." It was a miscellany of Charles's verse from the 1740s, much of it of the occasional variety: "For New Year's Day," "For a Lay Preacher," "Before Preaching to the Colliers in Leicestershire," and so forth. But the second volume of the collection carried two series of hymns that showed Charles's distinctive theological emphases. The first series was called "The Trial of Faith," fifteen hymns that described the purifying effects of inward anguish and outward suffering (*P.W.*, 5:139–62). Typically, these hymns looked to the suffering Christ as a pattern for a believer's own life and faith:

Thy every perfect servant, Lord,
Shall as his patient Master be,
To all Thine inward life restored,
And outwardly conform'd to Thee,
(*P.W.*, 5:149)

These hymns later drew strong editorial reaction from John Wesley because of their attempt to make sense of human suffering in the context of sanctification (*P.W.*, 5:160, 161–62).

A second major series (twenty-two hymns) in the 1749 hymnbook had bearing upon more characteristically Wesleyan emphases, the nature and timing of Christian perfection. Charles's "Hymns For Those That Wait For Full Redemption" brought his own distinctive views to the forefront in a way that distinguished his position from that of brother John. The title of the series is deliciously suggestive of its contents; the hymns are about "full redemption," a liberation from all sin (original and actual) and from the power of sin because Jesus rules within the faithful:

> Come, Jesus, and cleanse
>   My inbred offence,
> O take the occasion of stumbling from hence,
>   The infection within,
>   The *possible sin*
> Extirpate, by bringing Thy righteousness *in.*
>   (*P.W.*, 5:290).

John Rattenbury has appropriately identified this collection of hymns as one point where we see Charles pursuing an ideal conception of perfection (Christlikeness) at the same time his brother was emphasizing the practicable conception (freedom from willful sin).[5] Another word from the title of that series was similarly significant—*waiting*. While John taught the sudden realization of inner purity (in a somewhat qualified sense), Charles's adoption of an unqualified conception of perfection caused him to begin to emphasize the quest after perfection, more than its sudden realization. These latter hymns hunger and hope for "full redemption," but do not declare its final realization; in fact, the last two in the collection criticize "Any Who Think They Have Already Attained" (*P.W.*, 5:313–36).

These issues (the nature of perfection, the timing of perfection, and the role of suffering) did not reach their flash point for another twenty years; but it is clear from the series "Hymns For Those That Wait For Full Redemption" that explosive ideas were already in the air. Charles had begun pursuing his own theological concerns in the doctrine of Christian perfection by the mid-1740s. And although the debate over a qualified or unqualified concept of perfection would shake Methodism in later years, that dispute clearly had roots in this earlier period.

THE ARTICLE OF DEATH

The Minutes of the fourth Methodist Annual Conference, dated June 16, 1747, reflect a dispute brewing over the Wesleyan doctrine of Christian perfection. There was apparently a broad body of theological consensus among the Methodist preachers, but there was one significant point of division. John Wesley's record of the Minutes offered three points "allowed by our brethren who differ from us with regard to entire sanctification": The dissenting Methodists granted "(1) That every one must be entirely sanctified in the article of death. (2) That till then a believer daily grows in grace, comes nearer and nearer to perfection. (3) That we ought to be continually pressing after it, and to exhort all others so to do" (*J.W. Works,* 11:388). The question that separated the Methodists at the fourth Annual Conference was, "Should we expect to be saved from all sin before the article of death?" John Wesley's report indicated that he answered this question in the affirmative; but what of brother Charles?

Various commentators have drawn attention to Charles Wesley's "obsession" or "preoccupation" with death. Born several months prematurely, Charles was sickly much of his life. The Epworth manse knew its share of sadness as well as joy; of the nineteen children born to the rector and Susanna Wesley, nine died in infancy. Mabel Brailsford points to young Charles's attendance at the funeral of the famous poet Joseph Addison (1719) as a formative factor in his development. According to the custom of their school (Westminster), Addison was buried at midnight, and the "King's Scholars" of a new generation encircled his grave with candlesticks to light the service of interment.[6] A bright lad, Charles was on a King's Scholarship at Westminster and was probably present at the funeral.

His fragile health broke again and again under the rigors of his devotional "method" at Oxford and under the pace of his ministry thereafter. Moreover, that these were dismal times in England is well attested in the popularity of the so-called graveyard poets such as Thomas Gray ("Elegy Written in a Country Churchyard," 1751), Edward Young ("Night Thoughts," 1746), and Thomas Wharton ("The Pleasures of Melancholy," 1747). The combination of his sensitive nature, his sickly constitution, and the fashion in which his age romanticized death had an impact on Charles that can be traced in hymns such as the series entitled "Desiring to Be Dissolved" (*Moral and Sacred Poems*, 1744).[7] In these rather morbid poems, death becomes a "Soothing, soul-composing thought!" (*P.W.*, 3:162). It is eulogized as "my hope," "my immortality," "My longing heart's desire" (*P.W.*, 3:163) and personified in a long and lovely embrace:

> 2. Extend thy arms, and take me in,
>   Weary of life, and self, and sin;
>   Be thou my balm, my ease:
>   I languish till thy face appears;
>   No longer now the king of fears,
>   Thou art all loveliness.
>   (*P.W.*, 3:163)

Charles's correspondence and journal show his life-long struggle with the thought of death. A letter to his wife, dated January 3, 1760, suggests that thoughts of release from the pain and trials of earthly life crept into the mind of Mrs. Wesley as well: "My dear Sally's wish has been often mine,—to have died in my infancy. I escapted [*sic*] many such thoughts last Saturday, by forgetting it was my birthday" (*C.W. Journal*, 2:226).

Although it is perhaps difficult for us to identify with the Charles Wesleys' sentiments about death, it is clear that in this "obsession" they were pretty much people of their own era. Yet, there was one important difference. In Wesley, a preoccupation with death was ultimately "escapted" and death was no longer "the king of fears," because it signaled the coming of the Bridegroom, the end of time and sin, and the entrance into "my eternal home" (*P.W.*, 3:161–63). Charles's sensitive nature felt the threat of death keenly; but through his tenacious faith, he came to terms with the final enemy, even occasionally longing for its coming. With the apostle Paul, Wesley could boldly exclaim: "We are confident, I say, and willing rather to be absent from the body, and to be present with the Lord" (2 Cor. 5:8). It was a mark of the early Methodists that they "died well"—that is to say, they typically died full of peace and assurance because of their faith in the risen Christ. Charles celebrated this same victorious faith, which overcame sin and fear in life and in death, through the hundreds of "Hymns For Funerals" that he wrote to mark the passing of people under his pastoral care.[8]

We noted in an earlier chapter Charles's poignant reflections upon the deathbed testimony of a Mrs. Hooper. In a hymn composed for Mrs. Hooper's funeral, Charles described the mood at her passing: "Come, to the house of mourning come, / The house of serious, solemn joy" (v. 1), "Accomplish'd is our sister's strife, / Her happier soul is gone before" (v. 2), "The captive exile is released, / Is with her Lord in paradise" (v. 3; *P.W.*, 2:183–84). Nor was the soteriological impact of this experience lost on Charles:

4. In her no spot of sin remain'd,
   To shake her confidence in God;
   The victory here she more than gain'd,
   Triumphant through her Saviour's blood.

5. She now the fight of faith hath fought,
   Finish'd and won the Christian race;
   She found on earth the Lord she sought,
   And now beholds Him face to face.

6. She died in sure and steadfast hope,
   By Jesus wholly sanctified;
   Her perfect spirit she gave up,
   And sunk into His arms, and died.
   (2:184)

There seemed to be no doubt in Charles's mind that the Christian was wholly sanctified "in the article of death," that is, in the moment of resignation just prior to death. A terse journal entry that recorded the untimely death of the tiny daughter of his friend, Rev. William Grimshaw, evidenced a similar belief that she was perfected "in the article of death." What was most remarkable to Wesley was not the tragedy of the child's death, but that she was perfected in the span of so few years: "A daughter of our brother Grimshaw's [sic] was just departed in the Lord; being perfected in a short space" (C.W. Journal, 2:67). Another example of his belief that perfection occurred "in the article of death" emerged in Charles's record of his visitation of Mrs. Reed on August 3, 1741: "I visited our Sister Reed, on a bed of sickness. All her doubts and fears are vanished at the approach of death, and she rejoices in confident hope that the Lord will sanctify her wholly, before he takes her hence" (C.W. Journal, 1:292).

Charles's hymns, especially those that escaped John Wesley's editorial pen, also made this connection between death and entire sanctification. His unaltered *Hymns and Sacred Poems* (1749) carried numerous examples of Wesley's expectation of a full salvation that became a reality as one laid down one's life in death. The following verses "For One in a Declining State of Health" are illustrative of many others expressing similar sentiments:

> 3. The more the outward man decays,
>   The inner feels Thy strengthening grace,
>   And knows that Thou art mine:
>   Partaker of my glorious hope,
>   I here shall after Thee wake up,
>   Shall in Thine image shine.

> 4. Thou wilt not leave Thy work undone,
>   But finish what Thou hast begun,
>   Before I hence remove;
>   I shall be, Master, as Thou art,
>   Holy, and meek, and pure in heart,
>   And perfected in love.

> 5. Thou wilt cut short Thy work of grace,
>   And perfect in a babe Thy praise,
>   And strength for me ordain:
>   Thy blood shall make me thoroughly clean,

And not one spot of inbred sin
  Shall in my flesh remain.

6. Dear Lamb, if Thou for me couldst die,
  Thy love shall wholly sanctify,
    Thy love shall seal me Thine;
  Thou wilt from me no more depart,
  My all in life and death Thou art,
    Thou art for ever mine.[9]

In these verses, most of the characteristic Wesleyan sanctification themes (*imago Dei*, perfection in love, moral purity, becoming wholly sanctified) come into contact with Charles's conviction that the entire ramifications of the soteriological event become a reality in the moments before death. But one of Wesley's hymns from the 1749 collection seemed to offer a counterpoint; it was number twenty-nine in the series of hymns "Waiting for Full Redemption," based on Romans 3:4 ("Let God be true, and every man a liar"). The hymn sets up a dialogue between faithful and faithless spokesmen, with the faithless ones registering a long string of doubts about God's willingness "To finish sin" and about humanity's ability to "live to God alone." The doubter concludes,

"Live without sin! impossible!
  With God impossible is this:
At least He *will not* sanctify,
He will not cleanse us—till we die."
    (*P.W.*, 5:326)

The sixth verse of the same composition indicates the point of Wesley's polemic: The "faithless" are limiting the power of God in their lives now by believing that God can perfect them only "in the article of death":

6. The great salvation Thou has wrought,
  They cannot, will not *yet* receive,
Or bear the' intolerable thought,
  While living, without sin to live;
They keep it to their latest breath,
Sinners in life, saints in death.
    (*P.W.*, 5:326)

Thus, there is a bit of ambivalence in Charles's writings from the midpoint of his career. His most persistent point is that perfection certainly occurs "in the article of death"; but (in one hymn at least) he shows himself unwilling to say that sinlessness is a reality *only* on the threshold between life and death.

Nevertheless, over twenty years of "Waiting for Full Redemption" seemed to erode Charles's optimism about realizing the blessing he sought. As he continued his life pilgrimage toward his death, Charles Wesley remained convinced that Christian perfection was certainly met in the moments before death; and in his declining years, "the article of death" became an increasingly insistent theme in his hymns. In the manuscript versions of his "Short Hymns on Select Passages of Scripture" (published and unpublished), this increased emphasis is felt with force; these manuscripts also preserve John Wesley's editorial reactions to his brother's efforts to connect perfection with death. For example, Charles's poetic comment on 1 Kings 10:11 applied the contrast between Solomon's youth and old age to describe the long pilgrimage from the first flush of faith to the realization of "heavenly bliss":

> On the first early dawn of grace,
>   Alas! who can depend,
> When the wise monarch's youthful days
>   In shameful dotage end!
> O never, Lord, my soul forsake,
>   Nor let *me* rest secure
> Of heavenly bliss, till death shall make
>   My perseverance sure.*
>   (*P.W.*, 9:176–77, no. 554)

Charles's development of this passage contrasts the first work of grace with the last work, which made "rest" or "bliss" sure. John Wesley's editorial intervention occurred at the asterisk; he simply echoed the "Alas!" that Charles voiced in the second line of the stanza. John's "Alas" indicated his reaction against Charles's phrase, "till death shall make / My perseverance sure."

The younger Wesley's poetic comment on Joshua 6:20 elicited an even stronger reaction from John. The hymn looked into the Bible's explanation of the fall of Jericho to find a pattern for the Christian's life, and the seven marches around the pagan fortress became a metaphor of the long quest for sanctification:

> Then let us urge our way,
>   And work, and suffer on,
> Nor dream, the first, or second, day
>   Will throw the bulwarks down:
> We on the sacred morn
>   Our seventh toil repeat,
> Expecting that the latest turn
>   Our labour shall complete.*
>   (P.W., 9:121–22, no. 374)

Charles's application of the biblical imagery seemed to turn the fortress of Jericho into the citadel of the human heart, which is not early or easily completely won to God. The pilgrimage around the city is depicted as being full of toil, work, and suffering, completed only in death or "the latest turn." John Wesley's rebuke came at the point of the asterisk. "When God pleases!" he wrote. The parameters that Charles's hymn placed around Christian perfection were too restrictive for John Wesley. Where Charles expected to prolong perfection to the end of one's labors, John demanded that one might expect it at any time, "When God pleases!"

The most explicit example of John Wesley's written reaction to Charles's later hymns, with their affirmation of sanctification "in the article of death," is contained in his poetic comment on Matthew 20:22 ("Ye know not what ye ask"):

> 1. Advancement in Thy kingdom here
>   Whoe'er impatiently desire,
>   They know not, Lord, the pangs severe,
>   The trials which they *first* require:
>   They all *must* first Thy sufferings share,
>   Ambitious of their calling's prize,
>   And every day Thy burden bear,
>   And thus to *late* perfection rise.

2. Nature would fain evade, or flee
   That sad necessity of pain;
But who refuse to die with Thee,
   With Thee shall never, never reign:
The sorrow doth the joy ensure,
   The crown for conquerors prepared;
And all who to the end endure,
   Shall grasp through death the full reward.*
               (*P.W.*, 10:336, no. 512)

In this hymn, Charles's theology of suffering mingled with his expectation of sanctification in the purging process of death. John Wesley penned in a pointed question (at the asterisk), "Not until Death?" Again he seemed not to approve of Charles's suggestion that most "to late perfection rise" by pursuing it to the end and grasping "through death the full reward." John's editing of the hymns, as well as his own treatises, indicated that he wanted to leave open the possibility for Christian perfection in the midst of life, not only at the end.

One of Charles's most interesting descriptions of the process of perfection is found in a hymn that was not published during the lifetime of the Wesleys, and thus it escaped John's editorial emendations. It is based on the saying in 3 John 11, "Follow not that which is evil, but that which is good." Charles wrote:

Based on 3 John 11, a hymn not published during the Wesleys' lifetime and thus not emended by John, contains one of Charles's most interesting descriptions of the process of perfection:

1. The caution is not vain:
   We may unfaithful prove,
And turn from God to sin again,
   And fall from pardoning love:
Yet will we boldly press
   Toward our high calling's prize,
And follow after holiness,
   And to perfection rise.

2. Perfection is the good
   Which wrestling saints receive,
Worthy of all to be pursued
   Who in our Lord believe:

> Perfection is the goal
> Which terminates our race;
> And come to that, the spotless soul
> Expires in His embrace.
>   (*P.W.*, 13:215, no. 3432)

The first verse is full of fundamental emphases from the Wesleyan message: conditional election, the possibility of falling from "pardoning love," *love* as the constitutive definition of grace, and—most notable for our consideration here—perfection or holiness as a "prize" that one must press toward or "follow after." Here we meet Charles's characteristic emphasis upon the progressive character of sanctification.

The last four lines of verse two are also of particular interest. There Wesley evidenced the source of his perfectionist language by pairing *perfection* with "the goal," its equivalent in the Greek root word (*telos*). Then, pairing *teleios* with the Latin concept of completion (*finis*, "end," "finish," or "termination"), Charles moved from the theme of Christian perfection to death. The same transition is reinforced in his last two lines, which picturesquely present the return of the "spotless soul" to its source, in the comfort of our Lord's embrace, through death.

Charles Wesley's series of hymns, "Preparation for Death," some of which were published in 1772, represent the final stage in his development of the connection between Christian perfection and death. The title of the hymns aptly describes their context and content. They were written by Charles as he contemplated his death, using that situation to help others prepare for their end. His declining years were riddled with illness. Death often weighed heavily upon his mind, but not in fear; rather, he longed for death as a release from this life into a perfect "rest" in the arms of God. Wesley's craving for holiness and his hope for his removal were thoroughly mingled in the aspirations of a manuscript hymn from this collection:

> 1. Thou to Whom all hearts are known,
>   Attend the cry of mine
>   Hear in me Thy Spirit's groan

> For purity divine;
> Languishing for my remove [i.e., death]
>   I wait Thine image to retrieve;
> Fill me, Jesus, with Thy love,
>   And to Thyself receive.
>
> 2. Destitute of holiness,
>   I am not like my Lord,
>   Am not ready to possess
>   The stains' immense reward;
>   No; my God I cannot see,
>   Unless, before I hence depart,
>   Thou implant Thyself in me
>   And make me pure in heart.
>
> 3. Partner of Thy nature Thou,
>   And in Thine image found,
>   Saviour, call me up to reign
>   With life immortal crown'd,
>   With Thy glorious presence blest
>   In speechless ecstasies to gaze,
>   Folded in Thy arms to rest,
>   And breathe eternal praise.[10]

Reflecting the phraseology of Hebrews 12:14 ("holiness, without which no man shall see the Lord"), verse two raises the singer's lament of being unable to inherit the blessings Christ won in the victory of His cross ("The stains' immense reward"). The singer's double desire (perfection and death) is realized as he retrieves the *imago Dei* or is filled with love (verse one). The final stanza describes the transformation of nature ("Partner of Thy nature") that occurs with the transition from this life into the life to come ("call me up to reign").

It is not clear whether Charles Wesley was one of those who differed with John Wesley when the relationship between Christian perfection and death was debated at the annual meeting of Wesley preachers in 1747. It is, however, abundantly clear from his hymns and journal entries that from the 1740s onward, the younger Wesley came to expect the fullness of perfection at the moment of death. This emphasis did not signal a final breach between the brothers, but it did mark a difference of emphasis in their respective explanations of sanctification. The distinction also involves a matter of degree; that is to say, did Charles teach that perfection was to be attained *only* in the moment prior to death? His early hymns do not take that extreme position, since they place "the article of death" and "perfection here" side-by-side as possibilities in God's grace. But the hymns of Charles Wesley's declining years show an erosion of his hope for perfection in the midst of life, and they seem to meditate more and more upon the purification that would occur as the writer laid his painful body down in death. All of his journal's investigations into those who had received the gift of holiness placed the blessing in the immediate context of the death of the believer.

We cannot know for certain whether Charles Wesley was among those who differed from the majority in attendance at the 1747 Conference by insisting on "the article of death"; but by 1767 it had become apparent that the brothers Wesley differed on the doctrine of Christian perfection. John's letter to Charles penned on January 27 of that year intimated that the timing of entire sanctification was one of the issues that distinguished their respective views: "As to time," John wrote, "I believe this instrument *generally* is the instant of death, the moment before the soul leaves the body. But I believe it *may* be ten, twenty, or forty years before death. Do we agree or differ here?" (*J.W. Letters*, 5:39, italics added).

The language of this letter was much more conciliatory toward Charles's point of view than what was published in John's *Christian Perfection* of 1765; but in both accounts, it is clear that John was still insisting on a perfection that was possible before (perhaps even long before) the instant of death. There is no record of Charles's reply to the letter of 1767, but John may have already received his answer in the hymns his brother composed and published in 1762 and thereafter. Charles's latest hymns showed him gradually despairing of the possibility of perfection in this life and correspondingly turning more and more toward "the article of death." This development was surely colored by Wesley's own pilgrimage down paths of longing and pain toward his passage through the portal that separates this life from the full realization and enjoyment of life everlasting.

IN A MOMENT

John's chronicle of the development of the Wesleyan doctrine of Christian perfection points to the preface of the 1742 edition of *Hymns and Sacred Poems* to find a consensus of the views of the two brothers. Once again John's treatise, *A Plain Account of Christian Perfection*, emphasized the unified perspective held by him and Charles: "I have been the more large [extensive] in these extracts [from earlier works], because hence it appears, beyond all possibility of exception, that to this day both my brother and I maintained" (*J.W. Works*, 11:393). The angelic perfectionists sought to set one brother against the other, thereby dividing and conquering the revival for their own point of view; John's insistence on the fundamental unity he and Charles enjoyed in the doctrine of sanctification was his response to this climate of conflict and doubt. More importantly, however, the 1742 preface also declared what it was that the Wesleys had always "maintained" regarding Christian perfection. The older Wesley distilled the doctrine to four basic points:

> (1) . . . Christian perfection is that love of God and our neighbor, which implies deliverance from all sin. (2) That this is received merely of faith. (3) That it is given instantaneously, in one moment. (4) That we are to expect it, not at death, but any moment; that now is the accepted time, now is the day of this salvation (*J.W. Works*, 11:393).

Items three and four in John's list soon became an issue of debate among the Methodists and between the Wesley brothers.

Charles's hymns of the mid-1740s evidenced an interest in instantaneous renovation. He typically turned toward narratives describing Jesus' miraculous healings or toward healing imagery to describe this sudden work of perfection:

7. Lay but Thine hand upon my soul,
    And *instantaneously* made whole
       My soul by faith shall rise,
    Shall rise by faith and upright stand,
    And answer all Thy just command
       In all its faculties.
                    (*P.W.*, 4:381, italics added; cf. 4:376)

Charles's *Short Hymns on Select Passages of Scripture* (1762 and thereafter) suggest that the fanatics who disrupted the London society by claiming to be made as perfect as angels also claimed an instantaneous blessing. The *Short Hymns* offer a few pointed polemics against those who would claim a complete, instantaneous change, and they usually describe sanctification in images of growth or maturation. It was a message that Charles found written in the six days of Creation (Gen. 2:1):

Who madest thus the earth and skies,
    A world, a six days' work of Thine,
Thou bidd'st the new creation rise,
    Nobler effect of grace Divine!
We might spring up at Thy command,
    For glory in an instant meet;
But by Thy will at last we stand
    In *gradual holiness* complete.
                    (*P.W.*, 9:3, no. 7, italics added)

"Gradual holiness" became one of Charles's recurrent phrases in his later hymns. It emerged in his poem based on Proverbs 4:18; the "shining light" of the biblical passage became "the gradual light" in which we

More of His grace and more to know,
In faith and in experience grow,
Till all the life of Christ we prove,
And *lose ourselves* in perfect love!
                    (*P.W.*, 9:346)

John Wesley reacted to his brother's reference to "gradual light" and penned an editorial correction—"And THE SUDDEN"—into the margin of the manuscript. Considering the phraseology of James 5:7 ("Behold, the husbandman waiteth"), Charles's hymn voiced the question, "But may we not at once spring up, / In sudden holiness mature?" (*P.W.*, 13:175). His response was not long in coming:

> Nay; but we must the flattering hope
>   Renounce, and to the end endure;
> The ripest fruit *cannot* appear,
>   Until the latter rain come down,
> And faith's almighty Finisher
>   Our patience with perfection crown.
> (*P.W.*, 13:176)

Growth or maturation became one of Charles Wesley's favorite metaphors for describing the realization of Christian perfection, and in this (as in all other things), Jesus was Charles's primary example. One of his unpublished hymns looked into the language of Luke 2:40 ("And the child grew, and waxed strong in spirit, filled with wisdom") and found in the maturation of the Christ child a pattern for the Christian's perfection:

> Jesus the Child by growing shows
> That still He in His members grows,
>   His body here savours increase
>   In faith and love and holiness,
> No instantaneous starts we find,
> But more and more of Jesus' mind
>   Till our full stature we attain,
>   And rise into a Perfect man.[11]

Similar expositions abound throughout Charles's manuscript hymns based on the Lucan narratives, emerging for example in the healing work of the Good Samaritan (Luke 10:33), in the growth of the lilies of the field (Luke 12:27), or in the humility of Jesus (Luke 14:10).[12] Jesus' description of the kingdom of God as rising "by fast degrees" from a mustard seed (Matt. 13:31) made it an apt polemic against instantaneous holiness:

> 1. The Kingdom rises from a grain
>   Into a tree by fast degrees,
>   Our hasty nature to restrain,
>   To check our manifold forwardness
>   Which reaches for the when and how,
>   Which urges man *be perfect now*.

2. Our darkest ignorance of pride
   Our unbelief, O Lord, remove,
   Which sets Thine oracle aside
   Thy words and actions to improve,
   And demand at ONCE the hallowing leaven,
   And preach a shorter way to heaven.

3. O may I never teach my Lord,
   Wise above what is written be!
   We by the method of Thy Word
   Bring us to full maturity,
   Save us, when Thou hast purged my guilt,
   But save sure when and as Thou wilt.[13]

The second and third verses of this hymn are particularly important for understanding the attitude toward instantaneous sanctification as it was evidenced in Charles Wesley's later hymns. He had come to believe that it was through "Our darkest ignorance of pride" and through setting the Bible ("oracle") aside that one both demanded "at *once* the hallowing leaven" and preached "a shorter way to heaven" (*Ms. Matthew*, based on Matt. 13:31). Hebrews 6:1 ("Let us go on unto perfection") formed the foundation of Charles's contrast between the New Testament apostles and latter-day claimants of instantaneous holiness:

> Which of the *old* apostles taught
> Perfection in an instant caught,
> Show'd *our* compendious manner how,
> "Believe, and ye are perfect *now*;
> This moment wake, and seize the prize;
> Reeds, into sudden pillars rise;"
> Believe delusion's ranting sons,
> And all the work is done at once![14]

Charles concluded that self-love and ego are the pearls of great price sold to buy perfect love:

> The ascertaining terms I know,
>   And would with joy approve,
> Sell all; myself, my life forego,
>   To buy Thy perfect love.
>   (*P.W.*, 10:276, no. 348)

By way of contrast, he said that perfection and the kingdom of God are like leaven (Matt. 13:33) which gradually spreads throughout the heart and "slowly sanctifies the whole":

> That heavenly principle within,
> Doth it at once its power exert,
> At once root out the seed of sin,
> And spread perfection through the heart?
> No; but a gradual life it sends,
> Diffusive through the faithful soul,
> To actions, words, and thoughts extends,
> And slowly sanctifies the whole.
> (*P.W.*, 10:275, no. 345)

With the composition and publication of many of Charles's *Short Hymns* in 1762 and thereafter, it is small wonder that John Wesley's letter of June 27, 1766, suggests that he and his younger brother were emphasizing opposite ideas on the timing of Christian perfection, with one pressing "instantaneous blessings" and the other "enforcing the gradual work." In a subsequent piece of correspondence penned January 27, 1767, John indicated that he believed that perfection is "wrought . . . in an instant. But I believe in a gradual work both preceding and following that instant" (*J.W. Letters*, 5:39). Then John Wesley asked his brother Charles, "Do we agree or differ here?" The letter closed on a note of urgency. The doctrine of sanctification was dividing the Wesleys and the Methodists; hence, John seemed to plead: "If it be possible, let you and I come to a good understanding, both for our own sakes, and for the sake of the people."[15]

SINLESS PERFECTION?

The Wesleyan hymns that mark the pace of the earliest years of the revival, the poetical products of the brothers' joint authorship, trace a concern for salvation to the uttermost back to the very beginnings of their partnership (*P.W.*, 1:338). Many of the hymns of the first two editions of *Hymns and Sacred Poems* (1739, 1740) establish victory over the guilt and power of sin as a fundamental Wesleyan theological theme.[16] Occasionally employing the phraseology of 1 John, these hymns sing, "Born of God, I sin no more" (*P.W.*, 1:275). And Charles's famous hymn "For the Anniversary of One's Conversion" voiced similar sentiments: "He [Jesus] breaks the power of cancell'd sin" (*P.W.*, 1:300).[17] The brothers' "Prayer Against the Power of Sin" concluded with the same triumphant note: "I shall sin no more!" (*P.W.*, 1:269–71), and "The Believer's Triumph" was equally explicit that the triumph of Christ's sacrifice implies triumphant living for the Christian:

> 10. Carnal, and sold to sin, no more
>   I am; hell's tyranny is o'er:
>   The' immortal seed remains within,
>   And, born of God, I cannot sin.
>   (*P.W.*, 1:348)

The hymns that can be traced directly to Charles Wesley's hand (as in the series entitled "Waiting for Full Redemption," published in his *Hymns and Sacred Poems* of 1749) continued this insistence that redemption is "full," an "utmost" salvation from sin's "guilt and power" or its "indwelling" carnal character.[18] The renovation was to be realized through a destruction of "the old *Adam*" (*P.W.*, 5:296, 298) and a filling with perfect love (*P.W.*, 5:306, 308, 310). Christ, the second Adam, is the agent of restoration who bestows "perfect soundness" or "perfect holiness" upon Christians as they are "washed white as snow" and regain "the life of God" lost by the fall of the first Adam:

> 6. The loss I by the first sustain
>   The Second *Adam* shall repair:
>   I shall the life of God regain,
>   The image of the Heavenly bear.
>
> 7. Let others from themselves remove,
>   And chase salvation far away;
>   But Thou canst perfect *me* in love,
>   Canst perfect me in love *to-day*.
>
> 8. Let others madly hug their chains,
>   Their idol of inbeing sin;
>   I cannot plead for sin's remains,
>   When Thou hast said, Ye shall be clean.
>
> 9. If Thou hast power and will to save,

> Saved to the utmost I shall be,
> The fulness of the Godhead have;
> For all the Godhead is in Thee.
>   (*P.W.*, 5:310–11, no. 19;
>   cf. 5:311–13, no. 20)

Yet this same series of hymns, which voices Charles's expectation of an utter and unqualified salvation from all sin, carries seventeen hymns "For Any Who Think They Have Already Attained" this state of sinlessness.[19] The younger Wesley seemed unwilling to offer his unqualified conception of sanctification without a corresponding corrective for those who were apt to claim it in a facile or superficial fashion.

In these hymns, "For Any Who Think They Have Already Attained," Charles attempted to achieve a delicate balance between (1) his belief that God is able to bestow absolute deliverance from all sin and (2) the sort of spiritual pride that, upon beginning to experience deliverance from the power of sin, does not press on toward utter sinlessness. To those who would forestall the renovation of the inner person until the moment of death, Charles asserted the infinite power of God's grace, which could enable believers to "the promise prove / Saved into all perfection *here*, / Renew'd in sinless love" (*P.W.*, 5:325; cf. 5:319, 327, 328). Using language reminiscent of Hebrews 6:6, Wesley came to consider the rejection of full sanctification in this life as a form of apostasy, since it made void the sacrifice of Christ and cast doubt upon the redemptive power of God:

> 2. Alas! if their report be true,
>   Who teach that sin must still *remain*,
>   If sin we scarcely can subdue,
>   But never *full* redemption gain,
>   Where is Thy power, almighty Lord?
>   Where is Thine everlasting word?
>   (*P.W.*, 5:328, no. 30)

Those who block the power of God by filling the channels of faith with doubt are "abject souls" who get their faithless wish; they receive the full redemption that might have been theirs in life only on the threshold between life and death.

To those "Who Think They Have Already Attained," Charles urged inward discernment, based on the witness of Word and Spirit, that stripped away pretense and partial purity: "Behold us with Thine eyes of flame, / And tell *me* what by grace I am" (*P.W.*, 5:313, no. 21; cf. 5:315, no. 22). Under the penetrating gaze of God, one receives an accurate picture of "what by sin I am, / And what I am by grace" (*P.W.*, 5:315). The result of this spiritual X-ray is a humble self-evaluation: "We would not of ourselves conceive / Above what Thou hast done" (*P.W.*, 5:315); and this self-evaluation puts one on the path toward utter perfection in love:

> 6. We would not, Lord, ourselves conceal,
>   But walk in open day;
>   We pray Thee, all our sin reveal,
>   And purge it all away.
>
> 7. Whate'er offends Thy glorious eyes
>   Far from our hearts remove,
>   As dust before the whirlwind flies,
>   Disperse it by Thy love.
>
> 8. Then let us all Thy fulness know,
>   From every sin set free:
>   Saved, to the utmost saved below,
>   And perfectly like Thee.
>   (*P.W.*, 5:316, no. 22)

The Wesleyan Conference that met in Bristol in August 1758 focused its attention on the connection between sinlessness and Christian perfection. John Wesley's tract *A Plain Account of Christian Perfection* preserves a portion of those deliberations and indicates that the discussion revolved around a distinction between "mistakes" and "sinlessness." In his typical fashion, John seemed more comfortable with indicating what sinlessness was not; and he said that sinlessness did not imply freedom from mistakes, since "(1) Every one may mistake as long as he lives, (2) A mistake in opinion may occasion a mistake in practice, (3) Every such mistake is a transgres-

sion of the perfect law, therefore, (4) every such mistake
were it not for the blood of the atonement, would expose
[one] to eternal damnation" (*J.W. Works*, 11:393). The
difference between a sin and a mistake, therefore, does not
lie in the realm of responsibility, since one is morally
culpable for both; but there is a sense in which (according
to John Wesley's conception) one may be sinless and yet
able to make mistakes. Thus, as John wrote, "It follows
that the most perfect have continual need of the merits of
Christ even for their actual transgressions, and may say for
themselves as well as for their brethren, 'Forgive us our
trespasses'" (*J.W. Works*, 11:393).

A significant portion of the difficulty with understanding the Wesleyan doctrine of sinless perfection lay in John
Wesley's definition of *sin*, which emphasized its volitional
nature. One of his earliest expressions of this distinctive
doctrine appeared in his sermon, "The Great Privilege of
Those That Are Born of God," based on 1 John 3:9. The
"privilege" of which his title speaks was a sinlessness that
Wesley described as "being born of God." John's entire
theological construct for this sermon was based on a
volitional definition of sin: "By sin I here understand
outward sin, according to the plain common acceptation
[*sic*] of the word; an actual, voluntary, transgression of the
law; of the revealed, written law of God; and of any
commandment of God, acknowledged to be such at the
time that it is transgressed" (*J.W. Works*, 5:227).

According to John Wesley, *sin* is a voluntary transgression; it has nothing to do with finite knowledge,
foresight, or recollection. And in this sense, mistakes
(which certainly can lead to dire situations) are not "sin
properly so called," since they arise out of ignorance or
finitude, not out of a rebellious will. John Wesley believed
that sin is primarily a problem of the will, and a renovation
that restores the purity of the human will and reconciles it
with the divine will produces "sinless perfection" (in his
specialized understanding of those words). In distinguishing between sin and mistakes, Wesley emphasized that the
human will is the citadel of our rebellion against God, just

as it can become a tabernacle or shrine where Christ dwells in us. Thus, the Wesleyan hamartiology (doctrine of sin) emphasized the willful or spiritual dimensions of sin more than the outward (moral) or cognitive (theoretical knowledge) aspects of it. *Sinlessness* in this context was more a matter of willing God's will than replicating God's perfect knowledge, action, or holiness; *sin* was more directly a matter of knowledgeable and willful rebellion against God's will than a failure or lack of conformity to the glory of God.

Measured by Wesley's standard, those who know and love God are actuated by His love and pure motives, and they are to that degree "sinless"; yet this condition is not the same as becoming "perfect" as God is perfect. As John wrote, "'Whosoever is born of God,' while he abideth in faith and love, and in the spirit of prayer and thanksgiving, not only doth not, but cannot, thus commit sin. So long as he thus believeth in God through Christ, and loves him, and is pouring out his heart before him, he cannot voluntarily transgress any command of God, either by speaking or acting what he knows God hath forbidden" (*J.W. Works*, 5:227–8). So long as the person's inward life is open to and being renewed by the love of God, the channels of communication and relationship are also open. That person's inward life is characterized not by double-mindedness but by a "singleness of eye" that focuses the whole of one's intentions upon the divine intention. As John Wesley's *Minutes of the 1758 Conference* concluded, "'He that loveth, hath fulfilled the law; for love is the fulfilling of the law,' (Rom. 13:10). Now mistakes, and whatever infirmities necessarily flow from the corruptible state of the body, are no way contrary to love; nor, therefore, in the Scripture sense, sin."[20]

John's qualified conception of sin has biblical warrant in the distinction he makes between "sins of the high hand"—a rebellion of will—and unintentional transgression (Lev. 4–5; Jer. 28:16; 1 John 5:13–18). This qualified view of sin has the genius of locating the roots of the matter in the corruption of human will and inward life, rather than turning to ethics (and a corresponding danger of works righteousness or legalism) or human finitude (and evoking the dangers of ontological dualism) for the theological starting point for our understanding of sin. Wesley's emphasis on the volitional nature of sin and sinlessness also has precedent in the *Anglican Standard Homilies*, since Homily II, "On the Misery of Man," distinguished between "deliberate and indeliberate sins."[21]

John Rattenbury goes too far to term it "John's defective doctrine of sin";[22] but it is clear that when the older Wesley wrote on sin or sinless perfection, he had something in mind that did not directly correspond to the popular understanding of those words. His definition of sin was a qualified definition that did not include mistakes or infirmities. In a similar fashion, John's understanding of sin ("properly so-called") insinuated something about the use of the term *perfection*. He held to a concept of qualified "imperfect" perfection that did not exclude the frailties of humanity (e.g., physical infirmities, ignorance, or errors of judgment) (*J.W. Works*, 11:395).

In 1759, John's conception of a qualified Christian perfection became a topic of discussion at the Methodist Annual Conference. Wesley recalled: "Perceiving some danger that a diversity of sentiments should insensibly steal in among us, we again largely considered this doctrine" (*J.W. Works*, 11:395). Using their standard confessional format of question and answer, the Methodists at the 1759 Conference defined Christian perfection in terms of perfect love: "The loving God with all our heart, mind, soul, and strength. This idea implies, that no wrong temper [attitude], none contrary to love, remains in the soul; and that all the thoughts, words, and actions are governed by pure love."

"Perfection in love," or "perfection in the inward person," was distinguished from the sort of perfection that inheres in God's being (e.g., freedom from ignorance, infirmities, mistakes, and so on).[23] Because of the specialized meaning that John Wesley brought to the terms *sin* and *perfection*, he was able to affirm the sinlessness (no voluntary transgression) and perfection (pure love) of frail and finite believers in this world. He said, "I see no contradiction here: 'A man may be filled with pure love, and still be liable to mistake.' Indeed I do not expect to be freed from actual mistakes, till this mortal puts on immortality." But in explaining himself "a little farther on this head," John admitted that "sinless perfection is a phrase I never use, lest I seem to contradict myself."[24] His theological insights on sin and sanctification were crucial ones, yet Wesley also knew that his conception sounded self-contradictory and fraught with qualifications.

Charles Wesley's concept of Christian perfection was largely in agreement with John's statements and writings, but Charles was not as hesitant as John in describing a "sinless perfection." In fact, the younger Wesley did not seem to distinguish between perfection in love and sinlessness; this view was certainly consonant with his basic conception of sanctification as the restoration of the *imago Dei* or the "life of God" within a believer. Charles emphasized a correspondingly unqualified sort of perfection. This difference of emphasis in the work of the respective Wesley brothers became more pronounced toward the end of their lives, with Charles longing for a sort of perfection that seemed impossible—but one he affirmed as a possibility in this life. John preached a practicable perfection which dealt with the inner life and motivational centers of a person and did not directly claim sinlessness.

Charles's most extensive compositions of the late 1750s and early 1760s are his *Short Hymns*. They show that he had continued to maintain the unqualified conception of perfection established in his early hymns and sermons, even in the face of his growing despair at attaining it. Perfection in love implied removal of "Our strong propensity to sin" (*P.W.*, 9:12). Wrapped in holy love, the believer is "Kept by [God's] power from acting sin" (*P.W.*, 9:11, 16, 18, 25, 32, 54).

Charles's poetic comment on Genesis 49:18 ("I have waited for Thy salvation, O Lord") is a bit more autobiographical than is typical of his hymns. The phrase "my threescore years" is the product of the life situation of Wesley; it is not found in the biblical passage:

Jesus, throughout my threescore years
  I have for Thy salvation stay'd,
And leaving now the vale of tears,
  I dare not doubt Thy promised aid;
Kept by Thy power from acting sin,
  The end of faith I here shall see,
Thy perfect righteousness brought in,
  And pure in heart return to Thee.
                (P.W., 9:32, no. 104)

The mood communicated in this hymn is as important to the development of Charles's doctrine as is its statement regarding sinlessness. The hymn depicts the speaker as still waiting for full redemption, waiting now in a "vale of tears."

On September 15, 1762, John Wesley addressed a pastoral letter to Dorothy Furly of St. Ives, England. The topic at hand was Christian perfection, which John explained in terms of perfect love: "I want you to be all love. This is the perfection I believe and teach" (*J.W. Letters*, 4:188). The letter went on to distinguish between John's understanding of Christian perfection and another view that Wesley described as "high-strained perfection." The latter variety, John contended, led to "a thousand nervous disorders" and would be especially dangerous to a person of Dorothy's sensitive nature. Wesley characterized this unhealthy, "high-strained perfection" as one "set too high (so high as no man that we ever heard or read of attained [it])." This unattainable goal would have the "unsuspected" effect of "driving [Christian perfection] out of the world."

This same theme of setting perfection too high emerged in another of John's letters; four years after he warned Dorothy Furly, John penned a pointed letter to his brother Charles, warning him against the unattainable standard: "There is *no such perfection* here as *you* describe—at least, I never met an instance of it; and I doubt I ever shall. Therefore, I still think to set perfection *so high* is effectually to renounce it" (*J.W. Letters*, 5:20). The distinction between the Wesleys' respective doctrines of sanctification revealed in this letter is not wholly surprising. Their teachings about Christian perfection had long been characterized by different emphases, and these differences increased as the years wore on. Nor is John's blatant statement that he and his brother were preaching different doctrines of Christian perfection altogether unprecedented. John had certainly recognized that Charles was pursuing his own direction as he read and criticized the contents of Charles's *Hymns and Sacred Poems* (1749). But by the time the *Short Hymns* appeared in 1762, Charles's doctrine had the potential of producing divisive effects, and John's letter to Dorothy Furly warned her about his brother's most recent publication: "Take care you are not hurt by anything in the *Short Hymns* contrary to the doctrine you have long received" (*J.W. Letters*, 4:189).

The similarity of the phraseology used in these letters to describe the Christian perfection that was "high-strained" and "set too high" indicates that the older Wesley was aware of the increasing distance between him and Charles on the doctrine of Christian perfection. Certainly from the standpoint of John's qualified perfection, Charles's idealism might have seemed "high-strained" or "set too high"; and John's stern warning about Charles's *Short Hymns* seemed to fix the identification of John's unnamed opponent who was promoting the unhealthy variety of Christian perfection. But others besides Charles Wesley were setting perfection too high; so much turmoil was stirring about the doctrine that it is small wonder John warned Mrs. Furly with almost apostolic urgency against following a conception of sanctification that was different from his.

THE WAY OF SUFFERING

Charles's preface to his *Short Hymns* of 1762 began and ended by ascribing all glory to God. The opening lines offered a forlorn reminder of the way in which illness had affected Wesley's ministerial labors: "God, having graciously laid His hand upon my body, and disabled me for the principal work of the ministry, has thereby given me an unexpected occasion of writing the following hymns" (*P.W.*, 9:vii, italics added). The preface also closed on a plaintive note, both glorifying God and soliciting prayer for the continued strength (and perhaps comfort in impending death) of the poet: "Reader, if God ministers grace to thy soul through any of these hymns, give Him the glory, and offer up a prayer for the *weak instrument, that whenever I finish my course, I may depart in peace,* having seen in JESUS CHRIST His great salvation" (*P.W.*, 9:viii). The joy of Charles Wesley's latter years was plundered by a host of ailments, including "pleurisy, neuralgia, lumbago, dysentery, piles, rheumatism, gout, and scurvys."[25] His physical pain met with an anguish of spirit; as John Rattenbury observes, Charles "brooded much; . . . notwithstanding his spurts of joy, he was often the subject of melancholy moods."[26]

The melancholy side of Charles Wesley's spiritual odyssey is important for our understanding of his doctrine of sanctification, because the poet connected his painful life situation with his doctrine of Christian perfection. Struggling to make sense of his lot in later life, Charles linked present suffering (in body and soul) with the process of purging sin and selfishness out of a person. His painful life experience placed a theology of suffering side-by-side with his main theological concern, Christian perfection.

One of Charles Wesley's most effective poetic devices was juxtaposition. A fine example of this tool was his use of two biblical images, "the cross" and "the crown"—emblems of suffering and reward—to communicate the Wesleyan theology of full salvation. Both terms are biblical in the broadest sense; but Scripture does not connect them as directly as Charles Wesley did. The pairing of cross/crown was one of Charles's most frequent images for describing the way of Christian discipleship.[27] Charles thought the call to Christian discipleship was a call to share in Christ; it was also a call to participate in His cross and His crown: "Shout all on earth, whom Jesus' love / Hath call'd His cross and crown to share" (*P.W.*, 6:285). The follower of Christ must "Welcome alike the crown or cross" (*P.W.*, 5:163, no. 16). The cross was said to be "annex'd" or connected to the crown, so that one could not have the one without the other (*P.W.*, 10:237–38, no. 250; cf. 12:106, no. 2003). But a person's natural tendency would be to desire the crown, yet wish to flee the difficult discipline of the cross:

> 3. But who the dreadful word receive,
>   Or gladly take Thy burden up?
>   We dare not, Lord, the truth believe,
>   But soothed with self-flattering hope,
> To feeble men for succour run,
> The crown-ensuring cross to shun.
>   (*P.W.*, 5:154, no. 10)

Wesley's constant notes about the cross and the crown stressed Christian steadfastness in the face of suffering, and tenacious faith even in persecution: "And all that to the End endure/ The Cross, shall wear the Crown."[28] The "cross," an implement of torture and death, was an emblem of selfless commitment to Christ and suffering for Christ; but what of the "crown"? Its biblical implications run a gamut from "reward" to "authority,"[29] and this diversity of meanings was not lost on Wesley. He connected the cross and the crown to describe a believer's reception of the kingdom of God:

> And Jesus returning presented the crown.
> . . . Who his dereliction On *Calvary* bear,
> And share His affliction, His kingdom shall share.
>   (*P.W.*, 6:287, no. 43)

The coming of the kingdom could focus upon Jesus' victorious return, or the hymn's reference to the kingdom's coming could as easily suggest Christ's coming into the Christian, reigning there through perfect love (*P.W.*, 10:249, no. 280; 10:250, no. 281; 10:335–36, no. 511). Since "perfect love" and "full salvation" were roughly synonymous in Wesleyan soteriological language, it is not surprising to find Charles describing the "crown" received by way of the "cross" as "full salvation" (*P.W.*, 13:47, no. 3121).

This connection between the cross and the crown, between suffering and sanctification, emerged in a few Wesleyan hymns from the early years of the revival. A line from *Moral and Sacred Poems* (1744) described the death of a Methodist by saying,

> Her soul, *through sufferings perfect made*,
> With joy forsook the earthly clod,
> And sprang into the arms of God.
> (*P.W.*, 3:176, italics added)

The theme can be traced through the hymns of Charles's middle years (1749–62), but it was still presented with moderation:

> Then, when our sufferings all are past,
>   O! let us pure and perfect be,
> And gain our calling's prize at last
>   For ever sanctified in Thee.[30]

In Charles's *Short Hymns* of 1762, his emphasis on the connection between suffering and sanctification became more pronounced, presumably keeping pace with his declining health and bouts with depression. The following verse, based on Deuteronomy 9:7, shows how excessive a few of Charles's statements became; in this case, he prayed that God would put an end to his sin, but not his pain:

> 2. A rebel to this present hour!
>   Yet now for all Thy mercy's power
>   I ask with contrite sighs
>   To end my sin, *but not my pain*:
>   I would lament till death,* and then
>   Rejoice in paradise.
>   (*P.W.*, 9:100, no. 319, italics added)

The asterisk marks the place where John Wesley penned an editorial response into the manuscript; John wrote an emphatic "God forbid!" as a rejoinder to Charles's desire to "lament till death." The journal of the younger Wesley also carried suggestions that he tried to see beneficial effects in suffering: "My dearest friends,—you will learn obedience by the things you suffer" (*C.W. Journal*, 2:217). An unpublished short hymn based on Acts

5:12, which was left in manuscript either by Charles or his brother, connected suffering with Christlikeness and therefore with spiritual improvement:

> 1. Made out of weakness strong,
>   By suffering fortified,
> We preach Him all day long,
>   Who once for sinners died;
> 'Tis double joy to make Him known
> And to suffer for His sake alone.[31]

This development was particularly prominent in Charles's poetical comments on the Book of Job. He wrote of a "sanctified use of woe," suggesting that through suffering the Christian can be renewed inwardly and thereby prepared for heavenly glories.[32] Occasionally, Charles merged the concept of perfection through the purifying effects of suffering with another idea detected in his later hymns—an unqualified conception of sanctification that was realized "in the article of death":

> Better for me to live, if Thou
>   My tempted soul with strength supply,
> And *then* my hoary head to bow,
>   And perfected through sufferings, die.
>   (*P.W.*, 10:96, no. 1490)

Charles Wesley used various images to describe the connection between suffering and sanctification. In his commentary on John 15:2 ("Every branch in me that beareth not fruit he taketh away: and every branch that beareth fruit he purgeth it, that it may bring forth more fruit"), he referred to the chastisements by which God purifies those He loves so that they might bear fruit "unto perfection":

> 2. Kindly Thou dost chastise, reprove,
>   The objects of Thy choicest love,
> That thus we may thy mind express,
>   Partakers of Thy holiness,
> May meekly all Thy sufferings share,
>   And fruit unto perfection bear.
>   (*P.W.*, 12:18, no. 2104)

John Wesley's rejection of Charles's theology of suffering increased as Charles published more poems voicing these sentiments. The editorial comments on the following hymn, based on Hebrews 12:8, showed John's persistent reaction against Charles's association of the themes of sanctification and suffering:

> 3. In sorrow, as in grace, we grow,
>   With closer fellowship in pain,
> Our Lord more intimately know,
>   Till coming to a perfect man
> His sharpest agonies we share,*
> And all His marks of passion bear.
>
> 4. Partakers of His bitterest cup,
>   And burden'd with His heaviest load,
> We fill His after-sufferings up,
>   Conform'd to an expiring God;
> And only such our Father owns,*
> And seats on our appointed thrones.
>   (P.W., 13:157, no. 3321;
>   cf. 10:98, no. 1496)

At each point where an asterisk appears above, John Wesley wrote an emphatic "NO!" on the manuscript; he clearly did not approve of the way Charles associated growing in grace with growing in sorrow, or the suggestion that only those "Conform'd to an expiring God" would inherit paradise.

"The rod" was another of Charles's vivid images for developing his theology of suffering; both the "cross" and the "rod" were vehicles of purification in this life, which prepared the Christian for the life to come (P.W., 9:240, no. 745). The cross and the rod were certainly to be preferred to the "sword" which severs one's relationship with God, cutting off the offending sinner:

> Cut me not off, almighty Lord,
> But use Thy rod, and not Thy sword;
> The cross no longer I decline,
> But save me from the curse Divine,
> Let sorrow break this wretched heart,
> Let pain my soul and body part,
> But suffer not my soul to be

For ever separated from Thee.
 (*P.W.*, 9:240, 745)

In Charles's mind, divine punishment—designed to reno-
vate and return the sinner—was more welcome than
parental neglect from the heavenly Father. When this rod
of chastisement became the focus of one's close consideration, its meaning was clear:

To think, afflicted, I begin,
 Study, the meaning of Thy rod,
Review my life, renounce my sin,
 And turn with all my heart to God.
 (*P.W.*, 9:356, no. 1017)

In a similar vein, the rod had a language all its own:

O might my heart distinctly hear
 The language of the rod,
Answer Thy will, and always fear,
 And always love my God.
 (*P.W.*, 10:98, no. 1496)

The "language of the rod" was a word of correction, a
chastening that evidenced a Father's care and elicited
reverential love from those punished. Obedience is the
lesson the rod teaches; but it is not taught in a purely
prohibitive sense, meaning, "Don't do that!" Chastening
also turns the straying pilgrim back on the pathway to
perfection; it both wounds and cures:

Taught obedience to my God
 By the things I have endured,
Meekly now I kiss the rod,
 Wounded by the rod and cured;
Good for me the grief and pain,
 Let me but thy grace adore,
Keep the pardon I regain,
 Stand in awe and sin no more.
 (*P.W.*, 4:479, no. 111)

Charles's *Short Hymns* show the effects of his efforts to
understand his illness and depression in the context of
God's grace and purifying love. Although his basic images
and constructs were rooted in the Bible,[33] Charles extended
those metaphors of suffering and sanctification in ways that

went beyond their biblical basis. This development was probably one of the factors reflected in John Wesley's concern for Dorothy Furly as she studied the theology of perfection espoused in Charles's most recent collection of poems.

ANGELIC PERFECTION

The Wesleys' dialogue on the doctrine of Christian perfection must be set against the background of an "enthusiastic" schism that threatened to divide and destroy the London society in the early 1760s. The Wesleys' writings and actions should be interpreted as a part of their efforts to resolve their own personal differences about Christian perfection and to present a united front to the Methodists and to a watching world. It is also clear that these disputes and divisions among the Methodists about the doctrine created a stigma against it that continued long after the actual controversy was resolved. Even the most faithful Methodist preachers, such as William Grimshaw, seemed confused about the Wesleyan distinctive in the midst of the turmoil and public outcry. In his journal entry for July 1761, John Wesley reported: "At five I preached on the manner of waiting for 'perfect love;' rather to satisfy Mr. Grimshaw, whom many had laboured to puzzle and perplex about it" (*J.W. Journal*, 4:469). Later that same month, John Wesley found himself again struggling to clarify his distinction between sinlessness and mistakes, urging that everyone needed the atoning blood of Christ and that no one was so perfect that he no longer needed it (*J.W. Journal*, 4:471).

The perfectionist controversies among the Methodists, and the abuses they engendered, had become sufficiently public to cause John to write five letters to the editors of various London papers. These letters, published between 1760 and 1766, were rather obvious apologies for the Wesleyan perspective on sanctification, and they also sought to disassociate the Wesleys' position from that of the fanatical pretenders to perfection who had arisen in their midst (*J.W. Journal*, 4:418, 423, 427, 428, 434–39).

John Wesley's journal and correspondence indicated
that it was becoming increasingly clear to him that the
"enthusiasm" was reaching a dangerous point in the
Methodist society of London. In a letter to his brother
Charles dated December 26, 1761 John tried to sound
optimistic about the outcome of the disturbance: "We are
always in danger of enthusiasm; but I think no more now
than any time in these twenty years" (*J.W. Works*, 12:122).
The ensuing events would prove John's early analysis to be
wrong; the next few years would be among the most
precarious in early Methodism. Three days after he penned
this note to Charles, who was looking after the society in
Bristol, John tried to have a meeting with the schismatics
of London. In that attempt, Wesley found a foreshadowing
of things to come:

> Dec. 29, 1761. In order to remove some misunder-
> standings, I desired all parties concerned to meet me.
> They did so, all but T.[homas] M.[axfield], who flatly
> refused to come. Is this only the first step toward a
> separation? Alas, for the man! Alas, for the people!
> (*J.W. Journal*, 4:482).

A letter (now lost) from Charles must have urged
caution in John's handling of the affair. Maxfield and his
followers had been among the most effective Methodist
preachers; perhaps they need not be lost to the cause.
Hence, Charles's letter seems to have warned John not to
speak too summarily. John's reply of January 5, 1762,
indicated his hope for a fair hearing: "You take me right. I
am far from pronouncing my remarks *ex cathedra*. I only
desire they may be fairly considered."[34]

John Wesley, probably suspecting that a united front
could quell the disturbance in London, pressed Charles to
join him there (*J.W. Works*, 12:121). But pleading the
excuse of ill health, Charles refused to leave Bristol. One
can only conjecture whether it was truly Charles's frail
health that kept him out of the fray so long. He may have
been avoiding an awkward ideological situation, since
Maxfield's unqualified concept of perfection sounded

rather like an extreme version of Charles's own! It is clear that Charles Wesley and Thomas Maxfield had served together sporadically since 1740; and Charles's personal disappointment may have combined with ideological difficulties and ill health to intensify his resolve not to come to London (*C.W. Journal*, 1:201–4, 206–10, 212, 233, 237, 241, 264, 400; 2:86).

Both Wesleys published significant books in 1762, and each of these touched on the question of Christian perfection. John's *Blow at the Root: Christ Stabbed in the House of His Friends* appeared in that year, and its very title suggests the sense of betrayal he felt in the controversy (*J.W. Works*, 10:364–70). The sermon begins by attacking those who imagine that "some external forms, or glorious actions, would supply the place of inward holiness" (*J.W. Works*, 10:364). This approach is the avenue of "Heathenism" and "Romanists"; but John also saw a "Popery among the Protestants" who attend to the means of grace and good works but do not abstain from all evil. Those who lay their foundation on Christ alone are also in danger of "evasion"; they may become disciples of a new Simon Magus who "appeared again and taught, 'that Christ had done, as well as suffered, all; that his righteousness being imputed to us, we need none of our own; that seeing there was so much righteousness or holiness in Him, there needs be none in us'" (*J.W. Works*, 10:366). It is not clear whether John Wesley was attacking Maxfield and his group through the guise of the ancient heretic Simon Magus, since Maxfield's antinomianism was not directly traced to a heretical understanding of imputed righteousness, and since John addressed that topic in other tracts (*J.W. Works*, 10:306–16).

A Blow at the Root was a general defense and explication of the nature of true personal holiness, rather than a polemical attack upon the dissidents in London. But John's exasperation with the disciples of Magus, who separated inward and outward holiness, would reemerge in his conflict with the fanatical perfectionists: "O when will ye understand, that to oppose either inward or outward holiness, under the colour of exalting Christ, is directly to act the part of Judas, to 'betray the Son of God with a kiss?' Repent, repent! lest he cut you in sunder with the two-edged sword that cometh out of his mouth" (*J.W. Works,* 10:367–68).

Charles's preface to his *Short Hymns* (also published in 1762) pointed even more directly to the controversy about Christian perfection that was raging among the Methodists. In that writing, Charles indicated that "Several of the hymns [in the volume] are intended to prove, and several to guard, the doctrine of Christian Perfection. I durst not publish one without the other" (*P.W.,* 9:vii). Wesley recognized that in those hymns where he sought to guard the doctrine, "I use some severity; not against particular persons, but against Enthusiasts and Antinomians, who, by not living up to their profession, *give* abundant *occasion to them that seek it, and cause the truth to be evil spoken of.*"

Charles sought to distinguish the Methodist movement from the abuses of a few fanatics. At the same time, he pointed out that enthusiasm and antinomianism were not unique to the Wesleyan revival, "Such there have been, in every age, in every revival of religion." The seemingly inevitable appearance of "enthusiasm" and doctrinal aberrations among those earnestly pursuing vital piety did not, however, excuse those who rejected all vital religion because of the abuses of a few: "This does in no wise justify the men who put darkness for light, and light for darkness; who call the wisdom of God foolishness, and all real religion Enthusiasm."

The fact that "when the wheat springs up, the tares also appear, and both grew together until the harvest" (Matt. 13:25f.) demanded that Charles discern the "essential difference between them" and therefore address either type of Christian with "a difference in my expressions; and as a great a seeming contradiction, as when I declare with St. Paul, *A man is justified by faith, and not by works; and with St. James, A man is justified by works, and not by faith only*" (*P.W.,* 9:viii). Thus, Charles set himself to explaining Christian perfection to the seeker, as well as mounting a polemic against enthusiasts and antinomians. The emphasis and tone of his hymns depended upon the reader he had in mind, and the apparent contradictions some might find in his doctrine could be resolved by recalling his intention of addressing his hymns to two opposite types of readers. In essence, Charles found himself on the horns of a pastoral dilemma: "'Who can check the self-confident, without discouraging the self-diffident?' I trust in God, that none of the latter will take to themselves what belongs to the former only" (*P.W.*, 9:viii).

John Wesley's letter to his brother Charles dated January 5, 1762, located Thomas Maxfield at the eye of the hurricane brewing in London. John's optimism about the possibility of avoiding a schism was waning; but he believed that if he proceeded cautiously, the damage to Methodist unity might be minimized: "If Thomas Maxfield continues as he is, it is impossible he should long continue with us. But I lie in hope of better things. Meantime *festina lente!* [Hasten onward with caution!]" (*J.W. Works*, 12:122).

John's closing line, "Hasten onward," could easily be read as a second attempt to persuade Charles to leave his family, his home, and the Methodist society in Bristol and join his brother in London. The elder Wesley's correspondence from early 1762 indicates that the bishop of London was applying the force of his office to examine the Methodists' "regularity" in the doctrine of sanctification (*J.W. Works*, 12:121–25). By April 23, 1762, John declared that the breach with Maxfield and the other enthusiasts was complete and irreparable; but this was a private admission, not a public pronouncement (*J.W. Journal*, 5:10). By August 21, 1762, Charles arrived in London, and the brothers worked together to repair the schism thorough direct conversations with Thomas Maxfield. In characteristic fashion, the Wesleys "freely told him whatever we disliked. In some things we find he had been blamed without cause; others he promised to alter; so we were thoroughly satisfied with the conversation, believing all misunderstandings were now removed" (*J.W. Journal*, 4:526).

Assuming that the danger was now defused, John Wesley left London for ministerial duties elsewhere, leaving Charles in the city to shepherd the flock and keep watch over the enthusiasts. In his letter to Samuel Furly, written September 15, 1762, John Wesley said, "I have lost my taste for controversy. I have lost my readiness in disputing; and I take this to be a providential discharge from it" (*J.W. Letters*, 4:189). The same correspondence indicates that Furly questioned John's qualified conceptions of sin and perfection; Wesley replied by pointing to those who are "cleansed from all sin," or "from all pride, anger, evil desire, idolatry, and unbelief." These people are not puffed up in their perfection (as Maxfield and his followers were); their inward purification causes an ever-increasing humility since they "feel more than ever their own ignorance, littleness of grace, coming short of the full mind that was in Christ, and walking less accurately than they might have done after their Divine Pattern" (*J.W. Letters*, 4:189). Those truly renewed by God's grace feel more and more acutely their reliance upon Him for their inward liberation from sin and the attitudes it produces in them. Thomas Maxfield and Samuel Furly seemed to agree that John Wesley's teaching on sin was not sufficient; John retorted: "If Mr. Maxfield or you say that 'coming short is sin,' be it so; I contend not. But still I say: 'There are they whom I believe to be scripturally perfect. And yet these never felt their want [need] of Christ so deeply and strongly as they do now.'"

Wesley did not wish to contend for his volitional or attitudinal conception of sin; he preferred instead to point to the miracle of lives transformed by God's grace, lives that were also filled by godly humility. If John would contend for one term with Samuel Furly, it was the word *perfection*: "Here are persons exceedingly holy and happy; rejoicing evermore, praying always, and in everything giving thanks; feeling the love of God and man every moment; feeling no pride or other evil temper. If these are not perfect, that scriptural word has no meaning."

Wesley's resolve against contention was pushed aside

by his fervor for the doctrine of Christian perfection: "Stop! you must not cavil at that word [perfection]: you are not wiser than the Holy Ghost" (*J.W. Letters*, 4:189). As he closed the epistle to Samuel Furly, John distinguished *perfection* from *sinlessness*. Recognizing that he and Furly had different doctrines of sin, he asked two rhetorical questions: "'Are they [the perfect ones] not sinners?' Explain the term [sinners] one way, and I say, Yes; another, and I say, No. 'Are they cleansed from all sin?' I believe they are; meaning from all sinful tempers." Those who were perfected in love were sinless according to John Wesley's attitudinal definition of sin, but not according to Furly's unqualified conception of it ("coming short is sin").

Wesley was concerned to demonstrate that the sort of sinless perfection he advocated would not produce the arrogant extravagances of the London controversy; so he concluded his apologetic letter to Furly by reminding him that Wesley's doctrine of perfection "is no contradiction; it is consistent with itself, and I think consistent with right reason and the whole of the oracles of God." Then John exhorted Furly to continue in the way in which he had already begun: "O let you and I go on to perfection! God grant we may so run as to attain!"

John Wesley's belief that the meeting with Maxfield put an end to the misunderstandings proved to be an ill-founded belief; and in John's absence from London, the situation heated up again. Charles Wesley's journal for that period is silent, but the tenor of the time is preserved in a letter Maxfield wrote to John Wesley. Maxfield lamented Charles's handling of the dispute; rather than showing any sympathy for Maxfield's unqualified conception of Christian perfection (as Maxfield might have expected from Charles), Wesley took steps to silence the dissident preacher: "[Charles] is gone out of town. Had he stayed much longer and continued Sunday after Sunday, to hinder me from preaching, he would have forced me to have got [*sic*] a place to preach in, where I should not have to have heard what I think the highest truths contradicted" (*J.W. Journal*, 5:6).

Behind Maxfield's indignation and threat of separation lay a veiled concern for self-justification; if there was a violation of their truce, Maxfield wanted John to believe that it was Charles's doing. Maxfield's arrogance shone through his lines; he portrayed himself as one slighted and persecuted (for righteousness' sake) by the volatile younger Wesley. "Experience teaches me daily," confided Maxfield, "that they that preach salvation from the nature of sin will have the same treatment for the others as they have had from the world; but I am willing to bear it" (*J.W. Journal*, 5:6).

In a second letter, which Maxfield wrote on October 16, "Tommy" again depicted himself as one set upon from all sides because of the truthfulness of his doctrine of sanctification: "We have great opposition on every side. Nature, the world, and the devil will never be reconciled to Christian perfection. But the great wonder is that *Christians* will not be reconciled to it; all, almost every one who call themselves ministers of Christ or preachers of Christ contend for sin to remain in the heart as long as we live, as though it were the only things Christ delighted to behold in His members" (*J.W. Journal*, 5:6). John could have read between Maxfield's lines and recognized that Charles Wesley and a few of the Methodist preachers were opposing Thomas's fanatical perfection. Yet, Maxfield's letter closes with a rather condescending (though probably sincere) hope that John Wesley would soon have the sort of experience Maxfield and his associates preached: "I long to have your heart set at full liberty. I know you will then see things in a wonderful different light from what it is possible to see them before."

John Wesley did not write a reply to Maxfield's second letter; he responded with action, making a forced march from Bristol back to London, arriving there by October 29. There was no question in his mind that the situation in London was rapidly deteriorating (*J.W. Journal*, 4:535). By November 1, he left the city once again; this time traveling down to Canterbury. He probably used the distance between the problems of London and the serenity of Canterbury for spiritual reflection and consideration of how to deal with Maxfield and the others. Upon arriving at the Mecca of the Church of England, John penned a reply to Thomas Maxfield's letters. Wesley's epistle was full of his famous directness: "Without any preface or ceremony, which is needless between you and me, I will simply and plainly tell you what I dislike in your doctrine, spirit, or outward behaviour." The "your" of John's evaluation was plural: "When I say 'yours,' I include brother Bell, and Owen and those who are most closely connected with them."

The tone of John's letter to Maxfield was surprisingly moderate. He was willing to both affirm and deny elements of Thomas's doctrine; but it was also clear that the crux of the controversy was to be found in Maxfield's conception of Christian perfection. On the one hand, Wesley found much to approve in the lay preacher's proclamation: "I *like* your doctrine of Perfection, or pure love; love excluding all sin; your insisting that it is merely by faith; and consequently it is instantaneous (though preceeded and followed by a gradual work), and that it may be now, at this instant" (*J.W. Journal* 4:535–36, italics added). Certainly, John liked Maxfield's doctrine thus far; it was an almost exact duplicate of Wesley's own! It took the form and phraseology that John Wesley himself employed to describe Christian perfection.

The problems Wesley had with Maxfield's position were the reason for John's letter and writing from Canterbury, the seat of the English prelate. And in this instance, Wesley did seem to speak *ex cathedra*: "I *dislike* your supposing man may be perfect as an angel; that he can be absolutely perfect; that he can be infallible, or above being tempted; or that the moment he is pure in heart he cannot fall from it" (*J.W. Journal*, 4:536, italics added). Each of the three elements John identified as errors in the enthusiastic doctrine of perfection was connected with an absolute or unqualified conception of Christian perfection (as in Charles's view), though the enthusiasts supposed it was also practicable and received in a moment (as in John's doctrine).

There is a sense which Maxfield's dangerous doctrine may have been an attempt to combine (in an unsophisticated way) Charles's emphasis upon an unqualified conception of perfection with John's concern for a radical change of heart and soul, receivable in the here and now. Certainly, the combination was a volatile one, with Maxfield, Bell, and others walking around London claiming to be "as perfect as angels"; their claim was outrageous, and the public outcry against it was equally extreme.

Numerous practical failings were also delineated in John Wesley's epistle to Thomas Maxfield, including the matters of spiritual pride, enthusiasm, and Maxfield's outward behavior. But a second theological theme emerged for special consideration: "I *dislike* the saying, [Christian perfection] was not known or taught among us till within two or three years. I grant that you did not know it. You have over and over again denied instantaneous sanctification to me; but I have known and taught it (and so has my brother, as our writings show) above these twenty years" (*J.W. Journal*, 4:536, italics added).

Here we meet the impetus behind John's insistent phrase "my brother and I" in his published defense, *Christian Perfection*. The schism that Maxfield had generated forced John to affirm repeatedly the continuity of the Wesleyan doctrine and his unanimity with Charles in its explication. John's response to Maxfield was a bit overstated, since it seems possible to point to shifts in Charles's doctrine of Christian perfection that undermine John's claims of continuity.[35] Perhaps Charles's silence on this point was equally telling. All the statements of the brothers' consistent unity on Christian perfection were coming from John; perhaps he protested too much!

By December 11, 1762, John Wesley was back in London serving the Methodist society and opposing the enthusiasts in its midst. Charles was back home in Bristol, and his brother penned him a progress report on the situation in London. John still found what he termed "unscriptural, enthusiastic expressions" of sanctification there; these are probably likened to the "angelic" perfection Wesley chided in his letter of November 1. John's journal reports that he visited Methodist worship at the renovated Foundery in the heart of the London, and he was extremely displeased with the work of one of his lay preachers, George Bell: "I heard George Bell once more, and was convinced that he must not continue to pray at the Foundery. The reproach of Christ I am willing to bear, but not the reproach of enthusiasm, if I can help it."[36]

John's letter to Charles dated December 23, 1762, seemed to respond to an invitation to come north for the holidays: "This is too critical a time for me to be out of London" (*J.W. Works*, 12:124). The urgent reason for John's presence was clear; the heretical leaven of Maxfield had begun to affect the whole batch. Thus, John told Charles, "I believe several in London have imagined themselves saved from sin, 'upon the word of others,' and these are early known." His personal frustration with Maxfield was reaching new heights. "He is *mali caput et fons* [the head and fountain of evil]," wrote John (*J.W. Works*, 12:124, 125).

On January 7, 1763, John Wesley made one final attempt to bring George Bell back into the fold. In his journal, John recalled, "I desired George Bell with two or three others of his friends, to meet me with one or two others. We took pains to convince him of his mistakes, particularly that which he had lately adopted—that the end of the world was to be on February 28, [1763] which at first he earnestly withstood" (*J.W. Journal*, 5:4). But Wesley and his like-minded friends "could make no impression on him at all. He was unmoved as a rock."

Bell's eschatological date-setting was particularly embarrassing to Wesley, and as the lay preacher promoted his timetable more loudly, John wrote two letters to the editor of the *London Chronicle*. Certainly "the reproach of enthusiasm" would be upon all the Methodists, since Wesley could not seem to silence George Bell. So his first letter to the editor (January 7, 1763) made an emphatic and public disclaimer of Bell's views. John's second letter, written nearly a month later, reported that Mr. Bell was no longer a member of the Methodist society.

As the fallout from the explosion over Christian perfection rained down upon the Methodists, members began withdrawing from the societies. Some did so because of the public reproach; others, like Mrs. Coventry, did so because they would follow Maxfield and not the Wesleys down the path toward perfection. John's journal entry for January 23, 1763, records a painful confrontation:

> I was sitting with many of our Brethren, Mrs. Coventry . . . came in, threw down her [class] ticket, with those of her husband, daughters, and servants, and said they would hear two doctrines [of perfection] no longer. They had often said before Mr. M.[axfield] preached perfection, but Mr. W.[esley] pulled it down. So I did, that perfection of Benjamin Harris, G.[eorge] Bell and all who abated them (*J.W. Journal*, 5:5).

John's evaluation of the encounter and its significance was succinct: "So the breach is made!" His letter to Thomas Maxfield, penned that same day, was equally direct:

> For many years I and all the preachers in connexion with me have taught that every believer may and ought to grow in grace. Lately you have taught, or seemed to teach the contrary. The effect of this is, when I speak as I have done from the beginning, those who believe what you say will not bear it. Nay, they will renounce connexion with us, as Mr. and Mrs. Coventry did last night. This breach lies wholly upon you . . . (*J.W. Journal*, 5:7).

His letter ended with a searching question for Maxfield, "Is this for your honour, or to the glory of God?" And he gave a desperate word of fatherly advice: "Oh, Tommy, seek counsel, not from man, but God; not from brother B[ell], but Jesus Christ!" By February 21, "about thirty of those who thought they were saved from sin had separated from their brethren; but above four hundred, who witnessed the same confusion, seemed more united than ever" (*J.W. Journal*, 5:7).

As George Bell's date for the destruction of the world approached, John observed "the terror occasioned by that wonderful prophecy . . . spread far and wide." Seizing the excitement created by Bell's enthusiasm, John Wesley turned the fanatical eschatology into an opportunity for evangelism: "I endeavoured to draw some good therefrom by strongly exhorting the congregation at Wapping, to 'seek the Lord while He might be found.' But at the same time I thought it incumbent upon me to declare (as indeed I had done from the hour I heard it) that [Bell's prophecy] 'must be false, if the Bible be true.'"

On the appointed day, George Bell and his followers ascended a mound of earth near St. Luke's hospital, celebrating and waiting for the end of the world. Calmer spirits prevailed as Bell was arrested, presented to a magistrate, and committed to prison to await the fulfillment of his prophecy.[37] John Wesley was also preaching on the day of Bell's announcement; at Spitalfields he once again used the turmoil generated by the enthusiasts as a backdrop for a bit of doomsday evangelism from the text, "Prepare to meet thy God" (*J.W. Journal*, 5:9). Wesley also used that occasion to attack "the utter absurdity of the supposition that the world was to end that night. But notwithstanding all I could say, many were afraid to go to bed, and some wandered about in the fields, being persuaded that, if the world did not end, at least London would be swallowed up in an earthquake." Wesley wryly recorded his reaction to this terror by going "to bed at my usual time, and was fast asleep about ten o'clock."

John spent most of March and April on the road, first preaching his way to Norwich and back, then to Bristol, arriving back in London on April 23, 1763. He had left the care of the London society in Maxfield's hands, despite their doctrinal disagreement; but the latter refused to preach at the Foundery and the other places Wesley appointed: "So the breach is made; but I am clear, I have done all I possibly could to prevent it." John went himself to supply in Maxfield's place, and he demonstrated his own inner anguish over Maxfield's defection and the schism of the society by expounding the text, "If I am bereaved of my children, I am bereaved" (*J.W. Journal*, 5:10). That evening Wesley introduced a short history of his dealings with the enthusiasts into the journal account. The account charged Maxfield with encouraging the "dreams, visions, or impressions" the enthusiasts received ("they thought from God"). When Wesley left London, the visions returned; "herewith was joined a contempt of such as had them not, with a belief that they were proofs of the highest grace" (*J.W. Journal*, 5:11).

Using this newly acquired spiritual authority, Maxfield and Bell usurped the Wesleys' leadership in the society; as George Bell said, "Blind John is not capable of teaching us; we will keep to Mr. Maxfield" (*J.W. Journal*, 5:12). The dissenters set up a rival society in the Methodist Chapel at Snowfields, whereupon John forbade "Tommy" to preach there, adding, "If you do, you thereby renounce connexion with me." By serving the enthusiasts at Snowfields and neglecting the Wesleyan society at the Foundery, Maxfield formalized his separation from the Methodists—a rift that had been almost seven months in the making. John Wesley spent the first two weeks in May "visiting the society, and settling the minds of those who had been confused and distressed by a thousand misrepresentations" (*J.W. Journal*, 5:13). On May 16, he began his northern campaign (reaching into Scotland), a month later than usual.

Charles Wesley spent the winter of 1762–63 ill at home in Bristol; but by May of 1763 he was back in London to supply the pulpit of the society there in John's absence. Charles's letter to "Sally," his wife, dated May 17, suggests that John had left the Maxfield affair in his hands, and the younger Wesley thought that he could salvage the situation: "T.[homas] M.[axfield] (I suspect) begins to relent. 'Tis well my B.[rother] left him to me, and given [*sic*] his Promise, Not to receive him again without my Consent, i.e. Not till he is truly humbled."[38] John had returned to London by June 23; "finding it not expedient to leave London during the ferment which still continued by reason of Mr. M.[axfield]'s separation from us, I determined not to move from it before the Conference [July 19–23]" (*J.W. Journal*, 5:24). Charles Wesley remained in London for the conference, confiding in a letter to his wife: "I do not wonder that my brother trembles and quakes at the thought of coming to London. Immediately after the Conference I think of scampering away to Margate. The sea would save me, I believe, a painful winter, if I live so long" (*C.W. Journal 2:260, Letter 82*).

Although Charles's journal is missing for this period of time, his letters to John suggest that he did not go to the sea, but stayed on in London while brother John took to the road again on August 1.[39] After a campaign into Wales, Bristol, and Bath, then a second foray into East Anglia and Norwich, John returned to London, finally finding time to lay the Maxfield situation before the Methodist society on November 30, 1763 (*J.W. Journal*, 5:39). By December 18, John had taken stock of the damage done in London: "I finished visiting the classes, and observed that since February last a hundred and seventy-five persons have been separated from us. A hundred and six left us on Mr. M[axfield]'s account. Few of them will return till they are deeply humbled" (*J.W. Journal*, 5:40). The enthusiasm that divided the London society had far-reaching effects for British Methodism; as John wrote, "In the evening I preached at Yarm; but I found the good doctrine of Christian Perfection had not been heard of there for some time. The wildness of our poor brethren in London has put it out of countenance above two hundred miles off; so these strange advocates for perfection have given it a deeper wound than all its enemies together could do!" (*J.W. Journal*, 5:17).

Much of John's preaching that fall was intended to "confirm those who had been shaken as to the important doctrine of Christian Perfection, either by its wild defenders or wise opposers, who much availed themselves of that wildness" (*J.W. Journal*, 5:35). Well over two years after the controversy in London, John still met opposition about

Christian perfection as he headed north toward Hadding-ton: "The frightful stories from London had made all our preachers in the north afraid to even mutter about Perfection. . . . It is what I foresaw from the beginning; that the devil would strive by Thomas Maxfield and company to drive Perfection out of the kingdom" (*J.W. Works*, 12:126). In a letter written on January 22, 1767, John summarized the long-term effects of the controversy generated by Bell and Maxfield: "They made the very name of Perfection stink in the nostrils even of those who loved and honoured it before" (*J.W. Letters*, 5:38).

It remains an open question whether or not Charles and John Wesley had strained relations during the contro-versy over Christian perfection engendered by the enthu-siasts. We have already considered John's warning to Dorothy Furly regarding the contents of some of Charles's *Short Hymns* (*J.W. Letters*, 4:188–89). Charles traveled to London on at least two occasions to help put Maxfield and the others on the defensive, but John Wesley seemed to think his brother was not carrying his fair share of the burden. For example, after receiving several negative responses to his suggestion that Charles should come to London, John's letter of March 1, 1764 betrayed a hint of bitterness: "You know nothing of, 'venturing to London before May,' then I must indeed 'do the best I can" (*J.W. Works*, 12:126). In May of the same year, John wrote Charles again, apparently wondering if there was a wall going up between them: "Is there any reason why you and I should have no further intercourse [communication] with each other, I know of none; although possibly there are persons in the world, who would not be sorry for it" (*J.W. Works*, 12:126).

When Charles arrived in London in May 1764, John had already begun making his spring march to the societies in the north. Maxfield and his company were still on the scene in London, still disputing over Christian perfection. In a letter to his wife back in Bristol, Charles described the results of his preaching:

On Thursday night after my preaching Poverty of
Spirit, such a Spirit of humility fell upon the bands at
their meeting, as had not been known for months or
years past. Every mouth was stopt; not one boasting
word of Perfection. . . . One of Mr. M.[axfield]'s
Society, after hearing me, cried out: 'This poverty of
spirit will destroy all our perfection.'[40]

As he preached his way north to Scotland, John
inquired about the state of affairs in London: "But how do
Thomas Maxfield and his friends go on? Quietly, or
gladiatorio animo [In the spirit and temper of prize
fighters]?" (*J.W. Works*, 12:126). Charles Wesley and
Thomas Maxfield seem to have had some sort of confrontation during this period (though the incident may have
occurred while Charles was in London the previous year).[41]
This contention spilled over into print, as John Wesley's
December 7, 1764, letter to Charles suggests. "Indeed,"
John wrote Charles, "you ought to have said something to
T.[homas] M.[axfield]'s letter, had it been only what you
say now. He is T. M. still. *Cerebrum non habet* [He has no
brains]" (*J.W. Works*, 12:127).

Charles's *Short Hymns* of the 1760s were his response
to Maxfield and company. Although Wesley sought to state
his doctrine of sanctification constructively, publishing
poems that would both "prove" and "guard" the doctrine,
it is clear (as his preface admitted) that in a few of them
Charles used "some severity" (*P.W.*, 9:vii). The result of
the controversy over Christian perfection was that, as John
Wesley put it, "A flood of reproach came upon me from
almost every quarter" (*J.W. Works*, 11:407). This admission paralleled the concern Charles raised in his preface to
the 1762 collection of hymns: "Enthusiasts and Antinomians, who, by not living up to their profession, give
abundant occasion to them that seek it, and cause the truth
[about perfection] to be evil spoken of" (*P.W.*, 9:vii).

But Charles's opposition to strident claims of Christian perfection also predated these years of heated controversy. As we have seen, his *Hymns and Sacred Poems*
(1749) carried a section "For Any Who Think They Have

Already Attained" perfection (*P.W.*, 5:313–36). He urged those who thought that they had already arrived at perfection to look at themselves once again; certainly some sort of sin remained within them:

1. Omnipotent, omniscient Lord,
   Present in heaven, and earth, and hell,
   Spirit and soul-dividing Word,
   Searcher of hearts unsearchable,
   Behold us with Thine eyes of flame,
   And tell *me* what by grace I am.

2. We would not our own soul deceive,
   Or fondly rest in grace begun:
   Thy wise discerning unction give,
   And make us know as we are known;
   Search, and try out our hearts, and reins,
   And show if sin in us remains.
   (*P.W.*, 5:313–14, no. 31)

Charles's early approach with those who would "Think They Have Already Attained" was not to ridicule them or to cast doubt upon the possibility of receiving Christian perfection in the present life. He said it was a "foolish man" who said that "there's no perfection here below" (*P.W.*, 5:325–27, no. 29). His early hymns created a juxtaposition between the apparent impossibility of living a life of sinless perfection and the infinite possibilities of God's grace. To those who claimed perfection, Wesley counseled thorough self-examination; certainly they must still have sins that must be repented and purged. But Wesley warned those who doubted the possibility of receiving perfection in this life that, by their doubt and self-will, they blocked the realization of the very blessing they sought.

This tension between the apparent impossibility of living without sin and the infinite power and possibilities of God played a prominent role in Charles's *Short Hymns*. He found this juxtaposition as easily in the Law and the Prophets as in the Gospels.[42] Commenting on Matthew 5:48 ("Be ye perfect"), Charles wrote:

1. Wouldst Thou require what cannot be?

> The thing impossible to me
> Is possible with God:
> I trust Thy truth to make me just,
> The' omnipotence of love I trust,
> The virtue of Thy blood.
> (*P.W.*, 10:173, no. 95)

Charles's hymns of the 1760s (both published and unpublished) carried caustic criticisms for those "Who Think They Have Already Attained." In some instances, his denunciations were so strong that Wesley seemed to question the possibility of perfection in this life. The following hymn, for example, chided those who claim the "second gift" in this life:

> 3. Thou waitest still, when Thee I know,
>   A larger blessing to bestow,
>   A second gift impart,
>   (The sinless mind, the farther rest,)
>   And stamp Thine image on my breast,
>   And fill my emptied heart.

> 4. Yet till Thy time is fully come,
>   *I dare not hastily presume**
>   *To snatch the perfect grace,*
>   But humbly patient to the end,
>   And praying at Thy feet attend,
>   Till Thou unveil Thy face.
>   (*P.W.*, 9:396–97, no. 1112, italics added)

Since the lines that Charles aimed at the presumptuous perfectionist (italicized above) might have also halted the progress of the sincere pilgrim of faith, John Wesley added an editorial rejoinder at the asterisk: "I dare say Now is the accepted time!"

More typically, however, Charles opposed the boasting or spiritual pride (and not the timing) of the strident perfectionists. The following verse is typical of many others in which Wesley criticized the boasting as well as the unwillingness to continue to struggle against sin, which he observed in the pretenders to perfection:

> Scarce have we put the harness on,
> When nature thinks, the work is done,
>   Defies the world and Satan's hosts,

And of her own perfection boasts;
But veterans in the service know
Their work is never done below;
And when to Christ their spirits they give,
They cease at once to fight and live.
(*P.W.*, 9:182, no. 571, italics added)

In other instances, Charles urged the reader to test the fruit of those who witness to having received perfection. Words without deeds do not qualify as fruit, they are leaves at best. Boasting about perfection shows that "the small spark of pride" remains and thereby designates the boaster as a false witness to Christian perfection. Contrariwise, those who wait in "humblest meekest love" thereby proclaim their perfection:

1. Must we not then with patience wait,
   False to distinguish from sincere?
   Or can we on another's state
   Pronounce, *before* the fruits appear?
   Can we the witnesses receive
   Who of their own perfection boast,
   The fairest words as fruit receive?
   The fairest words are leaves at most.

2. How shall we then the Spirits prove?
   Their attitudes with their words compare,
   And wait—till humblest meekest love
   Their perfect nothingness declare:
   But if the small spark of pride,
   Or selfishness, break out at last,
   Set the false witness aside;
   Yet hold the truth for ever fast.
   (*P.W.*, 10:203–4, no. 163)

In boasting their own perfection, the enthusiasts revealed rank religious pride that would cause their downfall:

2. Whom God exalts, he humbles too:
   But devilish pride hath blinded you
   Who your own perfection boast:
   The fiend hath set you upon high,
   And casts you down in sin to die,
   To die forever lost.[43]

Thus, Charles characterized the pretenders of perfection as both "self-exalting" and "self-deluded."[44] Neither had they learned that perfection could be lost in self-center-edness:

> What saint dares in himself delight,
>   Or boast the grace and talents given,
> Or glory in perfection's height,
>   Who sees archangels fall from heaven?
>   (*P.W.*, 11:192–93, no. 1350)

This orientation to self was equally dangerous because of the way in which it reduced their concern for others:

> Proclaiming my own holiness,
>   Myself if perfect I esteem,
> And others far beneath in grace,
>   Myself I must prefer to them.
>   (*P.W.*, 13:78, no. 3184)

Charles's second point of attack against the strident perfectionists had to do with their impatience. He called them 'Simple souls, who fondly dream/ Of instantaneous holiness!" (*P.W.*, 10:14–15, no. 1296; cf. 10:69, no. 1420). His tendency in these latter hymns was to emphasize the quest or pilgrimage element of sanctification, suggesting that perfection was realized—most typically—at the end of one's life. His poetical comment based on Deuteronomy 8:16 shows the way in which Wesley sought to stifle the claims of a "novice" in perfection by pointing to the race or goal that lay ahead:

> 1. A novice, to myself unknown,
>   That endless good I could not prove,
>   Or, when my race was scarce begun,
>   Attain the goal of perfect love:
>   But on Thy promise I depend
>   But bless me *at my latter end*.
>   (*P.W.*, 9:98, no. 312)

Charles's unpublished manuscript poems were particularly pointed in their treatment of the fanatical preachers of Christian perfection. The following hymn, based on Matthew 9:13, attacked the "lunacy and haste" of certain preachers (such as Maxfield and Bell) who cry, "Be perfect now!" Although the hymn denounces the enthusiasts for the destruction they bring, it also shows the positive thrust of Wesley's conception of sanctification, which was more and more frequently stated in language of growth or maturation:

1. If while their heart's are unconvert'd
     Toward task we rigourously enjoin,
   And yokes impose our converts rude;
     To men of sin unconvert'd will
   Who doctrines from emotions explain
     Old bottles with new wine fill,
   With truths they cannot contain.

2. While warm with undiscerning zeal;
     We urge the novices on too fast,
   To scale at once the holiest hill,
     As his first labour were his last;
   He swell as so holy sanctified.
     As perfect in a moment's space,
   He bursts with self importional-pride [*sic*]
     And lose all his real grace.

3. Longer that all should forward press,
     Should see the summit with his eyes,
   Impatient for his own success
     Be perfect now, the preacher cries!
   He ruins by his headlong haste,
     The wealth is choak'd with Tares o'errun,
   And Satan lays the lunacy and waste.

4. Our only wisdom is to trace
     The faith whereby the Spirit leads,
   The usual course of saving grace
     Which step by step by grace proceeds,
   Instructs them more and more to grow,
     A people for their Father born;
   Till all his mind at last they know.
     And ripe for God, to God return.[45]

Charles distrusted an easy or simplistic approach to Christian perfection, which he described as "a shorter way to heaven." Reflecting on the phraseology of Hebrews 6:1 ("Go on unto perfection"), he voiced the sentiments of his opposition: "Go on? but how? from step to step? / No; let *us* to perfection *leap!*" This approach "Leaps o'er the cross" of discipline, self-denial, and suffering "to snatch the prize"; but the results of this shortcut to sanctity are short-lived, "Like *Jonah's* gourd, displays its bower / And blooms, and withers, in an hour!' (*P.W.*, 13:132, no. 3279).

One of Charles Wesley's most constructive developments in perfection theology emerged as his *Short Hymns* began to explore biblical passages and metaphors that describe the kingdom (or reign) of God. An unpublished hymn based on Matthew 13:44 ("The kingdom of heaven is like unto treasure hid in a field") pointed to the incongruity of having perfect love and then voicing that claim in a prideful way. The thrust of Charles Wesley's teaching on this point is that those who are truly sanctified are careful not to claim it, lest they might be overtaken by spiritual pride. Sanctification, in Charles's application of the concept, becomes the treasure to be hidden in a field through humility:

1. He did not proclaim to all that passed by,
    How happy I am, How sanctified I,
   But finding a measure of heavenly power
    Conceal'd the rich treasure and labour'd for more.

2. The gift who receives and hastens to tell
    He call on thieves his treasure to steal;
   Who plainly refuses our treasure to hide
    His riches he loses thro' folly and pride.

3. The grace I have found O Jesus with Thee,
    I hide in the ground for no man to see;
   The grace I confide in the treasure Thou art,
    Who loves to reside in a penitent heart.

4. Of pardon possesst my God I adore,
    Yet can I not rest impatient for more;
   A greater salvation I languish to prove,
    A deeper foundation, a solider love.

5. The grace to insure the treasure concealed,
    A mendicant poor I purchase the field,
   Sold all to obtain it and seek it I find
    And ask for it I gain it, In Jesus his mind.[46]

Charles's manuscript hymns on the Gospel of Luke, hundreds of which remain unpublished, were full of stinging barbs for the strident perfectionists. Often the boaster of perfection is described as an agent of the evil one: "But if thou boast thy perfect love / The dream of Lucifer is thine" (*Ms. Luke,* p. 194). In other instances, the hypocritical boaster becomes the "rotten painted sepulcher" or the "blind and proud" Pharisee smarting under Jesus' rebuke in Luke 16:15 (*Ms. Luke,* p. 235). Returning to the same theme in his comment on Luke 18:11, Charles compared the contemporary Pharisees with those of old, and he even projected some of the emotional extravagance ("enthusiasm") of the Maxfield group back into the biblical passage:

> The modern Pharisee is bold
> In boasting to surpass the old;
> Triumphant in himself, he stands,
> Conspicuous with extended hands,
> *With hideous screams and outcries loud*
> *Proclaims his goodness to the crowd,*
> Glories in his own perfect grace,
> And blasphemies presents for praise!
> 'Again I thank Thee, and again,
> That I am not as other men,
> But holy as Thyself and pure,
> And must, O God, like Thee endure;
> Thyself I now to witness call,
> That I am good, and cannot fall,
> Thee to exalt, repeat the word,
> And thus I glory in the Lord!'[47]

The parade of self-righteousness that Charles Wesley saw in Maxfield and his associates was intolerable to his understanding of Christian perfection. Since it was perfection in and through the love of God and neighbor, genuine perfection never gave way to boasting, presumptuous pride, or self-love; rather, it was an inward, personal matter, a treasure to be hidden in a field of humility.

The debate over Christian perfection, once brought to the forefront by Maxfield and his companions, did not quickly vanish. John Wesley's letter to Charles dated June

27, 1766, hinted that the brothers were still debating the proper approach for presenting Wesleyan soteriology. Christian perfection had proved to be a difficult doctrine, but it was not one that Methodism could afford to jettison: "I dare not preach otherwise than I do, either concerning faith, or love, or justification, or sanctification" (*J.W. Letters*, 5:16). As John's letter moved toward its close, he added an earnest exhortation for brother Charles:

> O insist everywhere on *full* redemption, receivable by *faith alone!* Consequently to be looked for *now.* You are *made*, as it were, for this very thing. Just here you are in your element. In connection I beat you; but in strong, pointed *sentences* you beat me. Go on, in your *own way*, what God has peculiarly called you to. Press the *instantaneous* blessing; then I shall have more time for my peculiar calling, enforcing the *gradual* work (*J.W. Letters*, 5:16).

John's statement offers an interesting insight into the comparative styles of the two brothers; John excelled in logical connections, Charles in soul-searching sentences. But this passage also gives important information about the Wesleys' respective approaches to Christian perfection in 1766. John urged Charles to "Press the *instantaneous* blessing," and he offered the counterpoint by observing that the older Wesley would "have more time for my peculiar calling, enforcing the gradual work." At first glance, nothing seems amiss. Each brother has a preference in describing the reception of Christian perfection; John seemed to imply that he preferred to stress the gradual emphasis, whereas Charles pressed an instantaneous change. But for John Wesley to be making this statement in June 1766 is very strange—especially in view of the shift of emphasis that had occurred in Charles's hymns of the mid-1760s!

Charles's early hymns did offer a few statements about an instantaneous blessing of the Holy Spirit (*P.W.*, 5:23, no. 127). But his *Short Hymns*, written under the impact of Maxfield's heresy of angelic perfection, moved away from that emphasis and even attacked it. The unpublished hymns from *Ms. Luke* were critical of those who claimed "instantaneous starts," rather than grow "in faith, love and holiness" as Jesus did (*Ms. Luke*, p. 35). Christ's slow and painful death on the cross became a pattern for the death of the sinful nature of a Christian:

> Nail'd to the cross where Jesus bled,
>   United with His sacrifice,
> (Not instantaneously struck dead)
>   A lingering death our nature dies.
>   (*P.W.*, 13:7, no. 3041)

The historical power of Calvary blended with the contemporary power of Christ's saving death as Charles said: "My actions, words, and thoughts impure, / Sin's members, all destroy'd shall be," by the victory of the cross, and through faith-union with the risen Christ. "Of full salvation sure, / I dwell in Christ, and Christ in me" (*P.W.*, 13:7, no. 3041).

During this same period, Charles composed three poems based on Hebrews 6:1 ("Let us go on unto perfection"). These were exemplary of his mature thought on the matter at hand. The first hymn enforced the command of Jesus, "Would my Saviour have me do / What He commands, in vain . . . ?" (*P.W.*, 13:132, no. 3278). Wesley linked the Hebrews 6 text to Christ's command in Matthew 5:48 in order to reinforce the necessity of perfection and draw attention to the fact that the Lord is able to bestow what He commands of His disciples. The second and third hymns of this group, after establishing the validity and vitality of Christian perfection, mounted stinging rebukes of instantaneous perfection.

The second hymn emphasized the biblical words "Go on" as having a progressive or developmental connotation: "Go on? but how? from step to step?" The rhetorical question was answered by the believers' carnal nature, saying, "No: let *us* to perfection *leap!*" Charles's phrase "from step to step" pressed a gradual conception of perfection, with polemical intent, he placed the instantaneous claim of perfection on the lips of the ungodly.

The third selection from *Short Hymns* that Wesley wrote on Hebrews 6:1 forced the question of finding a scriptural basis for the doctrine of instantaneous perfection: "Which of the *old* apostles taught / Perfection in an instant caught" (*P.W.*, 13:132–33, no. 3280). Contrariwise, the poem depicts "delusion's ranting sons" as saying "Ye are perfect *now;* / This moment . . . seize the prize; / . . . And all the work is done at once!"

Charles Wesley came to consider a cavalier claim to instantaneous Christian perfection to be an indication of a person's bondage to his fallen nature:

> Nature would the crown receive
> The first moment we believe,
> But we vainly think to seize
> Instantaneous holiness.
>
> (*P.W.*, 13:133, no. 3282;
> cf. 9:493, no. 1108)

In view of these protestations against instantaneous sanctification, how could John Wesley tell his brother, "Go on, in your own way, what God has peculiarly called you to. *Press the instantaneous blessing*; then I shall have more time for my peculiar calling, enforcing the *gradual work*"? Charles Wesley could not often be found pressing the instantaneous blessing, and his hymns from the period of John's letter indicate that he was not only preaching "the gradual work" but attacking the alternative. It seems that brother John wrote in heated hyperbole! He seemed to be saying, in effect, that if Charles could find time to say more about "the instantaneous blessing," John could find time to enforce "the gradual work"; but as things stood between them, with Charles repudiating "the instantaneous blessing" in published and unpublished materials, John had no time to enforce "the gradual work." This seems to be the thrust of John's exhortation to Charles; he hoped to shame his younger brother into a more moderate stance. But if that were John's intention, he failed, since the hymns of Charles's declining years continued to emphasize "the gradual work" almost at the complete neglect of "the instantaneous blessing."

Exactly ten days after John Wesley wrote Charles urging him to preach the instantaneous blessing, a second letter came to Charles from his older brother. John's letter of July 7, 1766, hints at another element in the dispute between the brothers. The issues—as well as we can reconstruct them from the scanty records—seem to revolve around John's treatment of one of the Methodist lay preachers and Charles's handling of the Maxfield situation in London. Thus John wrote: "I have set aside J.H. and will stand by it. But I expect to meet more critical cases than his" (*J.W. Letters*, 5:16). John was perhaps anticipating some sort of final action against Thomas Maxfield, since the latter's name emerged later in the same paragraph.

The second paragraph suggests that upon returning to Bristol, Charles moderated his opposition to the strident claimers of perfection. He may even have made some conciliatory statements about Maxfield's point of view.

This development is not as impossible as it might seem at first glance. Charles's unqualified conception of Christian perfection was a common ground between him and the extremists. It is clear, however, that Charles Wesley never claimed to have received this sinless perfection, though the enthusiasts made this claim. John's letter directly charges his brother with changing his views in the middle of the controversy over Christian perfection, though John concedes that Charles may have been "in the humour of contradiction"—that is to say, arguing for the sake of arguing:

> How apt you are to take the colour of your company! When you and I [talked] together, you *seemed* at least to be of the same mind with me, and now you are all off the hooks again!—unless you only talk because you are in the humour of contradiction; and if so, I might as well blow against the wind as talk with you (*J.W. Letters*, 5:19).

John's letter was full of self-justification in the most recent confrontation with Maxfield: "I was not mad, though Thomas Maxfield was. I did not talk nonsense on the head [of Christian perfection] as he did. I did not act contrary to all moral honesty." After placing most of the blame with Maxfield, John reserved some for his brother; apparently, Charles came to London begrudgingly to present a united front with John on the doctrine of Christian perfection. It was a move designed to squelch the rumors of dissension between the Wesleys. But later, either from Bristol or in London after John's absence, Charles seemed to modify his position. Charles may have also questioned his brother's handling of the whole affair, since he was confident that the dissidents would be won back to the cause; such a disagreement on strategy may have generated John's extensive vindication of his handling of the affair. But, more to the point, John felt that Charles's most recent hymns added fuel to the fires of controversy, and John directly charged Charles with part of the responsibility for the schism: "When your hymns were added to his [Maxfield's] talking and acting . . . what was likely to be the consequence?"

After running through a few details about the approaching Annual Conference, John's letter of July 7 returned to the theme of Christian perfection, this time apparently to clarify the issues that stood between him and Charles: "One word more, concerning setting perfection too high. That perfection which I believe, I can boldly preach, because I have seen five hundred witnesses of it. Of that perfection which you preach, you do not even think you see any witnesses at all. Why, then you must have far more courage than me, or you could not persist in preaching it" (*J.W. Letters*, 5:20). John's comments were a blend of wit and sarcasm. He gingerly pushed Charles toward what he deemed to be the practical implications of his brother's point of view: "I cordially assent to [Whitefield's] opinion that there is no such perfection here as you describe—at least, I never met with an instance of it; and I doubt I ever shall. Therefore I still think that to set perfection so high is effectively to renounce it."

Again we see that John's concept of perfection was

practicable; since perfect love overcomes sin in the will ("voluntary transgression of a known law of God") without delivering one from mistakes, one could actually observe witnesses of it. But by pressing an unqualified conception of perfection, Charles ran the risk of elevating Christian perfection to a height that made it meaningless on the experiential level, which (to John Wesley's mind at least) was virtually the same as renouncing it.

Charles Wesley's most constant theological image for describing Christian perfection was to connect it with the restoration of the paradisaical *imago Dei* which had been lost or effaced in the Fall; this "image of God" could be restored as Christ was formed within the Christian through the work of the Holy Spirit. This had been Charles's basic emphasis even in the preaching and poems produced prior to the pivotal year of his conversion (1738). The same image remained the center pole of Charles's understanding of sanctification as it was developed in the Wesleyan revival. Charles's agonies of body and soul taught him that holiness was not easily attained; this caused him to react strenuously against Thomas Maxfield and other fanatics who claimed "a short way to heaven" or holiness. The younger Wesley's later hymns spoke of the earnest quest for Christian perfection. He longed, struggled, and waited for perfection as an "impossible possibility." Thus, without accommodating his standard to what was practicable, Charles believed that perfection was possible in this life. He pressed "the gradual work" without losing sight of the hope of its realization; but it must be admitted that Charles's hopes for the realization of Christian perfection were consistently pushed toward "the article of death" or an eschatological fulfillment in the return of Jesus, as Charles Wesley himself moved toward the end of his life.

The preceding study of the Wesleys' development of their doctrines of holiness suggests that the differences between the brothers' respective conceptions of Christian perfection were exaggerated by the heated controversies of the 1760s. Controversy had the effect of radicalizing several of the fundamental emphases that Charles had propounded in his earliest writings. The foregoing analysis also suggests that Charles Wesley's view of Christian perfection, while largely in agreement with that of his brother John, was also fundamentally different from it in basic definition (restoration of the *imago Dei*), in nature (unqualified versus qualified), and in timing (usually "in the article of death"). John Wesley's frequent disclaimers in *A Plain Account of Christian Perfection* notwithstanding, the Wesleys did have rather different emphases when it came to the doctrine of sanctification.

The last extant letters written between John and Charles Wesley touching upon the topic of Christian perfection showed John Wesley finally admitting the depth of the chasm between him and his brother on that issue. John's letter dated January 27, 1767, explains that he wrote Charles because "it may be a means of our understanding each other clearly; that we may agree as far as we can, and then let the world know it" (*J.W. Letters*, 5:38). From these remarks, it is evident that the brothers did not completely agree and that the world knew it. John named the focus of their disagreement: "I was thinking on Christian Perfection, with regard to the thing, the manner, and the time."

The elder Wesley then proceeded to explain his own position on the three points delineated. "As to the thing," he wrote, "I mean the humble, gentle, patient love of God and man ruling all the tempers, words, and actions, the whole heart by the whole life." He retracted a few of his earlier statements on the definition of perfection, indicating that he would no longer "contend for the term 'sinless,' though I do not object against it." Charles would have accepted John's definition of Christian perfection, though he might have pressed it farther toward the unqualified ideal.

Considering the manner of receiving Christian perfection, John Wesley's January 27 letter emphasized that sanctification is received in "a simple act of faith, consequently in an instant." He also "believed a gradual work both preceeding and following that instant." One cannot help wondering whether John's awkward synthesis of the instantaneous and gradual works was in part a concession to the debates of the 1760s and to Charles's position as published in the *Short Hymns*.

When discussing the final element, the time of sanctification, John began his exposition on the ground closest to where Charles stood: "I believe this instant generally is in the article of death." Then John began filling in the space between him and Charles with his more characteristic emphasis: "But I believe it may be ten, twenty, or forty years before death." Charles's tension—between the impossible hope of attaining perfection in this life and the infinite power of God which makes all things possible—allowed him to agree with John that perfection may occur a long time before death. But Charles's more characteristic emphasis, especially in his later hymns, placed full salvation in the instant just prior to death.

John Wesley's letter of January 27 was a masterpiece of theological diplomacy. In it, he maximized the genuine areas of agreement between the Wesley brothers without obscuring the issues separating them on sanctification. The structure of the bridge that John built over the chasm was designed to draw Charles Wesley into dialogue. After each major point of his presentation of sanctification, John solicited (and we can only wonder whether he got) Charles's response. Three times John asked, "Do we agree or differ here?"

John's letter to Charles dated May 14, 1768, indicated that a dispute still swirled about the Wesleys over the doctrine; the older Wesley intimated: "I am at my wit's end with regard to two things,—the Church, and Christian Perfection. Unless both you and I stand in the gap in good and earnest, the Methodists will drop them both. Talking will not avail. We must do or be borne away" (*J.W. Works,* 12:135). Another letter from John exactly one month later suggests that Charles was back in London "labouring not in vain"; John Wesley was at Stockport, near Manchester, and the effects of the controversy did not seem to taint his desire to preach Christian perfection in that vicinity: "The

north of England suits me best, where so many are
groaning after full redemption" (*J.W. Works,* 12:136). But
John recognized that he and Charles had not come to a
consensus: "I think it is high time that you and I, at least,
should come to a point. Shall we go on in asserting
perfection against all the world. Or shall we quietly let it
drop? We really must do one or the other; and, I
apprehend, the sooner, the better." The issues under
consideration remained fixed: "What shall we jointly and
explicitly maintain, . . . concerning the nature, the time
(now or by and by?) and the manner of it? instantaneous,
or not?"

The controversy over Christian perfection produced
some of Charles Wesley's most pointed poems. He criticized the pretenders to perfection with the vigor of one who
cherished the doctrine. Their arrogant claims cheapened a
perspective that Charles had come to know as the path of
costly discipleship and suffering. While these hymns
present Charles's mature and unedited views on sanctification, they were also concerned with the more practical
dimensions of the dispute. His hymns sing of pride,
arrogance, impatience, slothfulness, and inconsistencies
that point to the failure of the enthusiasts, since their form
of perfection did not produce vital piety.

Charles's hymns of the latter period of his life also
indicate that he was becoming increasingly independent of
his brother's supervision as editor of the hymns and as
general superintendent of the Methodists. Charles's hymns
seemed to solidify his distinctive approach to the doctrine
of perfection and to distinguish his perspective from
brother John's. Although the controversy certainly affected
the tone of Charles's hymns, his emphasis upon an
unqualified conception of perfection that was diligently
pursued all along the stages of life's way, and finally
realized "in the article of death," had been characteristic of
Charles almost from the beginning of his ministry. Although Charles's brother argued that to "set perfection so
high" was to effectually renounce it, the younger Wesley
found in this undimmed ideal a perfection that produced

deep humility, love, and a tenacious faith to fight against all sin in this life in preparation for the life to come. Charles described his concept to William Grimshaw in a letter of March 27, 1760:

> My perfection is to see my own imperfection; my comfort, to feel that I have the world, flesh and devil to overthrow through the Spirit and merits of my dear Saviour; and my desire and hope is, to love God with all my heart, mind, soul, and strength, to the last gasp of my life. This is my perfection. I know no other, expecting to lay down my life and my sword together.[48]

CONCLUSION:

"The Everlasting Gospel"

Charles Wesley left us a short summary of his estimate of Christianity's central truths. In his journal entry for Sunday, July 12, 1741, the younger Wesley recorded: "I declared the two great truths of the everlasting gospel, universal redemption and Christian perfection" (*C.W. Journal*, 1:286). While it seems unadvisable to place too much weight on one journal entry, these "two great truths" do describe what was most crucial and emphatic in Charles Wesley's understanding of the gospel. Both elements are monuments to his optimism about the liberating power of God's love and provide theological structures that stood firm throughout Charles's life, even in the face of his realistic appreciation of the thoroughly debilitating effects of human sin and his personal recognition that the path of the "cross" was sometimes a painful way to the "crown"— both for Christ and for those who followed after Him.

The phrase "universal redemption" spoke of the unlimited dimensions of God's redemptive love. Christ's arms, extended painfully upon His cross in Charles Wesley's poetic imagination, were arms of love thrown open wide to embrace every wandering son of Adam and every wayward daughter of Eve. The potential scope of the reconciliation wrought in Christ was as broad as the cosmic separation that occurred in the Fall: "Know every child of *Adam's* race, / Thy Saviour died for thee!" (*P.W.*, 11:346, no. 1668). The basis of this unlimited application of the Atonement was found in the life-giving effectiveness of Jesus' death: "The Man who lived for all to die, / Who died in all to live" (*P.W.*, 11:381, 1756). Those who spurn God's love in Christ are self-condemned, recognizing "In ourselves the hindrance lies" (*P.W.*, 11:375, no. 1738). Walls of stubbornness and self-will are the only ultimate limitations on the extent of God's salvation.

This universal call or offer of salvation was the motivating force of Wesleyan evangelism up and down the British Isles. In his homilies and hymns, Charles proclaimed the unlimited victory of Christ and the need for every person to come out of dungeons of despair in order to enter into the "broad and open space" of salvation. It was this same recognition of God's love for all people, this vision of the potential effects reconciling love might have in any life, that made the Wesleyan revival a movement that reached beyond the pious disciplines of Oxford to touch condemned felons at Newgate and the rough coal miners of Kingswood. In Charles's hymns "On God's Everlasting Love," the great *all* of the gospel love opposed the "narrow spirit" of its Calvinistic counterpart; the preface to the Wesleys' first hymnal proclaimed that personal devotion created a life of practical piety: "The Gospel of Christ knows of no religion, but social; no holiness, but social holiness. Faith working by love is the length and breadth and depth and height of Christian perfection" (*P.W.*, 1:xxii). The Wesleys proclaimed that there is no corner of creation into which the love of God cannot shine with restorative and liberating light; and that light overcomes the darkness of sin.

Just as there was no divinely established boundary to God's love, Charles Wesley knew no limit to love's curative power. He believed that Christ's blood had healing effects that cured sick souls and restored withered inward lives to vitality:

Nature's impatient condition
Feels my paralytic soul
Finds in Christ a kind Physician;
By the word of faith made whole.
                    (*Ms. Acts*, p. 145)

Charles's optimism about the renewing power of God's grace came to expression in his earliest preaching; "The One Thing Needful" was the restitution of the paradisaical image of God, which produced a "single eye" that overcame the inner anguish of a divided heart and mixed intentions. An ongoing visitation of the love of Christ and His Holy Spirit marked out the way of sanctification. The inner life darkened by "bosom sin," or "my inbred foe," was restored to its intended luminance as Christ was formed within the Christian. This personal renovation was as boundless as the scope of God's love; it began as love purified the heart, will, and intention and launched toward the skies in Charles's aspiration for utter perfection (Christlikeness).

Thus, the younger Wesley's passing remarks about "the two great truths of the everlasting gospel" mark out an approach to the Christian faith that was certainly borne out in the larger context of his life and thought. It was a gospel of victorious love, extending ever outward without respect to person, class, or predetermined limits; it was a gospel of restoration that extended ever inward, healing human brokenness and restoring a luster to the human heart that enabled it to mirror its Maker's image—"the life of God in the soul."

Charles Wesley urged his hearers at Oxford to press toward the vital center of holiness: "Knowest thou, that 'in Jesus Christ, neither circumcision availeth any thing, nor uncircumcision; but faith that worketh by love'; but a new creation? Seest thou the necessity of that inward change, that spiritual birth, that life from the dead, that holiness?" (*J.W. Works*, 5:32). In Wesleyan soteriology, justification by faith marks a beginning point that must be followed by growth in sanctity.[1] Perfection lies beyond pardon. Hence, when one of Charles's hymns asked the question: "I have pardon—what can a *poor sinner* have more?" The answer was:

> He can have a new heart,
>   So as never to start
>   From Thy paths: he may be in the world as Thou art.
>   (*P.W.*, 5:26, no. 130)

Yet Charles knew that the path to perfection is not an easy one. It is a "working out Thy salvation with fear and trembling," "agonizing to enter in at the straight gate," or it is "the way of the cross." The faint of heart fall by the wayside, unable to bear the weight of costly discipleship or God's chastisement, that they "May meekly all [Christ's] sufferings share, / And fruit unto perfection bear" (*P.W.*, 12:18, no. 2104).

Having been "awakened" from his own spiritual slumber, Charles was "freely justified." Because he had received grace "unbounded and free" (imputed and imparted), his doctrine became vivified through experience. As religious formalism gave way to reformation, he pressed his hearers to reconsider the very nature of religion: "Dost thou know what religion is? That it is a participation in the divine nature, the life of God in the soul of man: Christ formed in the heart, 'Christ in thee, the hope of glory.' Happiness and holiness; heaven begun on earth. 'A kingdom of God within thee; . . . no outward thing; but righteousness, peace, and joy in the Holy Ghost'" (*J.W. Works*, 5:35). Personal piety overflowed into "experimental and practical divinity" (1780 Preface), as pardon was not only wrought in Christ's "blood" but also "sealed" upon the human heart through the indwelling of the Spirit and the presence of *agape* love.[2] As the biblical narratives direct, Wesley's concept of redemption was one of "full redemption"; it was freedom from the guilt and power of sin and freedom for being a new person, restored to one's created character, liberated in love for one's divinely intended personhood.

Sanctification, in its varied and interrelated forms of expression, lay at the center of the Wesleyan proclamation.

True to the biblical language and imagery, Charles Wesley knew that sanctification (in its etymological roots) meant utter consecration as well as a radically new standing before God. This demands that individuals understand themselves in terms of the potential and power of God's grace in them. Thus, sanctification is directly linked to moral and spiritual renovation (holiness), since God replicates His image in those who "desire to love" or "groan for full redemption." Perfection is the goal (*teleios*) of the process of sanctification; it is both the end and the means toward it, as love perfects (completes) the restorative process within those who resolutely forsake self-will and resign themselves into heavenly hands. This inner transformation is perfection of a sort, since the individual's divided mind is gradually overcome by willing the will of Him who made us and who desires to remake us in His image.

Søren Kierkegaard, Danish philosopher of a later generation, would write that "purity of heart is to will one thing." This phrase is highly suggestive of one side of the Wesleyan doctrine of Christian perfection: It is a perfection born of inner harmony with God's will and intention, even as the mind of Christ is being formed within us through the work of the Holy Spirit. Charles Wesley perceived that Christian perfection is a "circumcision" of the human heart, a removal of the "heart of stone" by an engrafting of the very "heart of God" into the human heart. The corrective surgery is a long process; it reaches its climax with a spiritual kind of open heart surgery (crisis), but life-giving transfusions and revitalizing therapies (process) are necessary to restore the patient's original vitality. Thus, as in John Wesley's view, Charles believed that the reception of "a new heart" could be considered Christian perfection; but unlike John, he believed that the outcome of this process would be a complete recovery of the patient's original health. And that—in Charles Wesley's conception—is ultimate Christian perfection. The Wesleyan vision of Christian perfection as an unqualified restoration of the Edenic ideal is an uncompromising goal for vital Christian life. John Rattenbury has wryly written that the idealistic Charles "always struggled to 'hitch his wagon to a star,' whereas John, practical organizer as he was, tried to pack the stars in his wagon."[3]

Charles Wesley's perspective on sanctification wed soteriology with disciplined and ethical life to produce a wholistic, balanced theology of redemption. "Holiness" meant wholeness. Positionally, it meant being included in a redemptive relationship with God by faith; practically, it meant having the love of Christ formed within one's life, producing inner rectitude and ethical obedience:

> 5. He died that we might be made whole,
>   Holy in body, spirit, soul;
>   Might do His will like those above,
>   Renew'd in all the life of love.
>   (*P.W.*, 5:317, no. 125)

Charles believed that sanctification was "full salvation" or "salvation to the uttermost," a renovation so pervasive that it anticipated wholeness of heart and life.

Charles Wesley's view of sanctification both complemented and contrasted that of his brother John. The Wesleys were united in their concern for "vital piety" and "scriptural holiness"; both emphasized the regeneration ("new birth") as the beginning of a radical, inward change that justification allowed God to work in us (sanctification). Charles shared his brother's interest in Christian perfection, which he typically described in terms of "perfect love": "This it is to be a perfect man, to be sanctified throughout, created anew in Jesus Christ; even 'to have a heart all flaming with the love of God, . . . so as continually offer up every thought, word, and work, as a spiritual sacrifice, acceptable unto God through Christ'" (*J.W. Works*, 14:330). For Charles, "perfect love" strained toward perfection itself, and his later hymns did not hesitate to say it was "sinless perfection"—an expression that caused John discomfort. As he came more and more out from under John's editorial control and personal shadow, Charles began to develop his own distinctive emphases in holiness doctrine.

First, his poetic and mystical temperament predisposed Charles to the quest after perfection. John was a more pragmatic man; he believed that to set holiness so high would undermine its practical and experiential vitality.

Second, clinging tenaciously to his unqualified conception of Christian perfection, Charles increasingly adopted progress language or developmental models for describing his doctrine.

Third, shaped by a certain sadness of the times and impressed by the testimonies of dying saints, Charles became convinced that perfection was certain "in the article of death." As his pilgrimage wore on, he became increasingly disillusioned with those who glibly claimed an instantaneous re-creation without having learned costly discipleship.

Each of these three emphases was intensified in Charles's later hymns because of his conflict with the "enthusiastic" Methodists of London who claimed to be as "perfect as angels" in their present life.

While each of Charles's distinctive emphases deviated slightly from what some would consider to be standard Wesleyan holiness theology, it is clear that they are as Wesleyan as Charles Wesley.[4] Historically, Methodist theology has followed John's option, embracing purity of intention and ethical holiness as the features of sanctification and perhaps differing a bit on the matter of timing and the mixture of instantaneous and progressive elements.[5] John's practicable emphasis is a powerful and helpful way of describing the restorative power of God's love. It is also fraught with the difficulties of John's "defective doctrine of sin" (distinguishing between sin "properly" and "improperly so called").[6] It separates Methodists from Protestants of other traditions who affirm a different doctrine of sin. Coupled with a Wesleyan insistence upon the "instantaneous work" of sanctification, it also holds the potential for what Reinhold Niebuhr described as the most heinous sort of sin—religious pride—among "Any Who Think They Have Already Attained."

Charles's view on sanctification holds out perfection as the believer's goal and walks the Christian toward perfection through sanctification, step by step into "gradual holiness grown." He aptly described perfection in his view as an "impossible possibility"—impossible insofar as utter sinlessness seems unlikely in this life, but a possibility in faith, in hope, and in the power of God's grace as one lays this life down in death. Charles's Christian perfection is no friend of the faint of faith and heart, nor is it amicable toward those who would set lower standards in order to "attain" or "step over the cross" to achieve the crown. His concept guards against exaggerated moral and spiritual claims, but supports the buoyant optimism of one who knows there are no limits on the power of God's love. Since Charles based his doctrine on the whispers of his own heart, as opposed to the testimony of "five hundred witnesses," a Wesleyan commentator the caliber of John Rattenbury finds Charles to be "the more reliable witness."[7]

We need not, in fact we should not, choose one Wesley at the expense of the other. The Wesleyan partnership in ministry produced the revival and over half the hymnals that undergirded it. It is not surprising that each brother had his "peculiar work" in preaching the doctrine of Christian perfection. Whether they realized it or not, the brothers balanced and honed each other's views on sanctification. Their dialogue kept both the practicable and the ultimate dimensions of perfection before eighteenth-century Methodism as live options. Their contrasting emphases seemed to be a divinely appointed process of checks and balances to keep the revival on a steady course; John's instantaneous, practicable perfection was saved from pettiness by Charles's vision of gradual, unqualified perfection, which allowed no one to "leap over the cross to snatch the crown. The pathos of Charles's lifelong "Groaning for Full Redemption" was softened and balanced by John's emphasis upon a perfection that was not "set so high as to effectively renounce it."

The truth about the Wesleyan doctrine of sanctification lies in the center of the dialogue between the Wesley brothers; it is found both in their fundamental agreement about Christian perfection and in their historical insistence that there are various Wesleyan options when it comes to the nuances of that essential doctrine.[8] It might be said that a portion of the difficulty contemporary Wesleyan theology has found with its distinctive doctrine—either walking resolutely away from it or enshrining it in canons of language and experiential expectations of another era—comes from our forgetfulness about the balance that the two Wesleys gave the doctrine of Christian perfection in their own lifetimes.

Christian perfection is not an elective element of theology done in the Wesleyan tradition; it was, at least in the minds of the founders of that tradition, Methodism's *raison d'être*. While this study is not the place for a full-scale restatement of the Wesleyan distinctive, it is clear that our inquiry into Charles Wesley's understanding of sanctification suggests theological trajectories for our contemporary consideration of Christian perfection.

First, we must seek to recover the Wesleys' sense of theological balance. Theirs is a theology of the both/and, instead of an either/or. Affirming all the classical Protestant doctrines, the Wesleys gave each doctrine their characteristic imprint: justification by faith *and* justification of life, grace imputed *and* imparted, salvation from the guilt *and* the power of sin. This sense of balance also enabled the Wesleys, both strongly enamored with the doctrine of Christian perfection, to insist that it was sudden *and* gradual, receivable "at any moment" *and* in the "article of death," in one sense a qualified perfection *and* in another sense an unqualified vision. Some would call this theological equivocation, but the Wesleys did not see it that way; their approach was not "speculative or practical latitudinarianism" or an "indifference to all opinions" (*J.W. Works,* 5:501–4). Their theological posture was "fixed . . . in the main branches of Christian doctrine," and yet it found its distinctive emphasis not primarily in creed, but in wholeness of heart and life (*J.W. Works,* 5:503). This pervasive theological mood took the Wesleys to Scripture, tradition, reason, and experience as resources for doing theology in the modern age.[9]

Nor should we lose sight of the fact that they were among the first Protestant theological leaders to live in the afterglow of the Enlightenment; they "plundered the Egyptians," as Albert Outler described their ability to draw upon a vast array of theological sources and ideas.[10] An ardent student of the Scriptures, Charles Wesley was also the sort of man who read with profit an unlikely pair such as Martin Luther and Henry Scougal and extended their work into his own.

The Wesleys' synthesis of life and faith demanded of them, as it does of their descendants, an approach to Christianity that was both biblically based and able to square with common sense. They turned from the bare formalism of their day without jettisoning the riches of the Christian past and the sacramental life of their church in pursuit of living religion. They avoided becoming "holy solitaries" like the mystics, or "enthusiasts" like those who discredited the revival in pursuit of religious experience for its own sake. This sense of balance pervaded the great Wesleyan doctrines and is certainly a factor in their staying power.

This eclectic, balanced theological mood found expression in the structures of Wesleyan theology. Creation and re-creation were like bookends to their theology of redemption, since salvation ultimately meant (especially for Charles) nothing less than a recapitulation of the Edenic perfection of humanity. In a similar display of symmetry, theirs was a theology of "full salvation," bringing about inner and outer rectitude, personal and social holiness.

Charles showed this same sense of balance in steering a middle course between the extremes of the "Christ only" emphasis (Christomonism) of popular Protestantism on the one hand and the "Spirit-centeredness (Pneumatocentrism)" of some Pentecostal or revivalist expressions of Christianity on the other. Wesley had an appreciation for the doctrine of the Trinity that went beyond merely mouthing the creed; he located this truth at the center of his theology of redemption. He affirmed that salvation (as justification and sanctification) was a work of the Son-sending love of the Father, of the self-giving love of the Son, and of the indwelling power of the Spirit. He further affirmed that Christ, who came at His Father's bidding, is formed within those who unite themselves with the triune God by faith, through the agency of the Word and Spirit of God.

Charles's appreciation of "love," as the motive behind and the power that flows from the Christ event, made love a vital force in his theology of sanctification. No hymnal hit society with a more explosive energy than Charles's *Hymns on God's Everlasting Love*; it opposed popular Calvinism, pietistic isolationism, and religious formalism by identifying God's *agape* as the vital power of the gospel. The Wesleyan theology of love holds great potential as an avenue to the heart of the Wesleyan tradition; it enables the descendants of Wesley to explain Christian perfection in ways intelligible to Christians of other traditions and in forms that reflect contemporary theological concerns.[11] Kindred souls as distant in history (though perhaps not in spirit) as the Wesleys and Martin Luther King, Jr., have found in *the strength to love* a force that goes beyond mere sentimentalism in the serious business of world shaking.[12]

The Wesleyan insistence that salvation means freedom from the guilt and power of sin as well as freedom for personal and social wholeness has implications for a Wesleyan world theology. Historically, the Wesleys' concern for the whole person placed them in the forefront of a movement for spiritual, moral, and social reform; hence, the heirs of the Wesleys have found themselves following their theology of redemption into deeds that touch the whole person through ministries of Word and sacrament, through avenues of mission, education, and social justice.[13] Modern Wesleyans will find in their traditional concern for the whole person—sanctification of heart and life—points of contact and mutual concern, as well as points of theological correction, for contemporary theologies of liberation.[14]

Finally, in Charles Wesley's distinctive emphases on sanctification, Wesleyans will find a barometer for spiritual complacency and a hedge against the arrogance of "Any Who Think They Have Already Attained." We meet in Charles Wesley a theological sweep as broad as Creation and redemption, which puts perfection in the beginning, middle, and end of Protestant soteriology. Further, Charles's definition of perfection—as a process that unites Christ and the Holy Spirit in a continuing work of restoration of the *imago Dei* within the believer—suggests a starting point for a new examination of the Wesleyan theological distinctive. The developmental models for sanctification that emerge in Charles's later hymns suggest points parallel with contemporary approaches to moral development and spiritual formation.[15]

Charles's suggestion that Christian perfection can be likened to the kingdom or "reign" of God offers us another model for describing holiness as an effective presence of Christ "in our midst" or "among us," which also strains toward its consummation in the eschatological future. Here Charles offers us an image that is profoundly biblical, central to the message of Jesus, full of the reality of His presence, yet one that extends our understanding of perfection toward the upward limits that Christian hope can anticipate. With the lesson he learned well among the enthusiasts, Charles Wesley also reminds us that perfection, like leaven or the pearl of great price, is most effective when humbly hidden in the midst of transformed lives. His theology of the kingdom merges personal and societal ethics (cf. Matt. 4–5) in a way that is characteristic of the Wesleyan tradition.[16] Charles Wesley's "everlasting gospel" holds enduring significance for his theological heirs!

NOTES

INTRODUCTION:
THE GRAND DEPOSITUM

1. Quotations from Charles Wesley's works are cited in the text using the following abbreviations; when lines are sufficiently located, by title of short poems or sections of poems, no citation appears:

C.W. Anthology	John R. Tyson, ed., *Charles Wesley: An Anthology of Readings* (New York: Oxford University Press, 1986).
C.W. Journal	Thomas Jackson, ed., *The Journal of Charles Wesley, M.A.*, 2 vols. (London: John Mason, 1849; Grand Rapids: Baker, 1980).
C.W. Letters	Frank Baker, *Charles Wesley as Revealed by His Letters* (London: Epworth, 1948).
C.W. Sermons	Charles Wesley, *Sermons by the Late Rev. Charles Wesley, A.M.* (London: Baldwin, Cradock, and Joy, 1816).
P.W.	George Osborn, ed., *The Poetical Works of John and Charles Wesley*, 13 vols. (London: Wesleyan-Methodist Conference Office, 1868–72).

Quotations from John Wesley's works are cited in the text using the following abbreviations:

J.W. Letters	John Telford, ed., *The Letters of the Rev. John Wesley, A.M.*, 8 vols. (London: Epworth, 1931).
J.W. Oxford Works	Frank Baker, ed., *The Works of John Wesley* (Oxford: Oxford University Press, 1980–83).
J.W. Works	Thomas Jackson, ed., *The Works of John Wesley*, 14 vols. (London: Wesleyan Conference Office, 1872; reprinted by various publishers).

2. Frank Baker, *A Union Catalogue of the Publications of John and Charles Wesley* (Durham, N.C.: Duke University, 1966), p. 205. Dr. Baker suggests that Mrs. Charles Wesley edited the collection of sermons; another possible identification would be Charles's daughter, also named Sarah Wesley.

3. The letter to William Chandler, April 28, 1785, is found in *Ms. Ordinations*. It will be published in *C.W. Anthology*. Mabel Brailsford, *A Tale of Two Brothers* (New York: Oxford University Press, 1954), has preserved a bit of Samuel Wesley, Jr.'s, reaction to Charles's "calling" to the New World: "Jack knew his strength and used it. . . . His will was strong enough to bend you [Charles] to go, though not me to consent. I freely own 'twas the will of Jack, but am not yet convinced 'twas the will of God" (p. 85).

4. The historical record of John's relationship with Grace Murray has been clouded by the jaundiced reporting of earlier biographers (cf. Luke Tyerman, *Life and Times of John Wesley*, 2:42–47). It is clear, however, that Mrs. Murray vacillated between the two suitors even after having entered into a formal agreement with Wesley. See Brailsford, *A Tale of Two Brothers*, pp. 175–88, for an account sympathetic to Grace Murray; *J.W. Journal*, 3:417–22, and Thomas Jackson, *The Life of the Rev. Charles Wesley*, 2 vols. (London: John Mason, 1841), 1:537–41, for rather straightforward reporting; and Richard Heitzenrater, *The Elusive Mr. Wesley*, 2 vols. (Nashville: Abingdon, 1984), 1:174–84 for John's recollection of how the events unraveled.

5. See *J.W. Works*, 12:114–16, for the letters that drew Charles's reaction.

6. Brailsford, *Tale of Two Brothers*, p. 167.

7. Jackson, *Life of Charles Wesley*, 1:iii–iv.

8. Ibid., p. iv.

9. Quite a bit of ink has been spilled over the issue of who began Methodism. In Charles's letter to William Chandler (April 1785), Charles claimed that he began the Oxford Holy Club while John was absent from the university; hence Frederick Gill's biography names *Charles Wesley: The First Methodist* (Nashville: Abingdon, 1964). Heitzenrater's *Elusive Mr. Wesley* observes that Gill's statement, "John was not the first Methodist; Charles Wesley founded the Holy Club before John returned to Oxford to take over the group," was one of those "astounding statements that might sound good (or even true) but do not coincide with reality" (2:206). The earliest of John's statements (November 1729) lists John and Charles Wesley and Richard Morgan as the first members of the Holy Club. Charles had been at college since 1726 and *his* letters suggest that the Holy Club began in the fall of that next year.

The matter is further complicated by the question of what the designation "the first Methodist" implies. If it means adhering to a "method" of spiritual formation, then John predates Charles. If by the designation one points to the Holy Club or evangelical conversion, then on those two counts Charles preceded John. The crux of the matter, however, does not lie with the question of when the Holy Club was founded, but with *why* it was begun. Therein we find the distinctive character of Methodist piety, and the reason for what the Wesleys termed "their partnership" in ministry.

10. John Julian, *A Dictionary of Hymnology*, 2d ed. (London: John Murray, 1915), pp. 1260–66, lists 482 Wesleyan hymns which appear in modern hymnals, indicating both their first lines and their location in the Wesleyan hymnological corpus.

11. Erik Routley, *The Musical Wesleys* (London: Jenkins, 1968).

12. John Earnest Rattenbury, *The Evangelical Doctrines of Charles Wesley's Hymns* (London: Epworth, 1941), p. 55.

13. Frank Baker, *Charles Wesley as Revealed by His Letters* (London: Epworth, 1948), pp. 35–36.

14. *P.W.*, 2:156–58, and *C.W. Journal*, 1:161, 204–5. Compare with *P.W.*, 4:378f., and *C.W Journal*, 1:208; *P.W.*, 6:153f., and *C.W. Journal*, 1:294f.; *P.W.*, 2:150f., and *C.W. Journal*, 2:185; *P.W.*, 2:173f., and *C.W. Journal*, 1:278, 367. See also Charles's manuscript shorthand sermon on John 8:1f.

15. See *P.W.*, 5:250–54, for Wesley's five hymns "For the Persecuted."

16. Funeral Hymns, *P.W.*, 6:188–365; "Come, Let Us Join Our Friends Above," *The Book of Hymns: The Official Hymnal of the United Methodist Church* (Nashville: United Methodist Publishing House, 1964), no. 302.

17. Rattenbury, *Evangelical Doctrines*, pp. 55, 132.

18. James H. Dale, "The Theological and Literary Qualities of the Poetry of Charles Wesley in Relation to the Standards of His Age," Ph.D. diss., Cambridge University, 1960, pp. 132–34, 180.

19. Rattenbury, *Evangelical Doctrines*, p. 62.

20. Albert Outler, ed., *John Wesley* (New York: Oxford University Press, 1964), p. 88.

21. Rattenbury, *Evangelical Doctrines*, pp. 85–107; chap. 4, "Charles Wesley Theologian."

22. Henry Bett, *The Hymns of Methodism in Their Literary Relations* (London: Epworth, 1913).

23. John W. Waterhouse, *The Bible In Charles Wesley's Hymns* (London: Epworth, 1954), examines the biblical allusions in several popular Wesleyan hymns. Also see Bett, *Hymns of Methodism*, pp. 71–98; Rattenbury, *Evangelical Doctrines*, pp. 46–54; R. Newton Flew, *The Hymns of Charles Wesley: A Study in Their Structure* (London: Epworth, 1953); Francis Frost, "Biblical Imagery and Religious Experiences in the Hymns of the Wesleys," *Proceedings of the Wesley Historical Society* 142 (December 1980):158–66; T. S. Gregory, "Charles Wesley's Hymns and Poems," *London Quarterly and Holborn Review* 182 (October

1957):253–62; and Bernard Manning, *The Hymns of Wesley and Watts* (London: Epworth, 1943).

24. Gregory, "Charles Wesley's Hymns and Poems," p. 261.

25. Manning, *Hymns of Wesley and Watts*, p. 42f.

26. See note #14 above.

27. Frederick J. Gilman, *Evolution of the English Hymn* (New York: Macmillan, 1927), p. 219.

CHAPTER ONE:
"AWAKE THOU THAT SLEEPEST!"

1. John Tyson, ed., *Charles Wesley: A Reader* (New York: Oxford University Press, 1986), "Letter to Dr. Chandler." Also see Leslie Church, "Charles Wesley—the Man," *London Quarterly and Holborn Review* 182 (October 1957): 247–53.

2. Gill, *First Methodist*, p. 36ff. Charles's recollection, in his letter to Dr. Chandler, traces the inception of the Holy Club to the period of John's absence. Yet, John Wesley's diary and correspondence indicate that he was practicing a "method" of spiritual formation at Oxford as early as March 26, 1725. Cf. Heitzenrater, *Elusive Mr. Wesley*, 1:51–55. Charles was probably more directly responsible for the establishment of a religious society at Oxford, John for development of the spiritual disciplines that would later characterize it. See note #9, "Introduction," for further discussion of this matter.

3. Ibid., p. 38.

4. George Whitefield, *Whitefield's Journals* (reprint London: Banner of Truth Trust, 1965), pp. 46–47.

5. Tyson, *Charles Wesley*, "Letter to Dr. Chandler."

6. Heitzenrater, *Elusive Mr. Wesley*, pp. 63–74; Robert Tuttle, Jr., *John Wesley: His Life and Theology* (Grand Rapids: Zondervan, 1978), pp. 113–26. Cf. George Tappert, ed., *Philip Spener, Pia Disideria* (Philadelphia: Fortress, 1964), pp. 89–97.

7. Winthrop Hudson, ed., *Henry Scougal's Life of God in the Soul of Man* (reprint Philadelphia: Westminster, 1976), p. 16.

8. Paul Stanwood, ed., *William Law* (New York: Paulist, 1978), p. 131.

9. Cf. Heitzenrater, *Elusive Mr. Wesley*, pp. 50–62.

10. Whitefield, *Journals*, pp. 46–47. Cf. Gill, *First Methodist*, p. 39; Tuttle, *John Wesley*, p. 139.

11. Eric Baker, *A Herald of the Evangelical Revival* (London: Epworth, 1948), and J. Brazier Green, *John Wesley and William Law* (London: Epworth, 1945). In his 1760 letter to the editor of the *London Chronicle*, John Wesley wrote: "It is true that Mr. Law, whom I love and reverence now, was once 'a kind of oracle' to me" (*J.W. Letters*, 4:106).

12. John R. Tyson, "John Wesley and William Law: A Reappraisal," *Wesleyan Theological Journal* 17 (Fall 1982): 58–79, gives a detailed examination of the connections and later disagreements between John Wesley and William Law.

13. Charles made an interesting play on words in this quotation by weaving William Law's surname into the phraseology of Galatians 3:24 (". . . the law was our schoolmaster to bring us unto Christ, that we might be justified by faith").

14. Cf. Tuttle, *John Wesley*, p. 124f., for examples of this "mysticism" in John's sermons.

15. For this reason, the Oxford years of Charles's life must be reconstructed out of his reminiscences and letters; John Wesley's diaries, journal, and letters; and a few recollections from Charles's friends.

16. *Ms. Ordinations,* to be published in Tyson, *Charles Wesley,* "Letter to Dr. Chandler."

17. Ibid., "Letter of the Atlantic Crossing."

18. Gill, *First Methodist*, p. 52.

19. This theme became the focus of Charles's 1746 hymnbook entitled *Hymns of Petition and Thanksgiving for the Promise of the Father.* Cf. *P.W.*, 4:163–204.

20. Peter Grant, "The Wesleys' Conversion Hymn," *Proceedings of the Wesley Historical Society* 35 (September 1966): 161–64, offers a fine discussion of the issues involved in the identification of the famous conversion hymn.

CHAPTER TWO:
"THE ONE THING NEEDFUL"

1. John R. Tyson, "Charles Wesley's Theology of the Cross: An Examination of the Theology and Method of Charles Wesley as seen in his Doctrine of the Atonement," Ph.D. diss., Drew University, 1983, pp. 58–66, discusses the extent of Charles's productivity.

2. B. C. Drury, "John Wesley Hymnologist," *Proceedings of the Wesley Historical Society* 32 (1959–60): 103.

3. Ibid.

4. Tyson, "Charles Wesley's Theology," pp. 60–61.

5. Frank Baker, ed., *The Representative Verse of Charles Wesley* (London: Epworth, 1962), p. lviii.

6. John R. Tyson, "Charles Wesley's Sentimental Language," *Evangelical Quarterly* 57:3 (July 1985): 269–75, offers a complete discussion of the editorial changes John Wesley made in Charles's compositions.

7. John R. Tyson, "Charles Wesley and the German Hymns," *The Hymn* 35 (July 1984): 153–58; cf. Drury, "John Wesley Hymnologist."

8. Baker, *Representative Verse*, p. 385, suggests that this *Collection* and its later *Supplement* contained over 623 hymns by Charles and no more than 30 composed by John.

9. James Dale, "The Theological and Literary Qualities of the Poetry of Charles Wesley in Relation to the Standards of His Age," Ph.D. diss., Cambridge University, 1960, p. 188.

10. Ibid., p. 132.

11. Rattenbury, *Evangelical Doctrines* (London: Epworth, 1941), p. 62.

12. Ibid., p. 60.

13. *Ms. Luke*(hymn based on John 17:6), pp. 93–94.

14. Ibid., p. 246.

15. N. Burwash, ed., *John Wesley's Doctrinal Standards: The Sermons With Introduction, Analysis and Notes* (reprint, Salem, Ohio: Schmul, 1967), p. 184. Cf. "The Privilege of the Children of God," *J.W. Sermons*, no. 19.

16. *J.W. Works*, 5:223–34; John's standard sermon no. 19 is based on the Bible text, "Whosoever is born of God doth not commit sin." Charles's manuscript shorthand sermon based on Titus 3:8 follows a similar line of development.

17. The fourth chapter will treat this theme more directly.

18. *Ms. Acts* (manuscript hymnbook), p. 210.

19. *Ms. Luke* (hymn on Luke 5:21), nos. 71–72; cf. *P.W.*, 12:224, no. 2536.

20. Gerhard Kittel and Gerhard Friedrich, ed. *Theological Dictionary of the New Testament*, trans. and ed. Geoffrey W. Bromiley, 10 vols. (Grand Rapids: Eerdmans, 1964–76) [hereinafter referred to as *TDNT*], s.v. "*sōzō*"; cf. George Arthur Buttrick, ed., *The Interpreter's Dictionary of the Bible*, 4 vols. (New York: Abingdon, 1962) [hereinafter referred to as *IDB*], s.v. "saved, salvation."

21. Ibid.; cf. William F. Arndt and F. Wilbur Gingrich, *A Greek-English Lexicon of the New Testament and Other Early Christian Literature*, 4th ed. (Chicago: University of Chicago Press, 1957), pp. 805–6.

22. *Ms. John* (hymn based on John 3:15), p. 39. Cf. *P.W.*, 152, no. 4.

23. Cf. *Ms. John*, p. 39; *P.W.*, 4:311; 4:373, no. 152; 10:102, no. 1508; 11:365, no. 1713; 13:22–23, no. 3073; 13:152, no. 3289.

24. "The One Thing Needful" (*C.W. Sermons*, no. 5), based on Luke 10:42, was preached Sunday, September 26, 1736 and October 30, 1737; "The Single Eye" (*C.W. Sermons*, no. 8), based on Matthew 6:22–23, was preached on Thursday, March 13, 1746; and "There the Wicked Cease From Troubling" (*C.W. Sermons*, no. 13), headed as "*John* Wesley's sermon," was preached by Charles on Sunday, October 3, 1736.

25. Richard Heitzenrater, "John Wesley's Early Sermons," *Proceedings of the Wesley Historical Society* 37 (February 1970): 110ff.

26. Ibid., p. 113. Dr. Heitzenrater's footnote no. 13 explains this mistake quite well. As he writes, "The editor of Charles Wesley's *Sermons* (1816) apparently was unfamiliar with Byrom's shorthand . . . indicated by some of the notes appended to the published sermons. The note on Sermon IX says, 'preached on board the London Galley, between Charlestown and Boston,' where the editor read as 'preached' was in fact five words in shorthand, 'transcribed from my brother's copies,' and applies to Sermons III and IV as well. The date of the transcriptions is noted at the end of the manuscript for Sermon V as the 4th September, 1736, 'off Boston,' and coincides with a reference in Charles's *Journal* on that date as 'writing by candel light'" (cf. *C.W. Journal*, 1:41). Another hint about these sermons is found in the Wesleys' Georgia correspondence. John's letter to Charles, March 22, 1736, indicates that John sent his younger brother a box that contained copies of his sermons: "You have now all my sermons, besides those which I have sent. Some are in the box . . . together with the Bible in quarto" (*J.W. Letters*, 1:198). Charles's letter of March 27 reports having received the "box" from John, and also laments it had been opened in transit (*C.W. Letters*, p. 24).

27. John Wesley, ed., *A Christian Library: Consisting of Extracts from and Abridgements of the Choicest Pieces of Practical Divinity which have been published in the English Tongue*, 50 vols. (1750; reprint, London: J. Kershaw, 1825). The title with its long subtitle aptly describes the contents of the large collection.

28. *P.W.*, 1:12, 15–20, 27, 32. Cf. Henry Bett, *The Hymns of Methodism*, pp. 71–169, for an outstanding survey of the sources utilized in the composition of the Wesleyan hymns.

29. Bett, *Hymns of Methodism*, pp. 168–69.

30. Tyson, *Charles Wesley*, "Letter to Dr. Chandler." Cf. Heitzenrater, "Early Sermons," pp. 112–13 and p. 32 above.

31. Irenaeus, "Against Heresies," in *The Ante-Nicene Fathers*, ed. by Alexander Roberts and James Donaldson, 10 vols. (Buffalo: Christian Literature, 1885–96; reprint, Grand Rapids: Eerdmans, 1950), 1:527.

32. Ibid., p. 526 (italics added). Cf. J. N. D. Kelley, *Early Christian Doctrines* (New York: Harper & Row, 1960), p. 173f., for a helpful discussion of Irenaeus's soteriology.

33. Outler, *John Wesley*, p. 10.

34. John R. Tyson and Douglas Lister, "Charles Wesley, Pastor: A Glimpse Inside His Shorthand Journal," *Quarterly Review* 4 (Spring 1984):14. This article cites several instances in which Charles's manuscript journal quotes Ignatius's letters and life as an example to follow in the midst of trials. Cf. Bett, *Hymns of Methodism*, pp. 98–112; Bett identified echoes of Augustine, Tertullian, and a host of others in Charles's writings. *Ms. Luke*, p. 296, introduces a poem based on "a

Saying of Chrysostom." Several letters between the Wesley brothers, included in *Ms. Ordinations*, debate Cyrian's saying about one's obligation to separate from a wicked overseer.

35. Verse 11 of the hymn "The Good Samaritan," *P.W.*, 2:156–58.

36. This Charles Wesley sermon should not be confused with John Wesley's sermon by the same title (*J.W. Works*, 7:297–305).

37. "Purity of affection" and "simplicity of intention" became standard Wesleyan descriptions for Christian perfection. As John Wesley wrote in his *Plain Account of Christian Perfection* (*J.W. Works*, 11:366–67), "In the year 1726 . . . I saw that 'simplicity of intention, and purity of affection' one design in all we speak or do, and one desire ruling all our tempers, are indeed, 'the wings of the soul' without which she can never ascend to the mount of God."

CHAPTER THREE:
"FREELY JUSTIFIED"

1. John R. Tyson, "John Wesley and William Law: A Reappraisal," *Wesleyan Theological Journal* 17 (Fall 1982) :58–79.

2. Thomas Albin, "Charles Wesley's Earliest Evangelical Sermons," *Methodist History* 21 (October 1982) :60–63, describes these sermons and their discovery, a process in which I played a small part.

3. *Ms. Sermon on Luke 18:9f.*, p. 5, italics added. The sermon is located in the Methodist Archives and Research Center, John Rylands Library of the University of Manchester, Manchester, England.

4. Thomas Albin and Oliver Beckerlegge have transcribed the Charles Wesley shorthand sermons mentioned above. The sermons will be published by the Wesley Historical Society (England) under the title *Charles Wesley's Earliest Sermons: Six Manuscript Shorthand Sermons Hitherto Unpublished and Now Deciphered*, edited by Thomas R. Albin and Oliver A. Beckerlegge. I am grateful to Albin and Beckerlegge for permission to cite this important documentary material from the manuscript of their transcription (hereafter referred to as *C.W. Ms. Sermons*). This quotation is found on p. 14 of their manuscript.

5. Ibid.

6. Ibid., p. 16.

7. Ibid., p. 18.

8. Ibid., p. 16.

9. Ibid., pp. 21–22.

10. *P.W.*, 4:409; 5:366, no. 162; *J.W. Works*, 5:33; Charles's sermon, "Awake Thou That Sleepest"; *Ms. Acts*, p. 44.

11. *C.W. Ms. Sermons*, p. 117.

12. "Waiting for Redemption," *Ms. Cheshunt*, p. 211.

13. *Ms. John*, pp. 367–68.

14. *Ms. Miscellaneous Hymns*, p. 81, no. 113. Cf. *P.W.*, 10:131, no. 1595.

15. Cf. *P.W.*, 4:416, 428, 436; 10:165; 11:192.

16. Cf. *P.W.*, 4:402–4; 5:39–42.

17. *Ms. Miscellaneous Hymns*, p. 275; cf. *P.W.*, 1:92; 4:208, no. 1; 5:70, no. 168; 9:309, no. 894; 10:163, no. 62.

18. Frank Whaling, ed., *John and Charles Wesley: Selected Writings* (New York: Paulist, 1981), p. xvi.; Timothy Smith, "The Holy Spirit in the Hymns of the Wesleys," *Wesleyan Theological Journal* 16 (Fall 1981): 20–48; T. Crichton Mitchell, "Response to Dr. Timothy Smith on the Wesleys' Hymns," *Wesleyan Theological Journal* 16 (Fall 1981): 49–58.

19. *C.W. Sermons*, p. 11; *C.W. Journal*, 1:90–92; *Ms. Luke*, p. 14; *Ms. Acts*, p. 145; *P.W.*, 4:165, 168, 190; 5:78; 7:374–75; 9:351, 462; 12:136.

20. *Ms. Luke*, p. 14; *P.W.*, 4:165, 168; 12:136; 13:43.

21. *P.W.*, 4:190, no. 272; 5:78; 9:462, no. 1258; 12:8, no. 2084.

22. *P.W.*, 4:288, 296, 307; 10:94, no. 1484; 10:419.

23. *Ms. Acts*, p. 198; *P.W.*, 7:108, no. 90; 7:463, no. 1260.

24. *P.W.*, 4:289, 310, 381; 10:119, no. 1553.

25. *Ms. John* (hymn based on John 3:4), p. 32; *P.W.*, 12:6, no. 5082.

26. *Ms. Clark*, p. 20; *P.W.*, 9:254, no. 778.

27. E. C. Blackman, "Faith," *IDB*, 2:22.

28. Ibid.

29. Arndt and Gingrich, *Lexicon*, pp. 665–67.

30. Ibid., p. 12.

31. Ephesians 1:7; Colossians 1:14; Hebrews 9:11–12.

32. *P.W.*, 12:295, no. 2683; cf. 6:407; 7:176; 12:172, no. 2424; *Ms. Miscellaneous Hymns*, p. 77, no. 113; *C.W. Journal*, 1:192, 307.

33. Arndt and Gingrich, *Lexicon*, pp. 816–18; Blackman, "Redemption," *IDB*, 4:16f.; Buschel, *"Allasso,"* *TDNT*, 1:251f.; William Barclay, *More New Testament Words* (London: SCM, 1958), pp. 103–4.

34. *C.W. Journal*, 1:280–81, 307; *P.W.*, 4:287; *P.W.*, 6:48.

35. Arndt and Gingrich, *Lexicon*, p. 415; J. Reuman, "Reconciliation," *IDB*, 5:728.

36. *Ms. Miscellaneous Hymns*, pp. 274–75; *P.W.*, 4:113, no. 8; 4:159, no. 6; 6:303; 6:454, no. 87; 6:456, no. 91; 7:22, no. 16; 7:31, no. 20; 7:56, no. 49; 7:92, no. 78; 7:136, no. 112; 7:215, no. 32; 7:332, no. 33; 7:341, no. 45; 9:53, no. 170; 9:65, no. 212; 9:144; 9:416, no. 1156; 10:40–41, no. 1352; 10:287, no. 384; 10:454; 11:502—3, no. 2047; 13:22, no. 3073; 13:180, no. 3366; 13:189, no. 3383.

37. *P.W.*, 4:113, 159; 6:303, 456; 7:31, 92, 136, 215, 332, 341; 10:287, no. 384; 13:22, no. 3073; 13:180, no. 3366.

38. See for example *Ms. Acts*, p. 202; *Ms. Preparation for Death*, p. 33, no. 69; *Ms. Miscellaneous Hymns*, p. 197; *P.W.*, 1:205; 4:40; 4:117, no. 11; 4:188, no. 19; 4:216, no. 8; 5:26, no. 130; 5:28, no. 131; 5:306, no. 14; 6:303; 6:374, no. 3; 7:217, no. 20; 7:381, no. 30; 9:256, no. 779; 9:339, no. 972; 9:352, no. 1007; 9:444, no. 1215; 10:264, no. 316; 11:44, no. 1020; 11:252, no. 1470; 12:158–59, no. 2398.

39. For Charles's use of other alliterative terms, see *P.W.*, 5:28; 10:182; 11:252.

40. *P.W.*, 7:381; 10:182, no. 109; *Ms. Miscellaneous Hymns*, p. 197.

41. Rattenbury, *Evangelical Doctrines*, p. 255.

42. Deuteronomy 33:34; 1 Kings 21:8; Nehemiah 9:38; Job 9:7, 33:16; Ezekiel 28:12; Daniel 12:9.

43. Cf. *P.W.*, 7:381; 10:10, no. 1286.

44. Arndt and Gingrich, *Lexicon*, p. 242; G. E. Mendenhall, *IDB*, 2:76.

45. G. Schrenk, *"Eloga," TDNT*, 4:176.

46. Arndt and Gingrich, *Lexicon*, p. 710; K. L. Schmidt, *"Proorizo," TDNT*, 5:456; G. E. Mendenhall, "Predestination," *IDB*, 3:869.

47. Frederick Luke Wiseman, *Charles Wesley and His Hymns* (London: Epworth, 1938), p. 178.

48. From the Hebrew *meim*, referring to the inward seat of deep emotions; cf. Song of Solomon 5:4; Jeremiah 31:20.

CHAPTER FOUR:
"AN INTEREST IN JESUS' BLOOD"

1. Leon Morris, *The Apostolic Preaching of the Cross* (Grand Rapids: Eerdmans, 1955), pp. 108–9.

2. Ibid.

3. Ibid., pp. 117–20.

4. Johannes Behm, *"Haima," TNDT*, 1:174.

5. Rattenbury, *Evangelical Doctrines*, p. 202.

6. D. J. McCarthy, "Blood," *IDB*, 1:115.

7. Morris, *Apostolic Preaching*, p. 122.

8. *P.W.*, 7:398, no. 44; 12:56, no. 2185; 12:59, no. 2191; 13:22, no. 3073; 13:164, no. 3331.

9. Walter Eichrodt, *Theology of the Old Testament*, trans. J. A. Baker (Philadelphia: Westminster, 1961), 1:155.

10. Ibid., 1:157–58.

11. Texts such as Leviticus 9:7f.; 10:17f.; 14:18f.; 15:15f.; 16:16f.; and 17:11f. bring *blood* and *atonement* into close proximity; and the phrase "blood maketh atonement" appears in Leviticus 16:27 and

17:11. But the exact phrase "atoning blood" does not appear in the Authorized Version of the Bible.

12. Johannes Hermann, *"Hilaskomai," TDNT*, 3:302–18. Cf. Morris, *Apostolic Preaching*, pp. 125–86, and R. Abba, "Expiation," *IDB*, 2:200–201.

13. C. L. Mitton, "Atonement," *IDB*, 1:310.

14. Claus-Runno Hunzinger, *"Rantizo," TDNT*, 6:981–83.

15. *P.W.*, 7:328, no. 31; 8:303; 10:11, no. 1291; 10:74, no. 1434; 10:80, no. 1449; 12:236, no. 2560; 12:243, no. 2576; *Ms. Acts*, p. 455.

16. *P.W.*, 3:111; 7:212, no. 13; 7:328, no. 31; 10:11, no. 129; 13:120, no. 3261.

17. *P.W.*, 10:11, no. 1291; cf. 4:349, 364; 5:266.

18. *P.W.*, 13:143; 4:45; *Ms. John*, p. 41.

19. *P.W.*, 13:43, no. 3115; cf. 7:397, no. 43; 13:33, no. 3092; 13:71, no. 3170.

20. *P.W.*, 4:166; cf. 4:279, no. 108; 12:300–301, no. 2693; 12:40, no. 2152; 12:298, no. 2690.

21. *P.W.*, 6:3, no. 1; 11:502, no. 2045; 12:157, no. 2386; 12:431, no. 2978.

22. *P.W.*, 7:384, no. 32; 7:403, no. 49; 10:23, no. 1311; 12:299, no. 2692; 13:173, no. 3352.

23. *P.W.*, 4:166, italics added; cf. 10:23, no. 1310; 12:83; 13:71, no. 3170.

24. *C.W. Journal*, 1:215; *P.W.*, 11:365, no. 1713; 12:109, no. 2300; 12:248, no. 2587; 12:258, no. 2610.

25. The use of the term *melted* in the KJV is interesting. In most instances (Josh. 5:1; 7:5; Isa. 19:1; Nah. 2:10), the term is used to communicate a deep sense of fear. On a few occasions, it connotes the related notion of being "faint in spirit" (as in Isa. 13:7; Ezek. 21:7). Charles's application of the term in his theology of redemption seemed to be based in a double sense of fear: On the one hand, this fear means a sense of dread; and on the other hand, it implies a sense of obedience and commitment to God (as in Prov. 1:7).

26. James A. Townsend, "Feelings Related to Assurance in Charles Wesley's Hymns" (Ph.D. diss., Fuller Theological Seminary, 1979). The main theme of this study is found in the connection between redemption, assurance, and feelings of comfort.

27. *Ms. Acts*, p. 292; cf. *P.W.*, 4:472, 375; 5:3, no. 114; 5:67, no. 148; 5:230, no. 62.

28. *Ms. Miscellaneous Hymns*, p. 77, no. 113; cf. *P.W.*, 6:456–57, no. 92; 7:108, no. 90; 8:379, no. 38; 12:109, no. 2300; 13:220, no. 3443.

29. *Ms. Acts* (hymn based on Acts 11:18), p. 210.

30. *Ms. Acts*, p. 297; cf. *P.W.*, 10:130, no. 1593; 13:70, no. 3168; 13:181, no. 3368.

31. *P.W.*, 13:164, no. 3331; cf. 7:212, no. 11; 7:235, no. 46.

32. *P.W.*, 5:57; cf. *Ms. Luke*, p. 342, no. 173; *P.W.*, 4:295–96; 7:160; 12:419–20.

33. *P.W.*, 12:192, no. 2467; 4:47, 52, 355; 5:274;

34. Arndt and Gingrich, *Lexicon*, p. 483.

35. Ibid., p. 484.

36. Rudolf Bultmann, "*Aphiēmi*," *TDNT*, 1:509–12.

37. A. C. Herbert, "Seal," *A Theological Word Book of the Bible*, ed. Alan Richardson (New York: Macmillan, 1950), p. 221–22. Cf. O. Tufell, "Seal," *IDB*, 4:25.

38. Gottfried Fitzer, "*Sphragis*," *TDNT*, 7:939ff.

39. Johannes Behm, "*Arrhabōn*," *TDNT*, 1:475. Behm offers *deposit, pledge,* or *guarantee* as synonyms for *seal*.

40. *Ms. Miscellaneous Hymns*, p. 28; *P.W.*, 4:355; 7:191; 11:16, no. 949; 13:117, no. 3258; 13:126, no. 3271.

41. This image is perhaps most famous for its role in Charles's hymn, "Arise, My Soul, Arise!" where "five bleeding wounds . . . pour effectual prayers" and "strongly plead for me." The metaphor is constant throughout the Charles Wesley corpus: *P.W.*, 4:470; 5:14, no. 120; 5:55, no. 148; 5:152; 5:317; 5:417, no. 714; 9:164, no. 512; 10:200–201; 11:223, no. 1413; 11:288, no. 1540.

42. *Ms. Miscellaneous Hymns*, p. 21, no. 113; no. 161; *P.W.*, 3:255; 7:379, no. 28; 13:161–62.

43. *Ms. Miscellaneous Hymns*, p. 21, no. 113; *P.W.*, 3:225; 5:55, no. 148; 11:288, no. 1540; 11:304, no. 1582.

44. *Ms. John*, p. 334; *P.W.*, 4:228; 7:108, 116, 154; 9:13; 10:417; 13:252.

45. *P.W.*, 4:158, no. 4; 4:171–72, no. 6; 4:203–4, no. 32; 7:370–71, no. 20; 13:235, no. 3473. This theme was especially important in Wesley's hymns "For the Promise of the Father," since he believed that the promise was the coming of the Holy Spirit.

46. *P.W.*, 4:261; 5:277; 11:269; 12:146; 13:161.

47. *Ms. John*, p. 334. Cf. *Ms. Miscellaneous Hymns*, pp. 21, 308; *P.W.*, 4:171–72; 4:328; 7:154; 7:379; 13:161–62; 13:235; 13:252.

48. *Ms. Miscellaneous Hymns*, p. 308.

49. *P.W.*, 3:225, no. 14; 3:242, no. 36; 4:157, no. 4; 13:136, no. 3286; 13:161, no. 3326; 13:192, no. 3387.

50. A. Skevington Wood, *The Burning Heart: John Wesley, Evangelist* (Exeter: Paternoster, 1967), p. 30.

51. Rattenbury, *Evangelical Doctrines*, p. 202.

CHAPTER FIVE:
"LOVE PERFECTED"

1. *C.W. Journal*, 1:92.

2. Ibid., p. 95.

3. Ibid., pp. 95–96.

4. Charles Wesley titled the hymn "Free Grace," but modern hymnals refer to it by its first line, "And Can It Be?" See *P.W.*, 1:105–6, for the full text.

5. *C.W. Journal*, 1:115, 121, 129, 139, 141, 149, 189.

6. Ibid., p. 181.

7. Ibid., p. 79. The sermon was reported six times in all, though Charles certainly preached it more frequently than that.

8. Barclay, *More New Testament Words*, pp. 9–24; C. E. B. Cranfield, "Love," *Theological Word Book*, pp. 131–36; E. M. Good, "Love in the Old Testament," *IDB*, 3:164–68; G. Johnston, "Love in the New Testament," *IDB*, 3:168–78; C. S. Lewis, *The Four Loves* (London: Geoffrey Bless, 1960); Anders Nygren, *Agape and Eros* (London: SPCK, 1957); and E. Stauffer, "*Agapao, Agape, Agapatos*," *TDNT*, 1:21–55.

9. *P.W.*, 2:74; 5:30–31, no. 134; 11:114.

10. *Ms. Acts*, p. 379.

11. *Ms. Preparation for Death*, p. 28, no. 53.

12. Romans 12:2; 2 Corinthians 4:16; 5:17; Ephesians 4:23–24; Colossians 3:10; Titus 3:5; Revelation 21:5.

13. *P.W.*, 6:404, no. 37; 7:235, no. 45; 7:236, no. 47; 7:355; 10:114, no. 1543; 13:167, no. 3336.

14. Arndt and Gingrich, *Lexicon*, p. 816.

15. *J.W. Works*, 7:1–22; 7:202–10; *P.W.*, 1:284; 2:126–34; 2:319–23.

16. Gerhard Delling, "*Teleios*," *TDNT*, 8:77f.

17. See J. P. Hyatt, "Circumcision," *IDB*, 1:629–31.

18. *P.W.*, 10:28, no. 1321; 12:58, no. 2189; *Ms. Luke*, p. 194.

19. *P.W.*, 13:95, no. 3215, commenting on 1 Thessalonians 5:25 ("Faithful is he that calleth you, who also will do it").

20. *P.W.*, 5:325–27, no. 29; cf. 5:328–33.

21. It is clear that John Wesley took significant theological and literary liberties with Charles's hymns as he prepared them for publication. See my article "Charles Wesley's Sentimental Language," *Evangelical Quarterly* 57:3 (July 1985): 269–75, for a discussion of some of the alterations John made in the Methodist hymns.

22. *Ms. Clark*, p. 27. The manuscript of this unpublished hymn is located in the Methodist Archives and Research Center, John Rylands Library of the University of Manchester, Manchester, England. It is cited here by permission of the Methodist Church Committee on Archives and History, England.

23. Otto Procksch, "*Hagios*," *TDNT*, 1:89; cf. James Mullenberg, "Holiness," *IDB*, 2:616–25; Eichrodt, *Theology of the Old Testament*, 1:270–71.

24. Edmund Jacob, *Theology of the Old Testament* (New York: Harper & Row, 1958), p. 87.

25. Eichrodt, *Theology of the Old Testament*, 1:272.

26. Ibid., 1:274–77; cf. E. C. Blackman, 'Sanctification," *IDB*, 4:210.

27. Ibid., p. 277.

28. Arndt and Gingrich, *Lexicon*, pp. 8–10.

29. Procksch, *"Hagios," TDNT*, pp. 100–12.

30. Only ten occurences in the New Testament are not based on a *teleios* form.

31. Arndt and Gingrich, *Lexicon*, pp. 816–17.

32. Compare the Pauline use of *sanctification* and related words with the preference in non-Pauline literature for *perfection* words: *sanctification/sanctify* (Rom. 15:16; 1 Cor. 1:2, 30; 5:23; 6:11; 7:14; Eph. 5:26; 1 Thess. 4:3; 2 Thess. 2:13; 1 Tim. 4:5; 2 Tim. 2:21); *perfection/perfect* (Heb. 2:10; 5:9; 6:1; 7:19; 9:9; 10:1, 14; 11:40; 12:23; James 2:22; 1 John 2:5; 4:17, 18).

33. J. C. K. Reid, "Sanctify," *Theological Word Book*, pp. 216–19.

34. *P.W.*, 4:169; 6:243; 10:33; 12:55, 216, 379.

35. Cf. *P.W.*, 7:243; 12:55, no. 2182; 12:216, no. 2620; 12:379, no. 2860.

CHAPTER SIX:
"THE LIFE OF GOD IN THE SOUL"

1. John L. Peters, *Christian Perfection and American Methodism*, 2d. ed. (Grand Rapids: Zondervan, 1985), pp. 15–19.

2. Scougal, *Life of God*, p. 5.

3. Adam Clarke, *Memoirs of the Wesley Family* (New York: Emory & Waugh, 1832), p. 222.

4. Whitefield, *Journals*, pp. 46–47.

5. Ibid., p. 47.

6. Scougal, *Life of God*, p. 30.

7. Ibid., p. 33.

8. Ibid. The "Divine Life" within the believer entails "love to God, charity to man, purity and humility" (pp. 33–34), as well as spiritual disciplines such as prayer, acts of devotion, and frequent communion (pp. 79–93).

9. John Wesley, ed., *The Life of God in the Soul of Man; or, The Nature and Excellency of the Christian Religion* (New Castle: J. Goodwin, 1744). See also John Wesley's *Christian Library*, 2d. ed.; volume 23:327–456 carries Scougal's sermons.

10. Scougal, *Life of God*, p. 49.

11. Ibid.

12. Ibid.

13. Ibid., pp. 49–62.

14. Ibid., pp. 83–90.

15. *P.W.*, 11:26, no. 969; cf. 4:371; 7:404, no. 49; 9:129, no. 396; 9:440, no. 1201; 10:141–42, no. 18; 10:235, no. 242.

16. Cf. *P.W.*, 4:309; 5:23–24, no. 127.

17. Smith, "The Holy Spirit in the Hymns of the Wesleys'; Mitchell, "Reply to Smith."

18. Smith, ibid., p. 34. Mitchell, "Reply to Smith," p. 44. Dr. Mitchell's first question of Dr. Smith—"Did Charles later modify his position?"—is a crucial one, since (as we shall see in chapter 7) the Methodist disputes over Christian perfection polarized the Wesleys' respective views of this doctrine.

19. What seems to be occurring in Charles's hymns of the 1740s is a subtle opposition to the revivalist pneumatology. The dangerously "enthusiastic" elements of the Wesleys' theology, which would cause problems in the 1760s, were restructured christologically in these hymns. This same point has been made from the more contemporary side of the discussion in Donald Dayton's "Doctrine of the Baptism of the Holy Spirit: Its Emergence and Significance," *Wesleyan Theological Journal* 13 (Spring 1978): 114–26. Dayton argues that a major shift occurred in nineteenth-century American Holiness theology's conception of the role of the Holy Spirit in Christian perfection. He identifies six major points descriptive of that transition, the first and sixth of which are most important for our discussion here: "(1) A basic shift from a fundamentally 'Christocentric' pattern of thought to one that might be called a fundamentally 'Pneumatocentric,' . . . (6) A shift from the goal of sanctification in 'Christian Perfection' to a greater emphasis on the event of the 'second blessing' " (p. 114). Dr. Thomas Langford's recent book, *Practical Divinity: Theology in the Wesleyan Tradition* (Nashville: Abingdon, 1983), seems to support Dayton's analysis (see pp. 134–35). Dr. Smith's tendency, in the article cited above, seems to be that of reading *Hymns of Petition and Thanksgiving for the Promise of the Father* from the contemporary side of this transition, whereas Charles's thought was more characteristically christocentric than pneumatocentric.

20. *Ms. John*, pp. 335–36. The hymn was probably written on August 30, 1764.

21. *Ms. Luke*, p. 126.

22. *P.W.*, 9:60, no. 194; 9:322, no. 928; 9:325, no. 934; 10:10–11, no. 1288; 11:43–44, no. 1019; 11:261, no. 1969.

23. *Ms. Luke*, p. 252.

24. Ibid., pp. 275–76. Cf. *P.W.*, 10:235, no. 242.

25. *P.W.*, 7:404, no. 49; cf. 9:110–11, no. 351; 9:233, no. 737; 9:304, no. 881; 9:335, no. 964.

26. *Ms. Luke*, p. 256.

27. Procksch, *"Hagios," TDNT*, 1:89; Eichrodt, *Theology of the Old Testament*, 1:270–76; Blackman, "Sanctification," *IDB*, 4:210f.

28. Arndt and Gingrich, *Lexicon*, p. 206.

29. James A Murray, ed., *A New English Dictionary on Historical Principles*, vol. 10, pt. 2 (Oxford: Clarendon, 1928), p. 238.

30. *P.W.*, 1:235; 6:402, no. 35; 7:27–28, no. 22; 7:114–15, no. 96; 12:260, no. 2614; 13:7–8, no. 3042; 13:126, no. 3270; 13:146, no. 3299; 13:235, no. 3473.

31. *P.W.*, 9:47, no. 151; 9:291, no. 849; 10:224, no. 215; 10:306, no. 435; 10:418, no. 718; 10:441, no. 775; 11:345, no. 1665; 12:91–92.

32. *Ms. Luke*, p. 98; *Ms. Acts*, p. 343; *P.W.*, 4:197; 7:23, no. 19; 7:49; 7:186, no. 154; 7:187; 9:115, no. 360; 9:421, no. 1164; 12:157, no. 2396.

33. Eichrodt, *Theology of the Old Testament*, 2:40.

34. *P.W.*, 4:477, no. 11, italics added; cf. 6:107; 6:383; 10:208–9; 10:432; 11:150, no. 1253.

35. *Ms. Acts*, p. 180.

36. *Ibid.*, pp. 180–81, 553–54; cf. *Ms. John*, p. 71; *P.W.*, 3:266, no. 70; 12:260, no. 2613.

37. *P.W.*, 11:150–51, no. 1253; cf. 10:225, no. 216; 11:345, no. 1665; 12:23, no. 19.

38. *P.W.*, 10:464, no. 821; cf. 9:231, no. 727; 10:455, no. 803.

39. *Ms. Luke*, pp. 341–42; *Ms. John*, pp. 71, 412; *P.W.*, 5:28–29, no. 321; 7:416, no. 64; 7:114–15, no. 96; 9:114; 9:115–16, no. 360; 9:193, no. 606; 9:279, no. 830; 9:421, no. 1164; 10:208–9, no. 171; 10:213–14, no. 187; 10:229–30, no. 868.

40. Harald Lindström, *Wesley and Sanctification* (Grand Rapids: Zondervan, 1980), pp. 99–102.

41. Wesley wrote: "This expression ['grow up in Him who is our Head'] of the Apostle admirably illustrates the difference between one and the other, and farther points out the exact analogy there is between natural and spiritual things. A child is born of a woman in a moment, or at least in a very short time: Afterward he gradually and slowly grows, till he attains to the stature of a man. In like manner, a child is born of God in a short time, if not in a moment. But it is by slow degrees that he afterward grows up to the measure of the full stature of Christ. The same relation, therefore, which there is between our natural birth and our growth, there is also between our new birth and our sanctification."

42. "Behemenish" refers to Jacob Boehme or "Behmen" (1575–1624), a German mystic whose writings had an increasing and—in Wesley's opinion—debilitating effect upon William Law.

43. The full text of John Wesley's criticism was as follows: "A late very eminent author, in his strange 'Treatise on Regeneration,' proceeds entirely on the supposition, that it is the whole gradual progress of sanctification. No; it is only the threshold of sanctification, the first entrance upon it. And as, in the natural birth, a man is born at once, and

then grows larger and stronger by degrees; so in the spiritual birth, a man is born at once, and then gradually increases in spiritual stature and strength. The new birth, therefore, is the first point of sanctification, which may increase more and more unto the perfect day."

44. Rattenbury, *Evangelical Doctrines*, pp. 308–9. Rattenbury writes: "While it must be admitted that some inconsistency remains in the uses of both brothers of the term, it would perhaps be fair to say that John employs it literally of Justification and metaphorically of Christian Perfection, and Charles literally of Perfection and metaphorically, . . . of Justification."

45. John Wesley, ed., *A Collection of Hymns for the Use of the People Called Methodists* (London: Paramore, 1780), pp. 211–22. John Rattenbury, in his *Evangelical Doctrines*, notes a similar alteration of Charles's hymn entitled "Lord I Believe a Rest Remains" (p. 264).

46. The last word in this line is a bit unclear; the manuscript reads either "unknown" or "are known."

47. *Ms. John*, pp. 32–33.

CHAPTER SEVEN:
"A BROTHERLY DEBATE"

1. Baker, *Representative Verse of Charles Wesley*, p. lviii.

2. Ibid. Cf. Drury, "John Wesley Hymnologist"; Gregory, "Charles Wesley's Hymns and Poems," pp. 253–62; Tyson, "Charles Wesley and the German Hymns," pp. 153–58.

3. *P.W.*, 1:34–35, based on Clement's *Stromata*, IV.

4. Ibid., p. 161. Freylinghausen's song was "Wer ist wol wie Du," no. 30 in the *Herrnhut Gesungbuch*.

5. Rattenbury, *Evangelical Doctrines*, pp. 286–88.

6. Brailsford, *Tale of Two Brothers*, pp. 29, 76–77.

7. *P.W.*, 3:161–67. Probably the most morbid hymn that Charles produced was "On the Sight of a Corpse" (*P.W.*, 6:193f.).

8. *P.W.*, 2:183–91; 3:107–28; 3:156–63; 3:171–80; 4:221–24; 4:245–51; 5:80–87; 5:199–228; 5:357–63; 6:188–367.

9. *P.W.*, 5:71–72; cf. 5:10, no. 118; 5:39, no. 139; 5:149, no. 6.

10. *Ms. Preparation for Death*, p. 33, no. 70; cf. *P.W.*, 8:268, 345, 398.

11. *Ms. Luke*, p. 35.

12. Ibid., pp. 157–58, 194, 210.

13. *Ms. Matthew* (hymn based on Matt. 13:31).

14. *P.W.*, 13:132–33, no. 3280; cf. 13:133, no. 3282; 13:134, no. 3283.

15. The letter outlines three points of contention: (1) sinlessness, (2) gradual or instantaneous perfection, and (3) the proximity of perfection to justification and to death.

16. *P.W.*, 1:109, 188, 243, 269, 273, 275, 300, 348.

17. This hymn is more commonly known by the title, "O For A Thousand Tongues to Sing."

18. *P.W.*, 5:289, 290, 291, 295, 296, 300, 301, 307, 308, 310, 312, 313.

19. *P.W.*, 5:325; cf. 5:321. Charles usually sets the word *love* in boldface or italics, suggesting "perfect love."

20. *J.W. Works*, 11:396, offers a helpful summary of John Wesley's position on perfection and the theological language he used to describe it.

21. Outler, *John Wesley*, p. 32.

22. Rattenbury, *Evangelical Doctrines*, p. 306.

23. "Q. Do you affirm, that this Perfection excludes all infirmities, ignorance, and mistakes?" A. "I continually affirm quite the contrary, and always have done so." (*J.W. Works*, 11:395).

24. John's definition of sin: "To explain myself a little farther on this head: (1) Not only sin, properly so called, (that is, a voluntary transgression of a known law,) but sin, improperly so called, (that is, an involuntary transgression of a divine law, known or unknown,) needs the atoning blood. (2) I believe there is no such perfection in this life as excludes these involuntary transgressions which I apprehend to be naturally consequent on the ignorance and mistakes inseparable from mortality. (3) Therefore *sinless perfection* is a phrase I never use, lest I seem to contradict myself. (4) I believe a person filled with the love of God is still liable to these involuntary transgressions. (5) Such transgressions you may call sins, if you please: I do not, for the reasons abovementioned" (*J.W. Works*, 11:396).

25. Baker, *Charles Wesley Letters*, p. 104.

26. Rattenbury, *Evangelical Doctrines*, p. 311.

27. See for example *Ms. Luke*, pp. 78, 276; *P.W.*, 3:331, no. 152; 4:32; 4:39, no. 9; 5:154, no. 10; 5:163, no. 16; 5:169, no. 22; 5:177, no. 27; 5:196, no. 42; 5:201, no. 45; 5:209, no. 50; 5:243, no. 71; 5:447, no. 336; 9:238, no. 250; 9:335–36; 9:408, no. 692; 11:38, no. 1004; 11:61, no. 1056; 11:62, no. 1058; 11:86, no. 1111; 12:37, no. 2146; 12:102, no. 2180; 12:127, no. 2338; 12:325–26, no. 2750; 13:47, no. 3121; 13:112, no. 3251; 13:126, no. 3270; 13:154, no. 3314; 13:228, no. 3460.

28. *Ms. Luke*, p. 78; cf. *P.W.*, 5:169, no. 22; 5:209, no. 50; 12:54, no. 2180.

29. E. Tooms, "Cross," *IDB*, 1:745–46.

30. *P.W.*, 5:233, no. 63; cf. 5:44, no. 28; 5:70–71, no. 161; 6:325, no. 2; 6:313, no. 13.

31. *Ms. Acts*, p. 97.

32. *P.W.*, 9:234; cf. 9:233, no. 733; 9:234, no. 734; 9:236, no. 736; 9:240, no. 744; 9:241, no. 749; 9:252, no. 771; 9:259–60, no. 787; 9:268, no. 805.

33. See Deuteronomy 8:5; Psalm 94:12; Zechariah 13:9; Malachi 3:2, 3; 1 Corinthians 11:12; 2 Corinthians 1:6, 7; Hebrews 2:10, 11; 5:8; 12:6, 7, 10; 1 Peter 2:19–23; 3:14–18; 4:15, 19; 5:4.

34. *J.W. Works*, 12:122. *Ex cathedra* is a Latin expression literally meaning "from the chair." It refers to the presumably infallible spiritual authority of a religious leader. Most typically it is used by Roman Catholics to describe papal infallibility when the pope makes official pronouncement on Catholic doctrine or practice.

35. *J.W. Journal*, 4:535. Cf. Jackson, *Life of Charles Wesley*, 2:210.

36. Ibid., pp. 535, 540, 541; cf. *J.W. Works*, 12:123.

37. Robert Southey, *The Life of Wesley: And the Rise and Progress of Methodism*, 2d American ed., 2 vols. (New York: Harper & Brothers, 1847), 2:180–86.

38. An unpublished letter, reported to the writer by Dr. Frank Baker in personal correspondence, May 24, 1983.

39. *C.W. Journal*, 2:260–64. Three letters appended to Charles's *Journal* may point to his continuation in London, but none of these letters carries the year of its composition, so his presence in the city cannot be established with complete certainty.

40. Ibid., p. 266. This letter was not dated with respect to the year of its composition; it may have been written the previous year.

41. An unpublished letter from Charles to his wife indicated that he intended to "humble" Maxfield.

42. *P.W.*, 10:100, no. 320; 11:23; 11:173, no. 95; 12:310, no. 2712.

43. *Ms. Luke* (hymn based on Luke 4:9), pp. 51–52.

44. *P.W.*, 9:374, no. 1062; 9:394, no. 1109; 10:27, no. 1320.

45. *Ms. Matthew*.

46. Ibid.

47. *Ms. Luke*, pp. 262–63, italics added.

48. Jackson, *Life of Charles Wesley*, 2:191–92.

CONCLUSION:
"THE EVERLASTING GOSPEL"

1. Charles exhorted his hearers: "I ask thee, in the name of Jesus, believest thou that his arm is not shortened at all? that he is still mighty to save? that he is the same yesterday, to-day, and forever? that he hath now the power on earth to forgive sins? 'Son, be of good cheer; thy sins are forgiven.' God, for Christ's sake, hath forgiven thee. Receive this, 'not as the word of man; but as it is indeed the word of God'; and thou art justified through faith. Thou shalt be sanctified also through faith which is in Jesus, and shalt set to thy seal, even thine, that 'God hath

given unto us eternal life, and this life is in his Son'" (*J.W. Works*, 5:32).

2. Charles described the experiential dimension of salvation in this fashion: "Your conscience beareth you witness in the Holy Ghost, that these things are so, if so be ye have tasted that the Lord is gracious. 'This is eternal life, to know the only true God, and Jesus Christ whom he hast sent.' This experimental knowledge, and this alone, is true Christianity. He is a Christian who hath received the Spirit of Christ. He is not a Christian who hath not received him. Neither is it possible to have received him, and not know it" (*J.W. Works*, 5:33).

3. Rattenbury, *Evangelical Doctrines*, pp. 298–99.

4. Thomas Langford, *Practical Divinity: Theology in the Wesleyan Tradition* (Nashville: Abingdon, 1983), pp. 131–46, offers a useful introduction to the salient themes and key figures of holiness theology.

5. American Methodism seems to have adopted the "gradual work," whereas "holiness theology" (as a distinct branch of the Wesleyan tradition) continues to insist upon a combination of instantaneous and gradual works of sanctifying grace. Cf. John L. Peters, *Christian Perfection and American Methodism*, 2d ed. (Grand Rapids: Zondervan, 1985), for a fine survey of the development of this doctrine in the American religious context.

6. *J.W. Works*, 11:295. Cf. Colin Williams, *John Wesley's Theology Today* (Nashville: Abingdon, 1960), pp. 126–40. Olin Curtis, a Methodist commentator of an earlier generation, lamented his inability to reconcile John's various statements on the nature of sin: "I have found no way of harmonizing all of Wesley's statements at this point; and I am inclined to think that he never entirely cleaned up his own thinking concerning the nature and scope of sin." Cf. *The Christian Faith* (reprint; Grand Rapids: Kregel, 1956), p. 378.

7. Rattenbury, *Evangelical Doctrines*, p. 306. Also note John's letter to Charles dated July 9, 1766: "One word more: Concerning setting perfection too high. That perfection which I believe, I can boldly preach; because I think I see five hundred witnesses of it. Of that perfection which you preach, you think you do not see any witnesses at all. . . . I wonder you do not, in this article, fall in plumb with Mr. Whitefield. For do not you, as well as he, ask, 'Where are the perfect ones?'" (*J.W. Works*, 12:131).

8. Both brothers taught that (1) holiness of heart and life (inward and outward) is the essence of vital Christianity; (2) holiness is a product of God's grace, a work of the Holy Spirit, and an enabled response of the human heart in love; (3) Christian perfection is the result of the purifying effects of love; it implies purity of intention and conformity to the mind of Christ, and it is the goal (*teleios*) of Christian existence; (4) sanctification is the process through which Christian perfection is realized; it is the simultaneous purging out of our sin and the formation of the mind of Christ, divine love, or the *imago Dei* within

the sanctified believer; (5) regeneration, or new birth, is an event of grace concomitant with justification, through which a person's essential nature or orientation is changed from sin and self to Christ and love; (6) the believer is to grow in grace or "go on unto perfection," although John continued to maintain that "entire sanctification" could occur "in an instant" and "at any moment," while Charles believed this was most likely to occur at death.

Charles's concept of Christian perfection began with "perfect love" and strained toward utter perfection. In a similar fashion, his understanding of the new birth, while beginning in regeneration, typically reserved the term for the end process of sanctification (restoration of the *imago Dei*), rather than located it at the beginning of that process as John did. Cf. Rattenbury, *Evangelical Doctrines*, pp. 298–308, for a useful discussion of the brothers' respective doctrines of Christian perfection.

9. For various perspectives on the importance of theological reexamination and restatement in our own age, see Thomas Oden, *Agenda for Theology* (New York: Harper & Row, 1979); Bernard Ramm, *After Fundamentalism* (New York: Harper & Row, 1983); Langford, *Practical Divinity*, pp. 197ff.; and *Wesleyan Theological Journal* 17 (Spring 1982). The last source takes its focus from Wayne McCown's presidential address, "Believing in the (Contemporary) Wesleyan Mode" (pp. 7–15), and carries eight essays that (as editor Alex Deasley wrote) "provide a synoptic view of the implications of Wesleyan theology for a wide variety of disciplines."

10. See Albert Outler, *Theology in the Wesleyan Spirit* (Nashville: Tidings, 1975), pp. 1–22, for a fine discussion of the eclectic nature of Wesleyan religious epistemology, described by this particular phrase.

11. Mildred Bangs Wynkoop, *A Theology of Love* (Kansas City: Beacon Hill, 1972), has demonstrated that *love* is a theological theme well able to serve as a center point for traditional Wesleyan theology. Norman Pittenger, *Unbounded Love: God and Man in Process* (New York: Seabury, 1976), gave *love* the integrative role in his process theology.

12. Martin Luther King, Jr., *Strength to Love* (Philadelphia: Fortress, 1982).

13. William Warren Sweet, *Revivalism in America* (Nashville: Abingdon, 1944), esp. pp. 144f.; Frederick Norwood, *The Story of American Methodism* (Nashville: Abingdon, 1974), esp. pp. 292f.; Timothy Smith, *Revivalism and Social Reform* (New York: Harper & Row, 1957); Donald W. Dayton, *Discovering An Evangelical Heritage* (New York: Harper & Row, 1976).

14. Theodore Runyon, ed., *Sanctification and Liberation* (Nashville: Abingdon, 1981), has opened the door to dialogue on the correlation between liberation theologies and the Wesleyan tradition. On the growing interest in a "wholistic" understanding of human life, see

John Cobb, *Theology and Pastoral Care* (Philadelphia: Fortress, 1977); Elizabeth Skouglund, *The Whole Christian* (New York: Harper & Row, 1976); and Paul Tournier, *The Meaning of Persons* (New York: Harper & Row, 1957).

   15. For a review of current thought on moral development, see Jean Piaget and Barbel Inhelder, *The Psychology of a Child* (New York: Basic Books, 1969); Lawrence Kohlberg, *The Philosophy of Moral Development* (New York: Harper & Row, 1981); and Brenda Munsey, ed., *Moral Development, Education and Kohlberg* (Birmingham: Religious Education Press, 1980). See Maxie Dunnam, *Alive in Christ* (Nashville: Abingdon, 1982), and Richard J. Foster, *Celebration of Discipline* (New York: Harper & Row, 1978), on the process of spiritual formation. Thomas H. Groome, *Christian Education: Sharing Our Story and Vision* (New York: Harper & Row, 1980) gives a synthesis of the modern views of moral and spiritual development for the teaching ministry of the church.

   16. Thirteen of John Wesley's fifty-two "standard sermons" are based "Upon our Lord's Sermon on the Mount," and they participate in this faith-life synthesis to form a kingdom ethic (*J.W. Works*, 5:247–443). This was also a point of departure for major modern works on theological ethics, such as Walter Rauschenbusch, *The Righteousness of the Kingdom of God* (Nashville: Abingdon, 1968), and Wolfhart Pannenberg, *Theology and the Kingdom of God* (Philadelphia: Westminster, 1975).

SELECT BIBLIOGRAPHY

I. Unpublished Primary Sources*

Ms. Acts
Ms. Cheshunt, held by the Cheshunt College Foundation, Westminster College, Cambridge, England.
Ms. John
Ms. Luke
Ms. Matthew
Ms. Miscellaneous Hymns
Ms. Ordinations
Ms. Preparation for Death
Ms. Scripture Hymns

II. Published Primary Sources

Albin, Thomas A., and Oliver A. Beckerlegge, eds. *Charles Wesley's Earliest Sermons: Six Manuscript Shorthand Sermons Hitherto Unpublished*. A forthcoming occasional publication of the Wesley Historical Society (England).

Baker, Frank. *Charles Wesley as Revealed by His Letters*. London: Epworth, 1948.

Baker, Frank, ed. *The Representative Verse of Charles Wesley*. London: Epworth, 1962.

Curnock, Nehemiah, ed. *The Journal of John Wesley*. 8 vols. London: Epworth, 1909–16.

Heitzenrater, Richard. *The Elusive Mr. Wesley*. 2 vols. Nashville: Abingdon, 1984.

Jackson, Thomas, ed. *The Journal of Charles Wesley, M.A.* 2 vols. London: John Mason, 1849; Grand Rapids: Baker, 1980.

*All of these manuscripts, unless otherwise indicated, are located in the Methodist Archives and Research Center, John Rylands Library, University of Manchester, England.

————. *The Works of John Wesley*, 14 vols. London: Wesleyan Conference Office, 1872; Grand Rapids: Baker, n.d.

Kay, J. Alan, ed. *Fifty Hymns by Charles Wesley*. London: Epworth, 1957.

Osborn, George, ed. *The Poetical Works of John and Charles Wesley*. 13 vols. London: Wesleyan-Methodist Conference, 1868–72.

Telford, John, ed. *The Letters of the Rev. John Wesley, A.M.* 8 vols. London: Epworth, 1931.

Tyson, John R., ed. *Charles Wesley: An Anthology of Readings*. New York: Oxford University Press, 1986.

III. Secondary Sources

Adams, Charles. *The Poet Preacher*. New York: Carlton & Porter, 1859.

Ayling, Stanley. *John Wesley*. New York: William Collins, 1979.

Baker, Frank. *Charles Wesley's Verse: An Introduction*. London: Epworth, 1964.

Beckerlegge, Oliver A. "Charles Wesley's Vocabulary," *London Quarterly and Holborn Review* 182 (October 1957): 280–90.

————. "John Wesley and the German Hymns." *London Quarterly and Holborn Review* 165 (1940): 430–39.

Bett, Henry. *The Hymns of Methodism in Their Literary Relations*. 3d ed. London: Epworth, 1956.

Bowmer, John C. "The Churchmanship of Charles Wesley." *Proceedings of the Wesley Historical Society* 31 (December 1957): 78–80.

Brailsford, Mabel Richmond. *A Tale of Two Brothers*. London: Hart-Davis, 1954.

Cannon, William R. *The Theology of John Wesley*. Nashville: Abingdon, 1946.

Church, Leslie F. "Charles Wesley—the Man." *London Quarterly and Holborn Review* 182 (October 1957): 247–53.

Curtis, Olin A. *The Christian Faith*. New York: Eaton & Mains, 1905.

Dale, James. "The Theological and Literary Qualities of the Poetry of Charles Wesley in Relation to the Standards of His Age." Ph.D. diss., Cambridge University, 1960.

Dayton, Donald W. "The Doctrine of the Baptism of the Holy Spirit: Its Emergence and Significance." *Wesleyan Theological Journal* 12 (Spring 1978): 114–26.

Dixon, Neil. "The Wesleys' Conversion Hymn." *Proceedings of the Wesley Historical Society* 37 (February 1969): 43–47.

Doughty, W. L. "Charles Wesley, Preacher." *London Quarterly and Holborn Review* 182 (1957): 263–67.

Drury, B. C. "John Wesley Hymnologist." *Proceedings of the Wesley Historical Society* 32 (March 1960): 102–8; (June 1960): 132–35.

Edwards, Maldwyn. *Family Circle*. London: Epworth, 1949.

———. *Sons to Samuel*. London: Epworth, 1961.

England, Martha Winburn, and Sparrow, John. *Hymns Unbidden*. New York: New York Public Library, 1966.

Findlay, George. *Christ's Standard Bearer*. London: Epworth, 1956.

Flew, R. Newton. *The Hymns of Charles Wesley: A Study in Their Structure*. London: Epworth, 1953.

———. *The Idea of Perfection in Christian Theology*. London: Oxford University Press, 1934.

Gill, Frederick. *Charles Wesley: The First Methodist*. Nashville: Abingdon, 1964.

Green, Richard. *The Works of John and Charles Wesley—A Bibliography*. London: C. H. Kelley, 1896.

Gregory, Arthur S. *Praises With Understanding*. London: Epworth, 1936.

Heitzenrater, Richard. "John Wesley's Early Sermons." *Proceedings of the Wesley Historical Society* 37 (February 1970): 110–28.

Hildebrandt, Franz. *Christianity According to the Wesleys*. London: Epworth, 1956.

———. *From Luther to Wesley*. London: Epworth, 1951.

———. *I Offered Christ*. London: Epworth, 1967.

Hodgson, E. M. "John or Charles?" *Proceedings of the Wesley Historical Society* 41 (October 1977): 73–76.

Holland, Bernard. "The Conversions of John and Charles Wesley." *Proceedings of the Wesley Historical Society* 38:2–3 (1971–72): 46–53, 51–65.

Hudson, Winthrop, ed. *Henry Scougal's Life of God in the Soul of Man*. Minneapolis: Bethany House, 1946.

Jackson, Thomas. *The Life of the Rev. Charles Wesley*. 2 vols. London: John Mason, 1841.

Jones, D. M. *Charles Wesley: A Study*. London: Epworth, n.d.

Langford, Thomas. *Practical Divinity: Theology in the Wesleyan Tradition*. Nashville: Abingdon, 1983.

Lawson, John. *Introduction to Christian Doctrine*. Grand Rapids: Zondervan, 1980.

Lindström, Harald. *Wesley and Sanctification*. Grand Rapids: Zondervan, 1980.

Manning, Bernard. *The Hymns of Wesley and Watts*. London: Epworth, 1943.

Mitchell, T. Crichton. "Response to Dr. Timothy Smith on the Wesleys' Hymns." *Wesleyan Theological Journal* 16 (Fall 1981): 49–58.

Noll, Mark A. "Romanticism and the Hymns of Charles Wesley." *Evangelical Quarterly* 46 (April–June 1974): 195–223.

Nuelson, John Louis. *John Wesley and the German Hymns*. Claverly, England: A. S. Holbrook, 1977.

Outler, Albert C. *Theology in the Wesleyan Spirit*. Nashville: Tidings, 1975.

Outler, Albert C., ed. *John Wesley*. New York: Oxford University Press, 1964.

Peters, John L. *Christian Perfection and American Methodism*. 2d ed. Grand Rapids: Zondervan, 1985.

Rattenbury, John Earnest. *The Conversions of the Wesleys*. London: Epworth, 1938.

———. *The Eucharist Hymns of John and Charles Wesley*. London: Epworth, 1948.

———. *The Evangelical Doctrines of Charles Wesley's Hymns*. London: Epworth, 1941.

———. *Wesley's Legacy to the World*. Nashville: Cokesbury, 1928.

Routley, Erik. *The Musical Wesleys*. London: Jenkins, 1968.

Rowe, Kenneth, ed. *Wesley in the Christian Tradition*. Metuchen, N.J.: Scarecrow, 1976.

Runyon, Theodore, ed. *Sanctification and Liberation: Liberation Theologies in Light of the Wesleyan Tradition*. Nashville: Abingdon, 1981.

Sangster, W. E. *The Path to Perfection*. Nashville: Abingdon-Cokesbury, 1943.

———. *The Pure in Heart*. London: Epworth, 1954.

Schmidt, Martin. *John Wesley: A Theological Biography*. 3 vols. Nashville: Abingdon, n.d.

Smith, Timothy L. "The Holy Spirit in the Hymns of the Wesleys." *Wesleyan Theological Journal* 16 (Fall 1981): 20–48.

Snyder, Howard. *The Radical Wesley: Patterns for Church Renewal*. Downers Grove: InterVarsity, 1980.

Southey, Robert. *The Life of Wesley and the Rise and Progress of Methodism*. 2 vols. New York: Harper & Brothers, 1847.

Standford, Paul, ed. *William Law*. Ramsey, N.J.: Paulist, 1978.

Steele, Daniel. *Love Enthroned: Essays on Evangelical Perfection*. New York: Hunt & Eaton, 1875.

Swift, Wesley. "Brothers Charles and John." *London Quarterly and Holborn Review* 182 (October 1957): 275–80.

Telford, John. *The Life of Charles Wesley*. London: Wesleyan Book Room, 1900.

Townsend, James A. "Feelings Related to Assurance in Charles Wesley's Hymns." Ph.D. diss., Fuller Theological Seminary, 1979.

Tuttle, Robert G., Jr. *John Wesley: His Life and Theology*. Grand Rapids: Zondervan, 1978.

Tyerman, Luke. *The Life and Times of Rev. John Wesley, A.M.* 3 vols. New York: Harper, 1872.

Tyson, John R. "Charles Wesley and the German Hymns." *The Hymn* 35 (July 1984): 153–58.

_____. "John Wesley and William Law: A Reappraisal." *Wesleyan Theological Journal* 17 (Fall 1982): 58–79.

Tyson, John R., and Douglas Lister. "Charles Wesley, Pastor: A Glimpse Inside His Shorthand Journal." *Quarterly Review* 4 (Spring 1984): 9–22.

Watson, Philip. *The Message of the Wesleys.* Grand Rapids: Zondervan, 1984.

Welch, Barbara Ann. "Charles Wesley and the Celebrations of Evangelical Experience." Ph.D. diss., University of Michigan, 1971.

Whitefield, George. *George Whitefield's Journals.* London: Banner of Truth Trust, n.d.

Whitehead, John. *The Life of the Rev. Charles Wesley.* Dublin: J. Jones, 1805.

Wiley, H. Orton, and Paul T. Culbertson. *Introduction to Christian Theology.* Kansas City: Beacon Hill, 1946.

Williams, Colin W. *John Wesley's Theology Today.* Nashville: Abingdon, 1960.

Wiseman, Frederick Luke. *Charles Wesley, Evangelist and Poet.* New York: Abingdon, 1932.

Wood, A. Skevington. *The Burning Heart: John Wesley, Evangelist.* Exeter: Paternoster, 1967.

Wood, Laurence W. *Pentecostal Grace.* Grand Rapids: Zondervan, 1984.

Wynkoop, Mildred Bangs. *A Theology of Love: The Dynamic of Wesleyanism.* Kansas City: Beacon Hill, 1972.

Index of Hymn and Sermon Titles

Index

Jesus' name 207–8
John the Baptist 228
Judge, God as 108–9
Justification 32, 41, 51, 62, 65, 71–73, 75, 80–82, 85, 89, 103, 110, 113, 129, 134, 143, 157, 163, 196, 211, 219, 292, 305, 308; by faith 39, 45; Charles's concept of 69–76
Juxtaposition, poetic use of 262

Kennington-Common 15
Kierkegaard, Søren 307
King, Martin Luther Jr. 313
Kingdom of God 77, 100, 128, 141, 189, 201, 217, 251, 262, 290, 306

Law, William 16, 31–32, 61, 63, 181–82, 217–19, 224; Charles's disaffection for 32; soteriology of 32, 71–72
Lay preachers 18
Liberation 99, 139–41, 162, 228–29, 303, 313
Life of God. *See* "Divine Life.'
Life of God in the Soul of Man, The 30, 32, 182, 184, 192
Lindström, [Harald] 214
London 110, 227, 249, 269–70, 272–73, 275, 278, 280–84, 296, 299; bishop of 111–12; Methodist society of 268–300
London Chronicle 278
Lord's Supper 127, 157, 200, 208–10
Love 40, 60, 91, 108, 122, 155, 157–64, 165, 179, 185–86, 200–201, 203–4, 208, 219, 257–58, 291–92, 303–4, 306–7, 313. *See also* Perfect love.
Luther, Martin 24, 43, 72, 312

Manchester 299
Margate 282
Marriage, Charles's 38; John's 18

Maturation 171, 216, 221, 225, 250
Maxfield, Thomas 269–70, 273–72, 274–84, 289, 291
Means of grace. *See* Baptism; Grace; Lord's Supper.
Melancholy 262, 264, 297; Charles's 35
Mercy 77, 88, 98–99
Methodism, birth of 20, 29–30, 217–18
Middleton, Dr. 42
Milton, John 25
Minutes of the Conference (1744) 233; (1747) 237; (1758) 257; (1759) 177, 258
Mitton, C. L. 121
Moorfields 15, 113
Moral and Sacred Poems (1744) 234, 264
Moravians 39, 43, 58, 67, 208, 231
Morris, Leon 116
Music 20–21. *See also* Hymnology; Hymns.
Mysticism 16

Name, Jesus' 207–8
New Birth 186, 214–25, 308; the Wesleys' differing views of 219–24
Newcastle 18
Newgate Prison 110, 304
Niebuhr, Reinhold 309
"Night Thoughts" 238
Notes Upon the Old and New Testaments 25

Ogelthorpe, General 33, 35–38
Ogelthorpe, Mrs. 48
Outler, Albert 61, 312
Oxford 24, 29, 31, 35, 39, 65, 112, 181–82, 304–5

Pardon 98–102, 122, 139, 141, 143–45, 150, 305
Peace 43, 89–90, 139, 177, 233
Pentecost 43